HEAVEN'S DESIGN TEAM

VOL.03

BY ➤ **HEBI-ZOU & TSUTA SUZUKI**

ART BY ➤ **TARAKO**

HEAVEN'S DESIGN TEAM

CHARACTER PROFILES

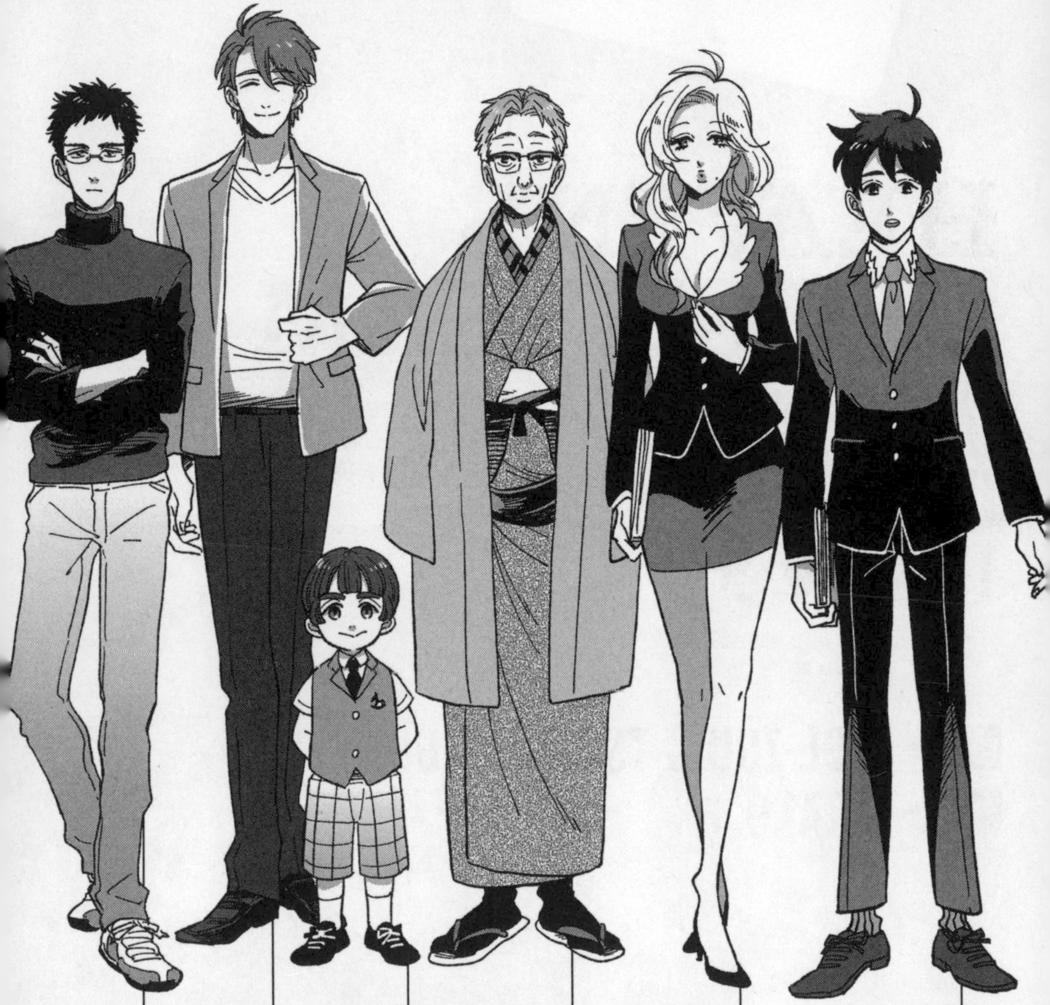

MERCURY

A designer. His masterpiece: the snake.

JUPITER

A designer. His masterpiece: the cow.

MR. SATURN'S GRANDSON

Mr. Saturn's grandson, Kenta. A horse fan, just like his grandpa.

MR. SATURN

A designer and the head of the Design Department. His masterpiece: the horse.

UEDA

Shimoda's supervisor. An angel who acts as a liaison between God and the Design Department.

SHIMODA

The new angel. Serves as the liaison between God (the client) and the Design Department.

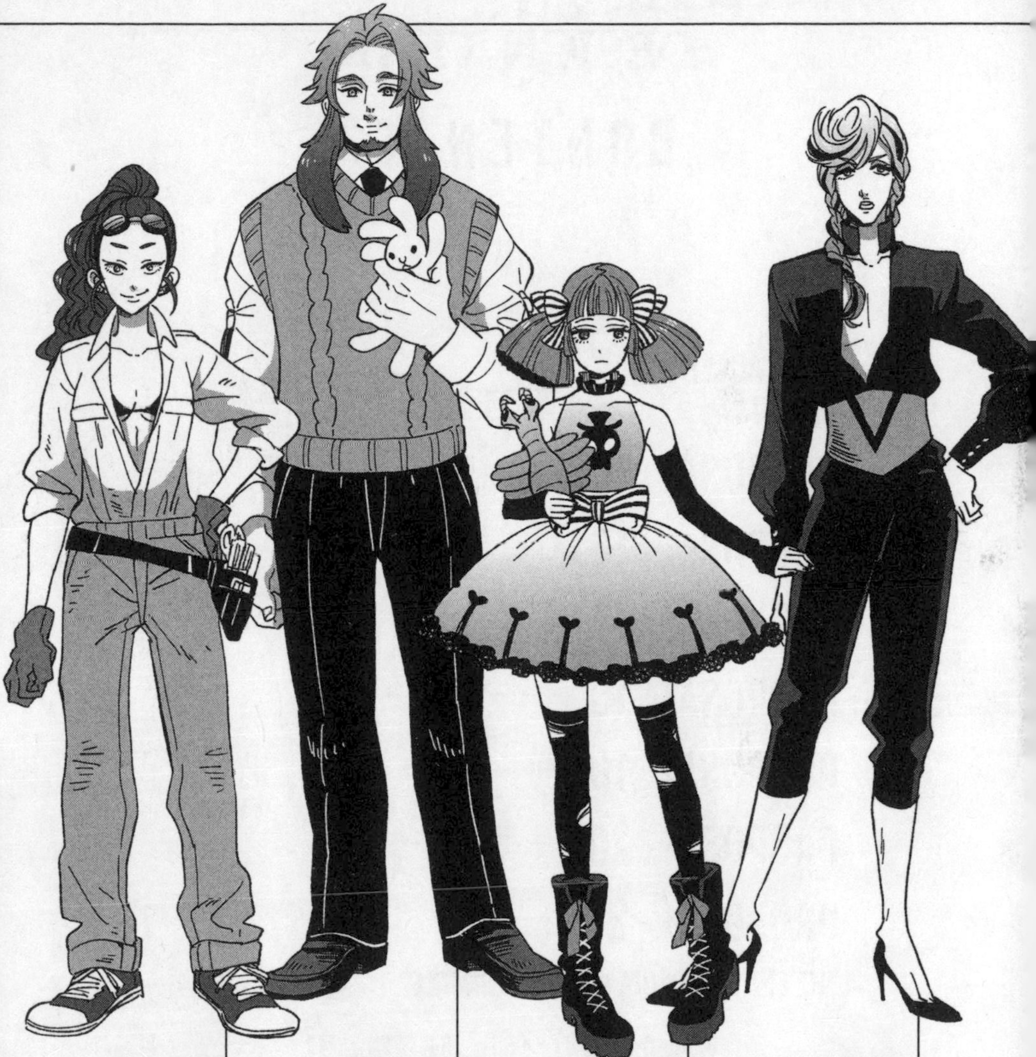

MARS

An engineer. Tests whether the animal designs will actually function in the physical world. The hardest worker in the office.

NEPTUNE

A designer. His masterpiece: the kangaroo.

PLUTO

A designer. Her masterpiece: the poisonous frog.

VENUS

A designer. Nicknamed "Ven." Their masterpiece: the bird.

HEAVEN'S DESIGN TEAM

CONTENTS

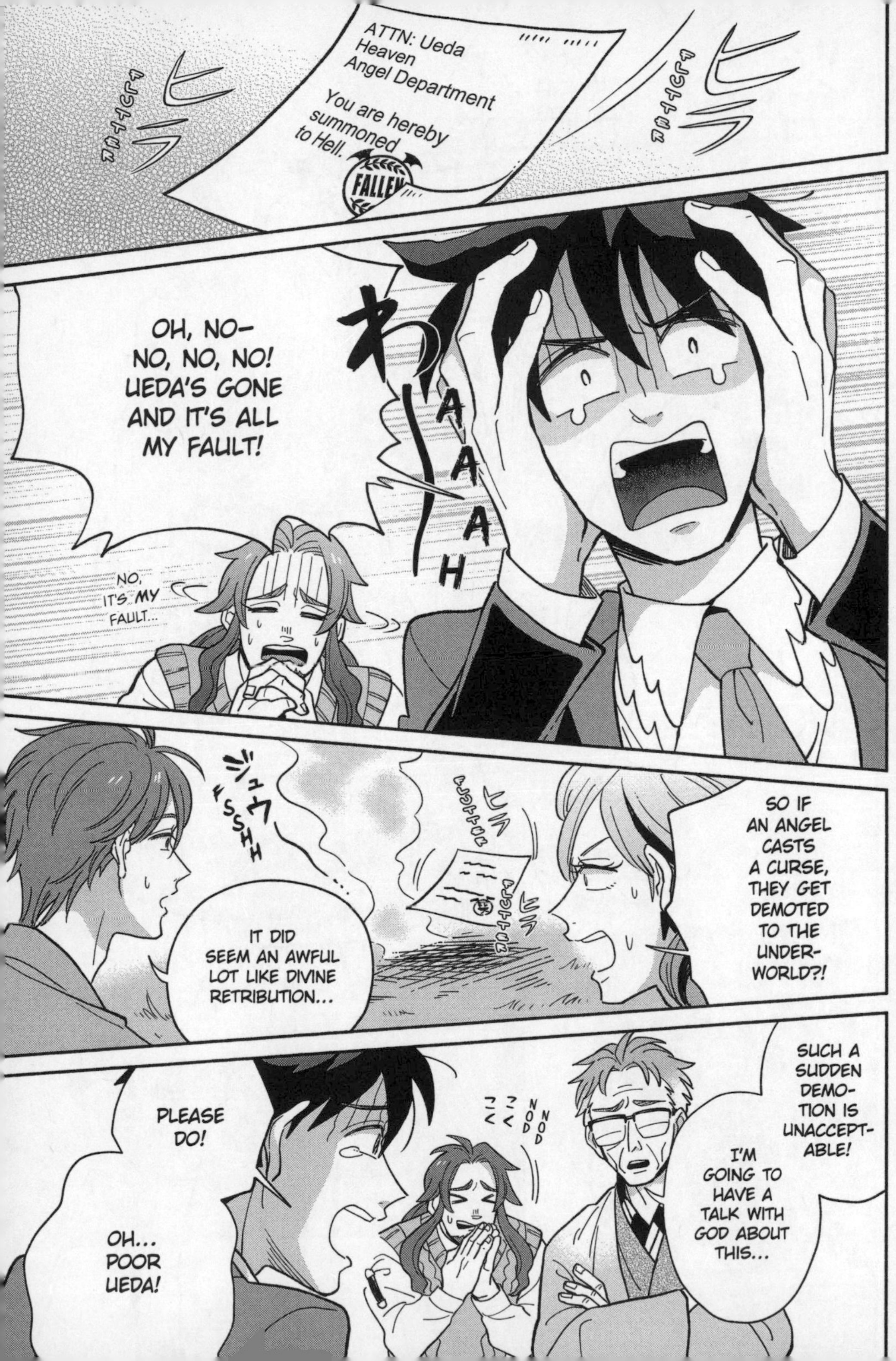
ATTN: Ueda
Heaven
Angel Department
You are hereby summoned to Hell.
FALLEN
ヒラ
FLUTTER
ヒラ
FLUTTER
OH, NO– NO, NO, NO! UEDA'S GONE AND IT'S ALL MY FAULT!
わー
AAAAH
NO, IT'S MY FAULT...
SO IF AN ANGEL CASTS A CURSE, THEY GET DEMOTED TO THE UNDER-WORLD?!
ヒラ
FLUTTER
ヒラ
FLUTTER
ジュウ
FSSHH
IT DID SEEM AN AWFUL LOT LIKE DIVINE RETRIBUTION...
SUCH A SUDDEN DEMO-TION IS UNACCEPT-ABLE!
I'M GOING TO HAVE A TALK WITH GOD ABOUT THIS...
こくこく
NOD NOD
PLEASE DO!
OH... POOR UEDA!

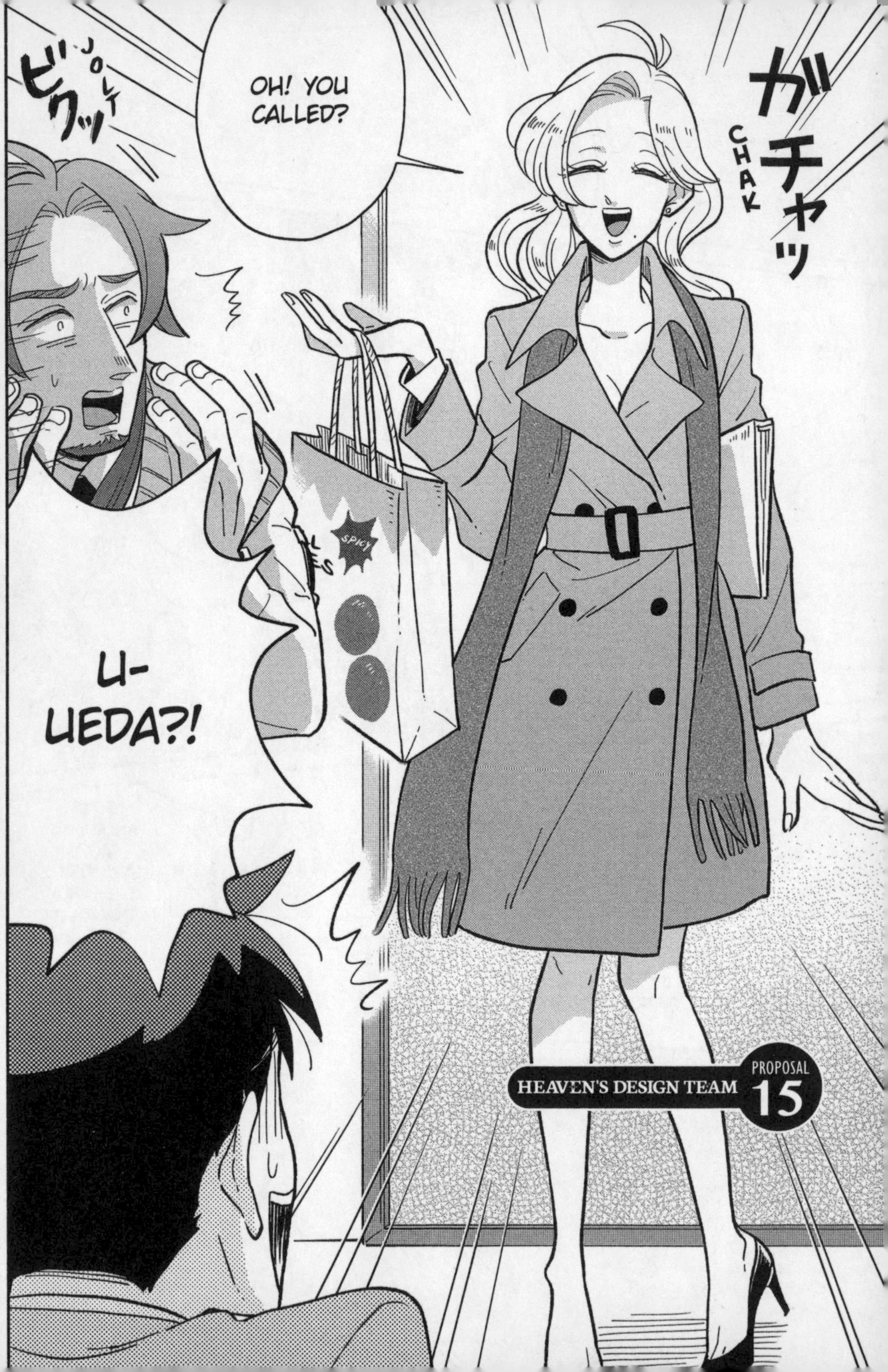
ガチャッ
CHAK
OH! YOU CALLED?
ビクッ
JOLT
SPIKY
U-UEDA?!
HEAVEN'S DESIGN TEAM
PROPOSAL 15

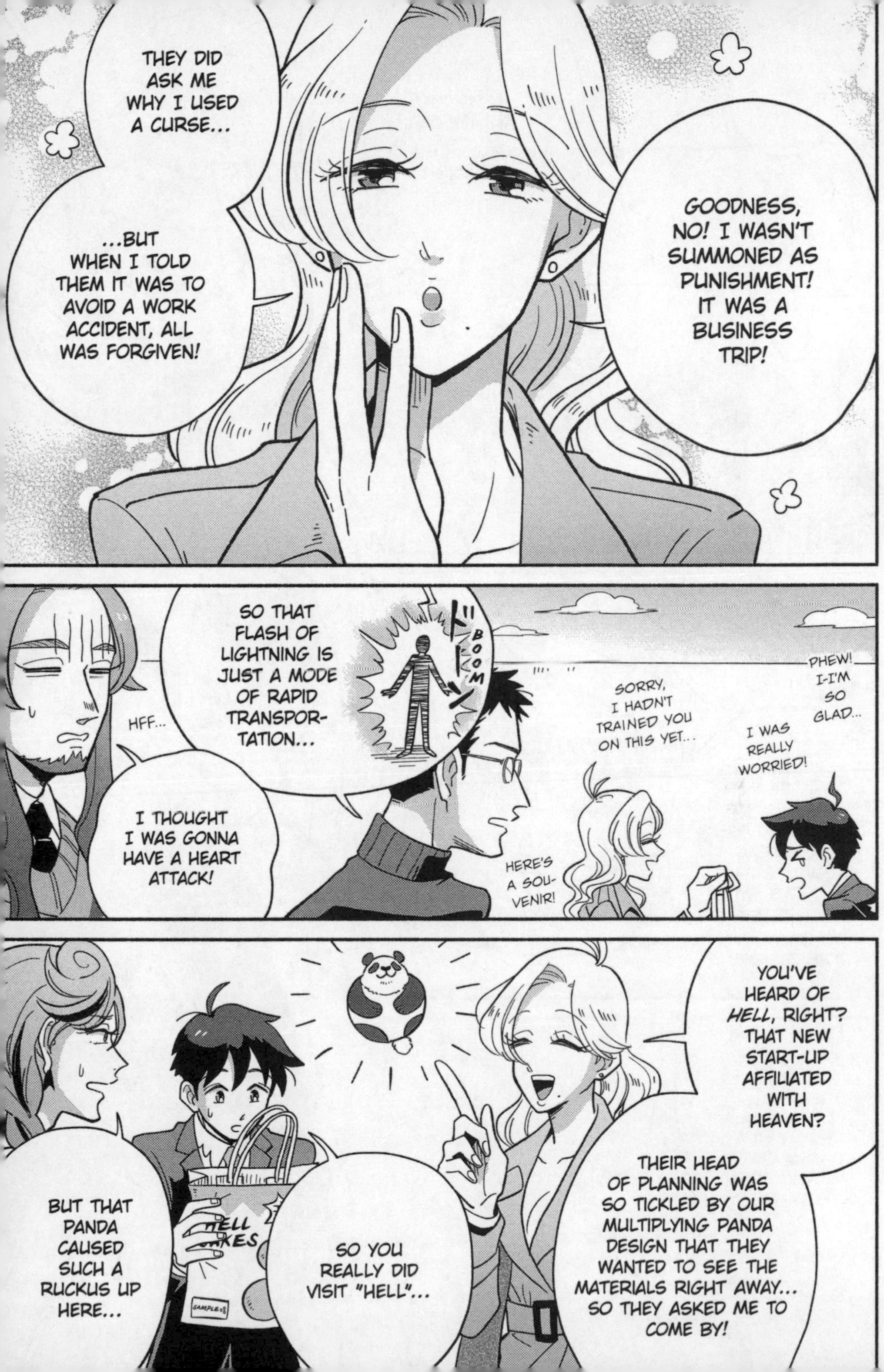
GOODNESS, NO! I WASN'T SUMMONED AS PUNISHMENT! IT WAS A BUSINESS TRIP!
THEY DID ASK ME WHY I USED A CURSE...
...BUT WHEN I TOLD THEM IT WAS TO AVOID A WORK ACCIDENT, ALL WAS FORGIVEN!
PHEW! I-I'M SO GLAD...
I WAS REALLY WORRIED!
SORRY, I HADN'T TRAINED YOU ON THIS YET...
HERE'S A SOU-VENIR!
BOOM
SO THAT FLASH OF LIGHTNING IS JUST A MODE OF RAPID TRANSPOR-TATION...
I THOUGHT I WAS GONNA HAVE A HEART ATTACK!
HFF...
YOU'VE HEARD OF *HELL*, RIGHT? THAT NEW START-UP AFFILIATED WITH HEAVEN?
THEIR HEAD OF PLANNING WAS SO TICKLED BY OUR MULTIPLYING PANDA DESIGN THAT THEY WANTED TO SEE THE MATERIALS RIGHT AWAY... SO THEY ASKED ME TO COME BY!
SO YOU REALLY DID VISIT "HELL"...
BUT THAT PANDA CAUSED SUCH A RUCKUS UP HERE...

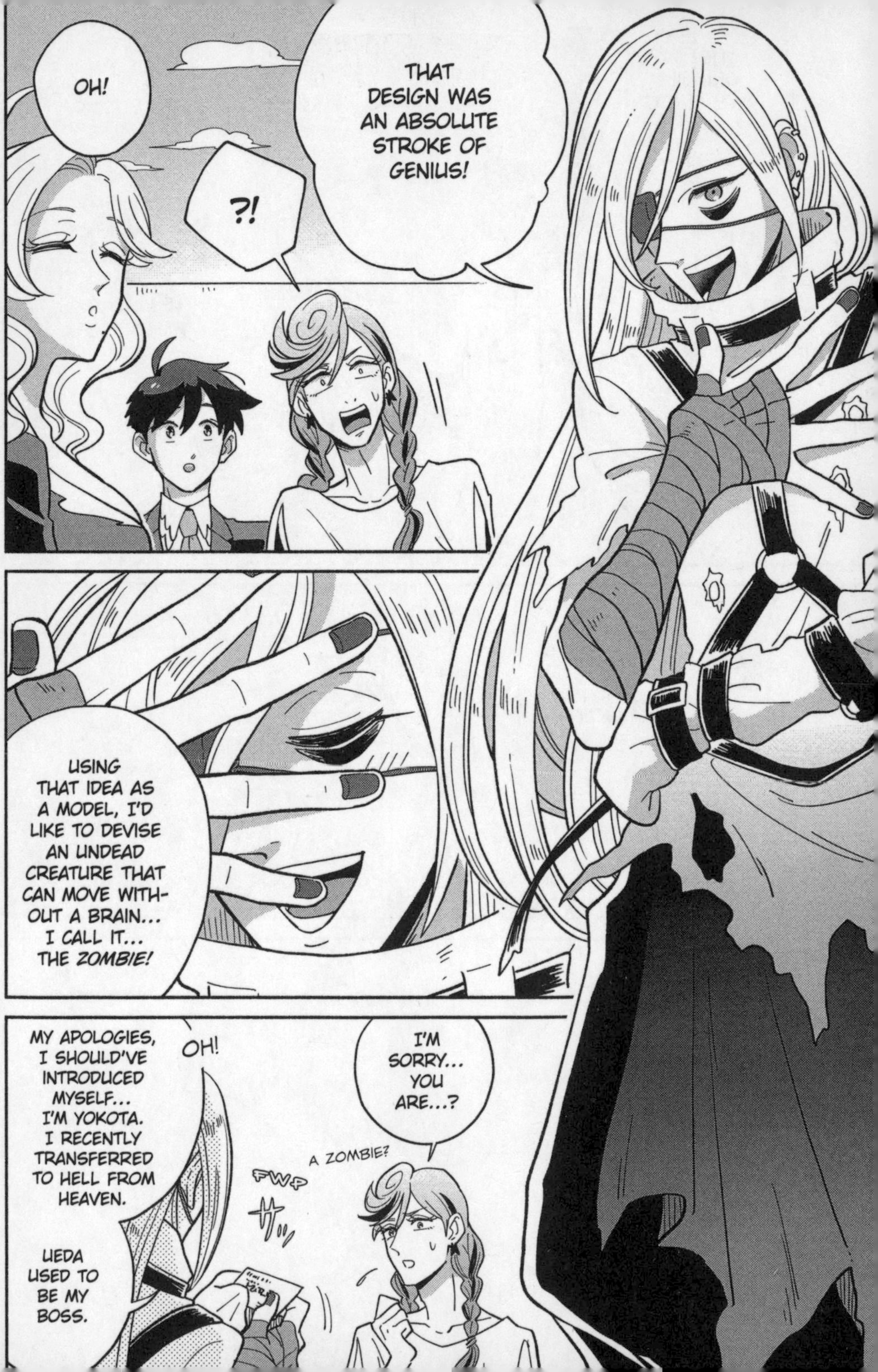
THAT DESIGN WAS AN ABSOLUTE STROKE OF GENIUS!
OH!
?!
USING THAT IDEA AS A MODEL, I'D LIKE TO DEVISE AN UNDEAD CREATURE THAT CAN MOVE WITH-OUT A BRAIN... I CALL IT... THE *ZOMBIE*!
I'M SORRY... YOU ARE...?
A ZOMBIE?
OH!
FWP
MY APOLOGIES, I SHOULD'VE INTRODUCED MYSELF... I'M YOKOTA. I RECENTLY TRANSFERRED TO HELL FROM HEAVEN.
UEDA USED TO BE MY BOSS.

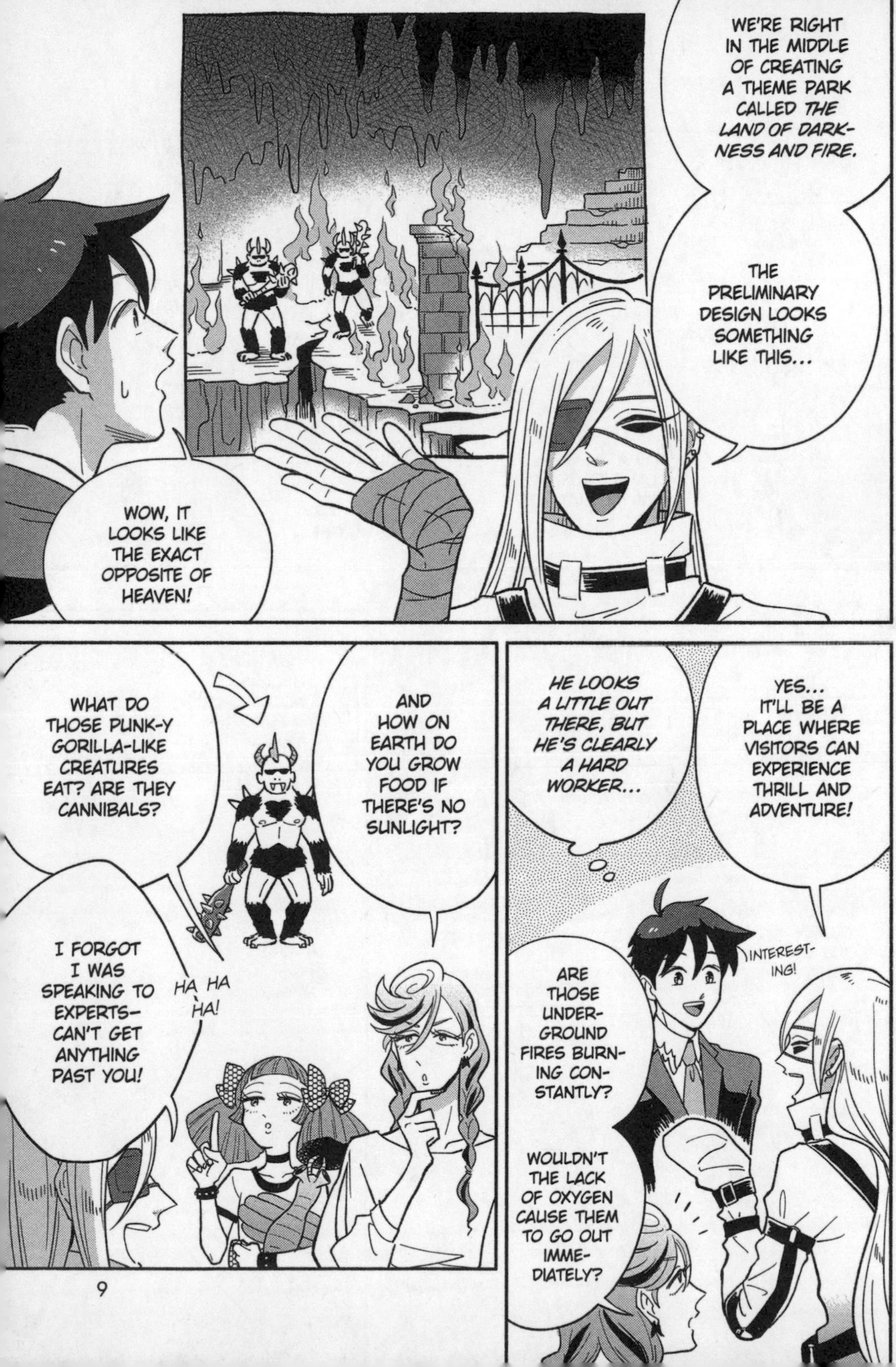
WE'RE RIGHT IN THE MIDDLE OF CREATING A THEME PARK CALLED *THE LAND OF DARKNESS AND FIRE.*
THE PRELIMINARY DESIGN LOOKS SOMETHING LIKE THIS...
WOW, IT LOOKS LIKE THE EXACT OPPOSITE OF HEAVEN!
YES... IT'LL BE A PLACE WHERE VISITORS CAN EXPERIENCE THRILL AND ADVENTURE!
HE LOOKS A LITTLE OUT THERE, BUT HE'S CLEARLY A HARD WORKER...
INTERESTING!
ARE THOSE UNDERGROUND FIRES BURNING CONSTANTLY?
WOULDN'T THE LACK OF OXYGEN CAUSE THEM TO GO OUT IMMEDIATELY?
AND HOW ON EARTH DO YOU GROW FOOD IF THERE'S NO SUNLIGHT?
WHAT DO THOSE PUNK-Y GORILLA-LIKE CREATURES EAT? ARE THEY CANNIBALS?
I FORGOT I WAS SPEAKING TO EXPERTS— CAN'T GET ANYTHING PAST YOU!
HA HA HA!

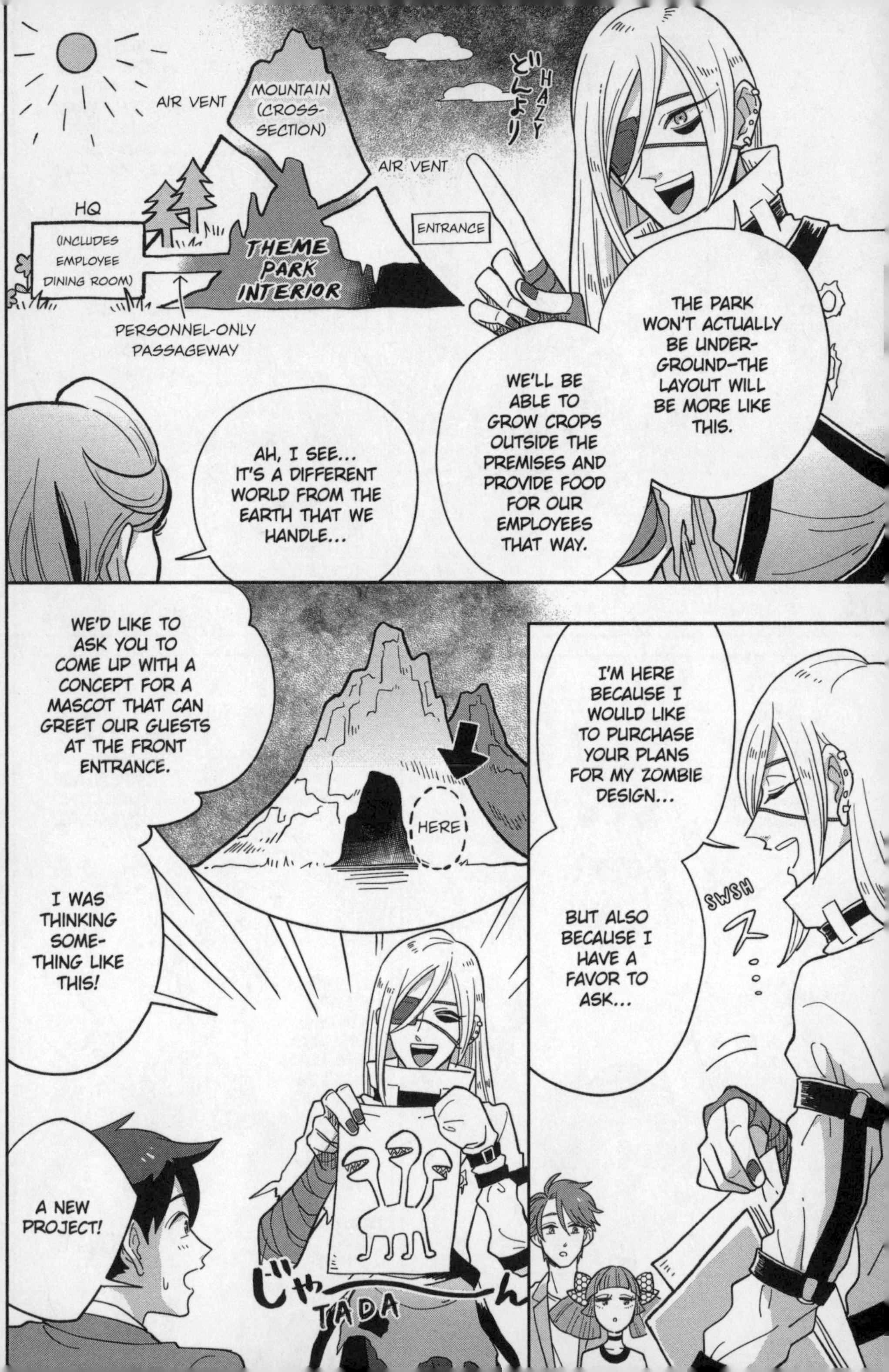

どんより HAZY
MOUNTAIN (CROSS-SECTION)
AIR VENT
AIR VENT
ENTRANCE
THEME PARK INTERIOR
HQ (INCLUDES EMPLOYEE DINING ROOM)
PERSONNEL-ONLY PASSAGEWAY
THE PARK WON'T ACTUALLY BE UNDER-GROUND—THE LAYOUT WILL BE MORE LIKE THIS.
WE'LL BE ABLE TO GROW CROPS OUTSIDE THE PREMISES AND PROVIDE FOOD FOR OUR EMPLOYEES THAT WAY.
AH, I SEE... IT'S A DIFFERENT WORLD FROM THE EARTH THAT WE HANDLE...
I'M HERE BECAUSE I WOULD LIKE TO PURCHASE YOUR PLANS FOR MY ZOMBIE DESIGN...
SWSH
BUT ALSO BECAUSE I HAVE A FAVOR TO ASK...
WE'D LIKE TO ASK YOU TO COME UP WITH A CONCEPT FOR A MASCOT THAT CAN GREET OUR GUESTS AT THE FRONT ENTRANCE.
HERE
I WAS THINKING SOME-THING LIKE THIS!
じゃーん TADA
A NEW PROJECT!

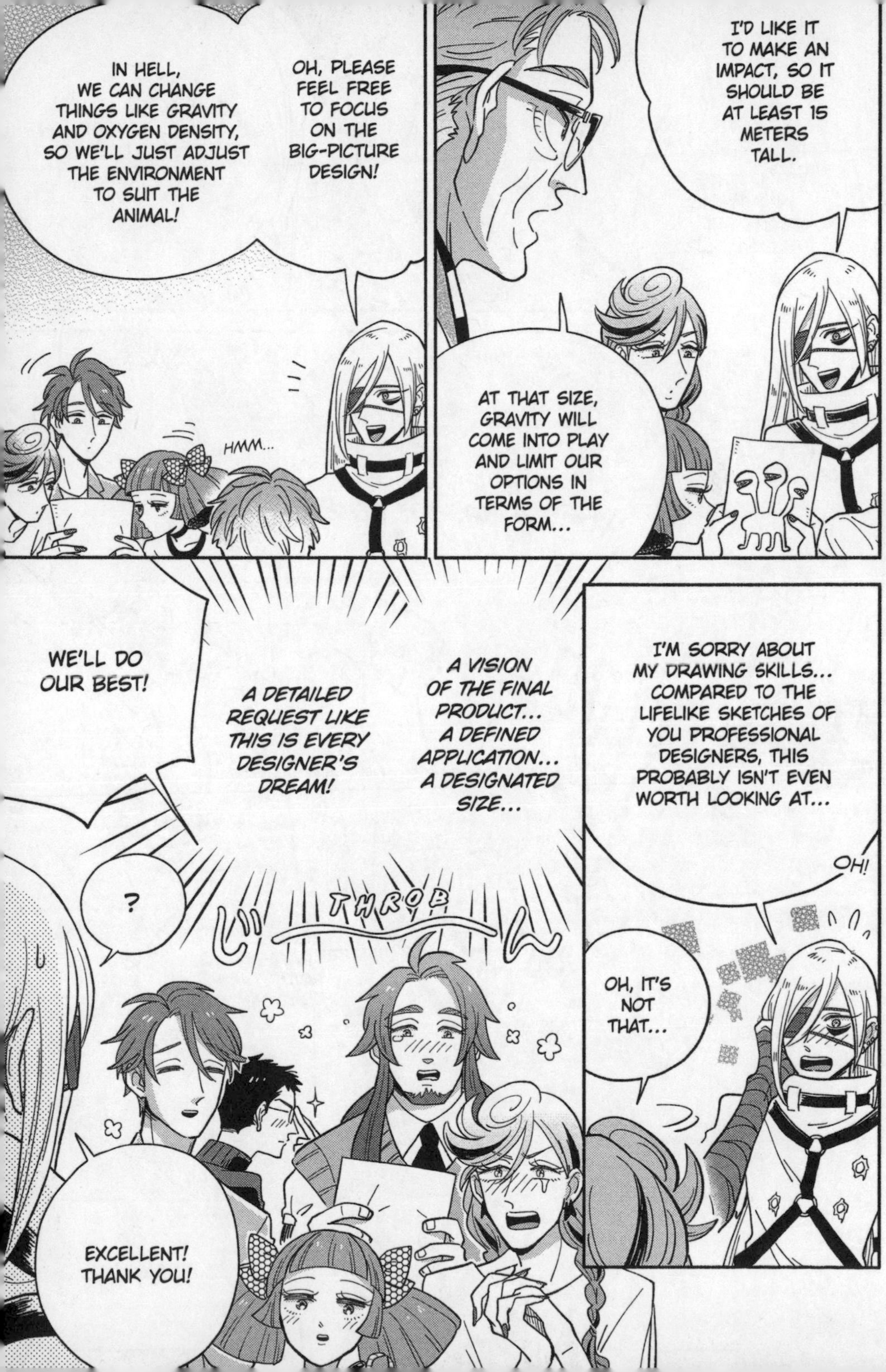
I'D LIKE IT TO MAKE AN IMPACT, SO IT SHOULD BE AT LEAST 15 METERS TALL.
AT THAT SIZE, GRAVITY WILL COME INTO PLAY AND LIMIT OUR OPTIONS IN TERMS OF THE FORM...
IN HELL, WE CAN CHANGE THINGS LIKE GRAVITY AND OXYGEN DENSITY, SO WE'LL JUST ADJUST THE ENVIRONMENT TO SUIT THE ANIMAL!
OH, PLEASE FEEL FREE TO FOCUS ON THE BIG-PICTURE DESIGN!
HMM...
I'M SORRY ABOUT MY DRAWING SKILLS... COMPARED TO THE LIFELIKE SKETCHES OF YOU PROFESSIONAL DESIGNERS, THIS PROBABLY ISN'T EVEN WORTH LOOKING AT...
OH!
OH, IT'S NOT THAT...
A VISION OF THE FINAL PRODUCT... A DEFINED APPLICATION... A DESIGNATED SIZE...
A DETAILED REQUEST LIKE THIS IS EVERY DESIGNER'S DREAM!
WE'LL DO OUR BEST!
?
THROB
EXCELLENT! THANK YOU!

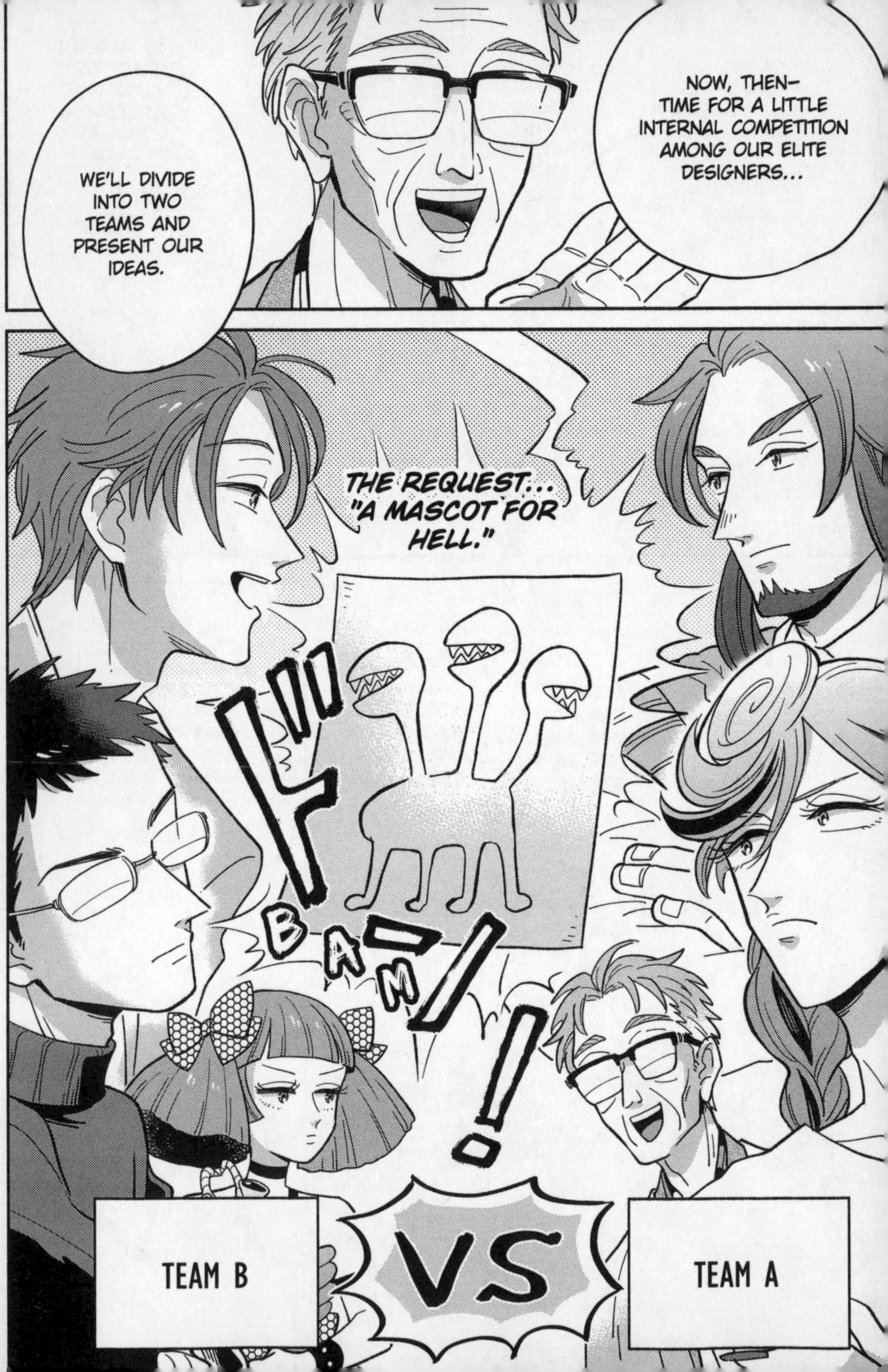
NOW, THEN— TIME FOR A LITTLE INTERNAL COMPETITION AMONG OUR ELITE DESIGNERS...
WE'LL DIVIDE INTO TWO TEAMS AND PRESENT OUR IDEAS.
THE REQUEST... "A MASCOT FOR HELL."
BAM!
TEAM A
VS
TEAM B

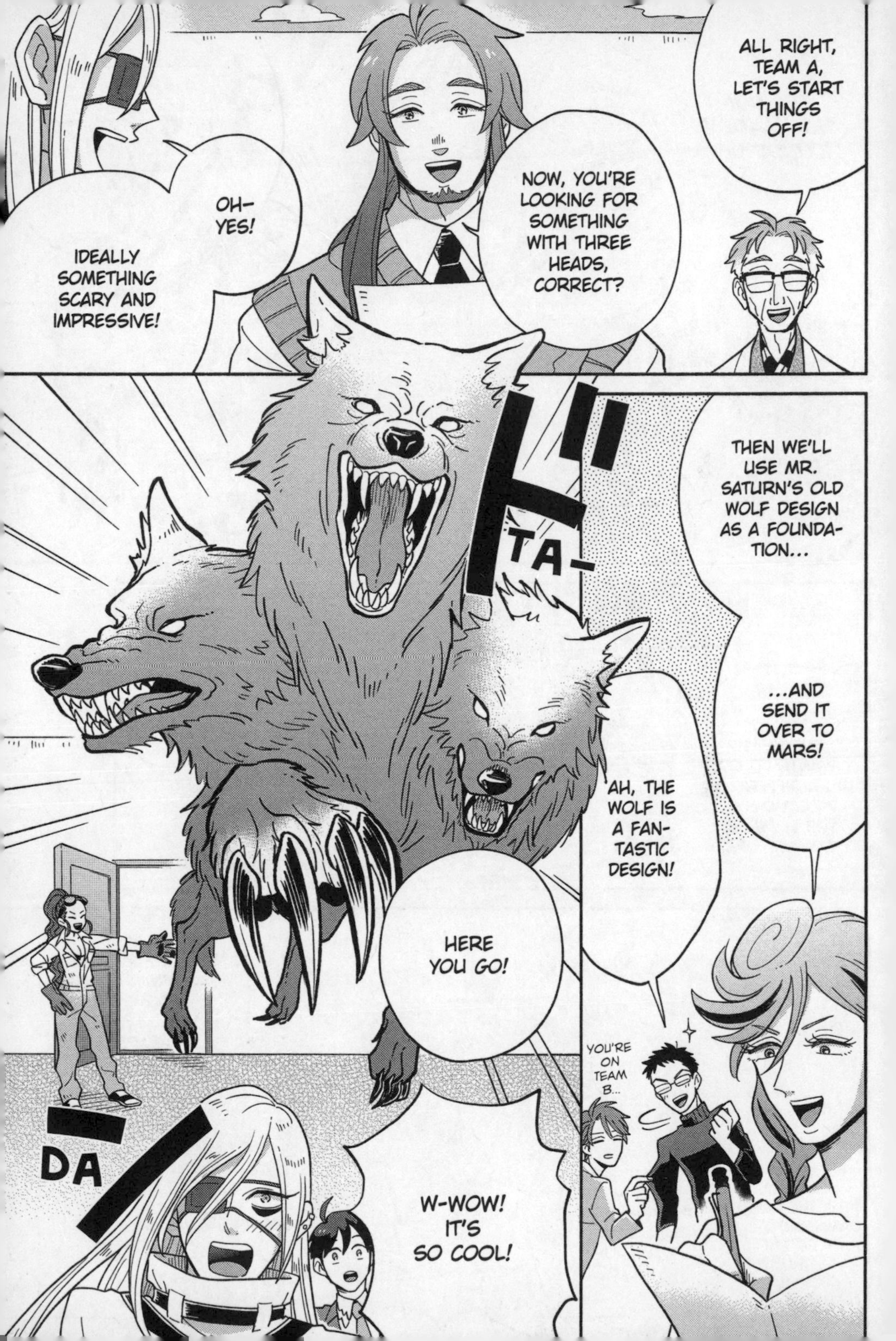
ALL RIGHT, TEAM A, LET'S START THINGS OFF!
NOW, YOU'RE LOOKING FOR SOMETHING WITH THREE HEADS, CORRECT?
OH— YES!
IDEALLY SOMETHING SCARY AND IMPRESSIVE!
THEN WE'LL USE MR. SATURN'S OLD WOLF DESIGN AS A FOUNDATION...
...AND SEND IT OVER TO MARS!
YOU'RE ON TEAM B...
TA—
AH, THE WOLF IS A FAN-TASTIC DESIGN!
HERE YOU GO!
W-WOW! IT'S SO COOL!
DA

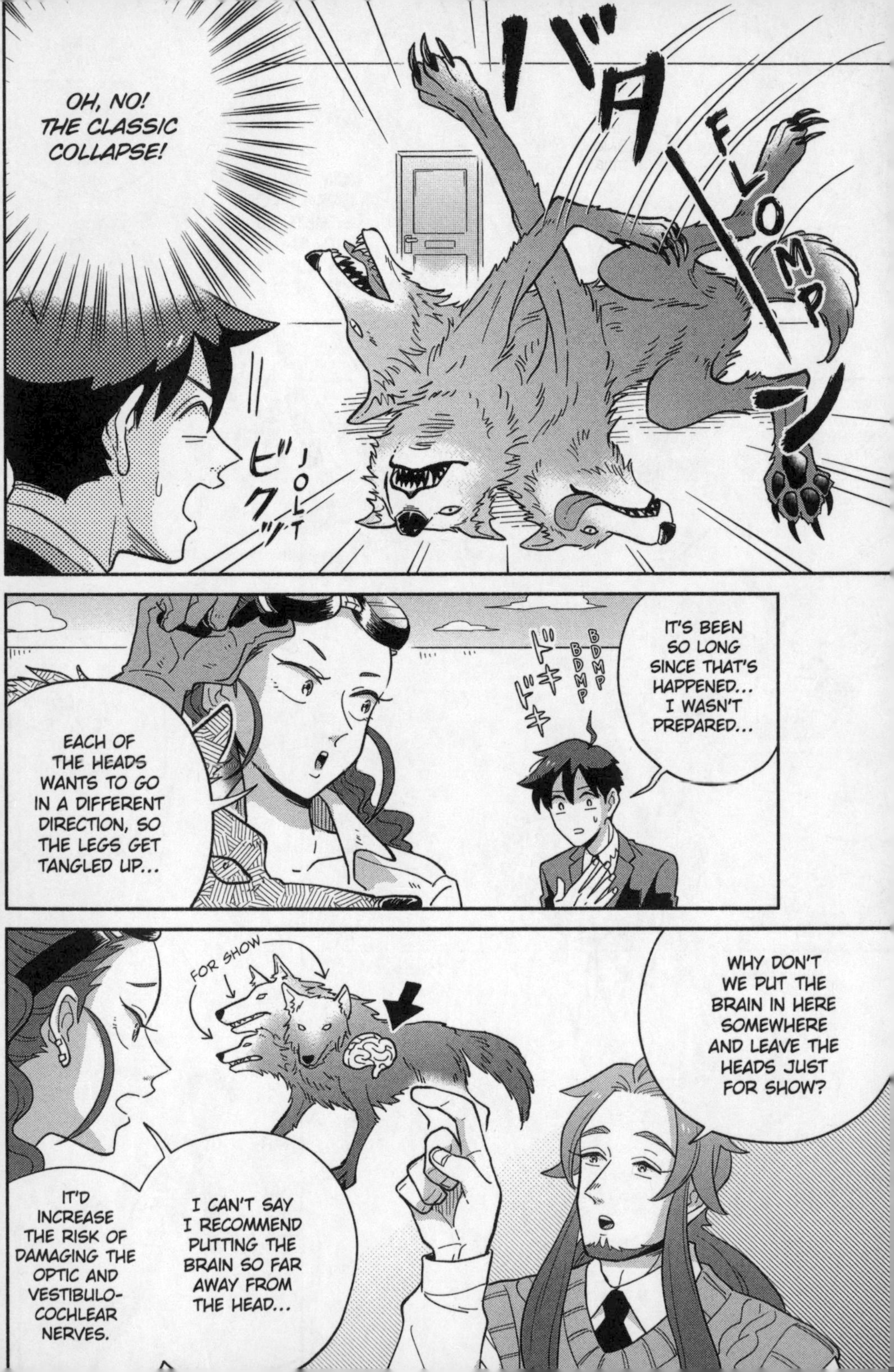
バタ
FLOMP
OH, NO! THE CLASSIC COLLAPSE!
ビクッ
JOLT
IT'S BEEN SO LONG SINCE THAT'S HAPPENED... I WASN'T PREPARED...
ドキドキ
BDMP BDMP
EACH OF THE HEADS WANTS TO GO IN A DIFFERENT DIRECTION, SO THE LEGS GET TANGLED UP...
WHY DON'T WE PUT THE BRAIN IN HERE SOMEWHERE AND LEAVE THE HEADS JUST FOR SHOW?
FOR SHOW
I CAN'T SAY I RECOMMEND PUTTING THE BRAIN SO FAR AWAY FROM THE HEAD...
IT'D INCREASE THE RISK OF DAMAGING THE OPTIC AND VESTIBULO-COCHLEAR NERVES.

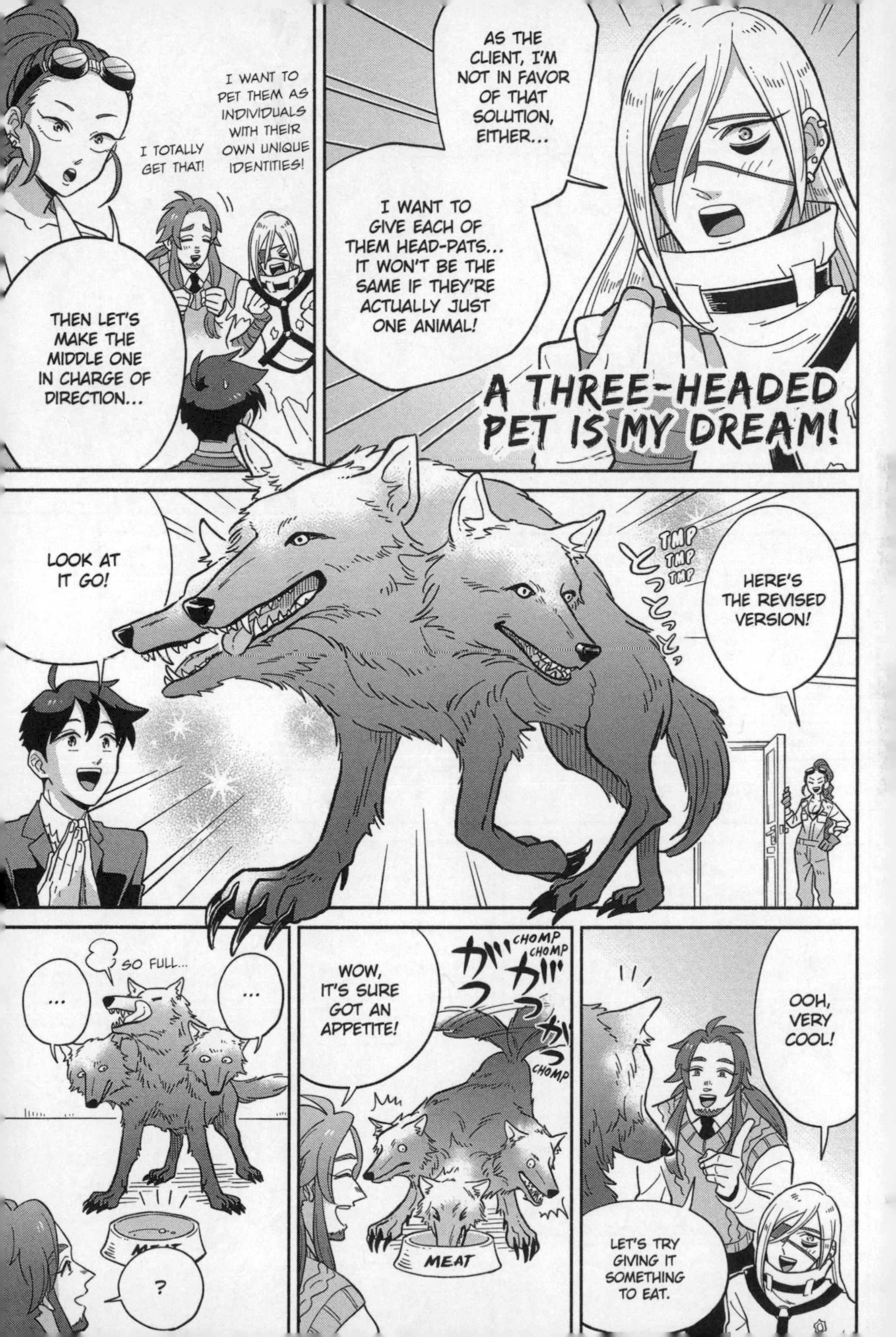
AS THE CLIENT, I'M NOT IN FAVOR OF THAT SOLUTION, EITHER...
I WANT TO GIVE EACH OF THEM HEAD-PATS... IT WON'T BE THE SAME IF THEY'RE ACTUALLY JUST ONE ANIMAL!
A THREE-HEADED PET IS MY DREAM!
I WANT TO PET THEM AS INDIVIDUALS WITH THEIR OWN UNIQUE IDENTITIES!
I TOTALLY GET THAT!
THEN LET'S MAKE THE MIDDLE ONE IN CHARGE OF DIRECTION...
TMP TMP TMP
HERE'S THE REVISED VERSION!
LOOK AT IT GO!
OOH, VERY COOL!
LET'S TRY GIVING IT SOMETHING TO EAT.
CHOMP CHOMP
CHOMP
WOW, IT'S SURE GOT AN APPETITE!
MEAT
SO FULL...
...
...
MEAT
?

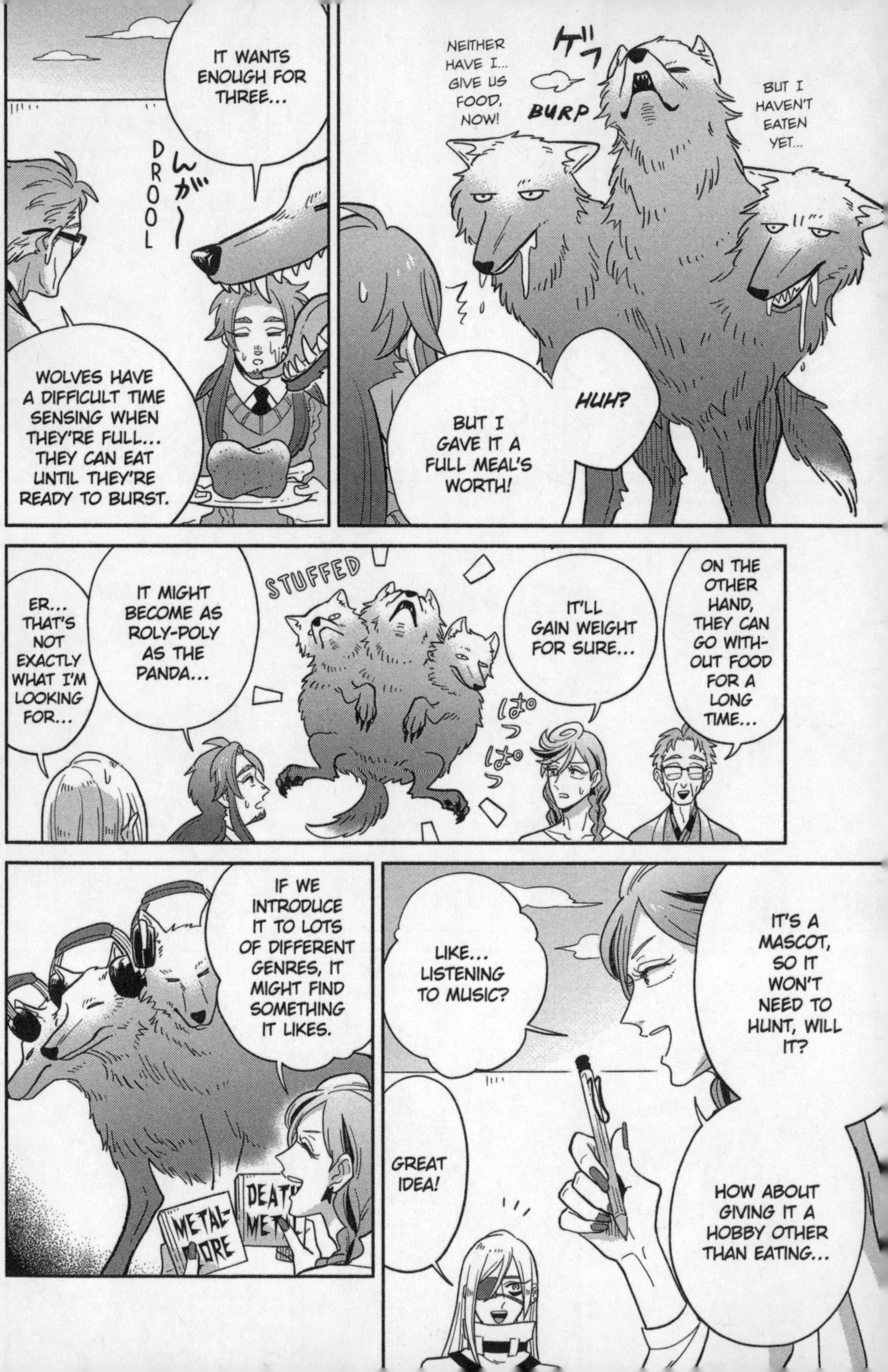
BUT I HAVEN'T EATEN YET...
ゲフ
BURP
NEITHER HAVE I... GIVE US FOOD, NOW!
HUH?
BUT I GAVE IT A FULL MEAL'S WORTH!
IT WANTS ENOUGH FOR THREE...
んガ～
DROOL
WOLVES HAVE A DIFFICULT TIME SENSING WHEN THEY'RE FULL... THEY CAN EAT UNTIL THEY'RE READY TO BURST.
ON THE OTHER HAND, THEY CAN GO WITH-OUT FOOD FOR A LONG TIME...
IT'LL GAIN WEIGHT FOR SURE...
ぱっぱっ
STUFFED
IT MIGHT BECOME AS ROLY-POLY AS THE PANDA...
ER... THAT'S NOT EXACTLY WHAT I'M LOOKING FOR...
IT'S A MASCOT, SO IT WON'T NEED TO HUNT, WILL IT?
LIKE... LISTENING TO MUSIC?
HOW ABOUT GIVING IT A HOBBY OTHER THAN EATING...
GREAT IDEA!
IF WE INTRODUCE IT TO LOTS OF DIFFERENT GENRES, IT MIGHT FIND SOMETHING IT LIKES.

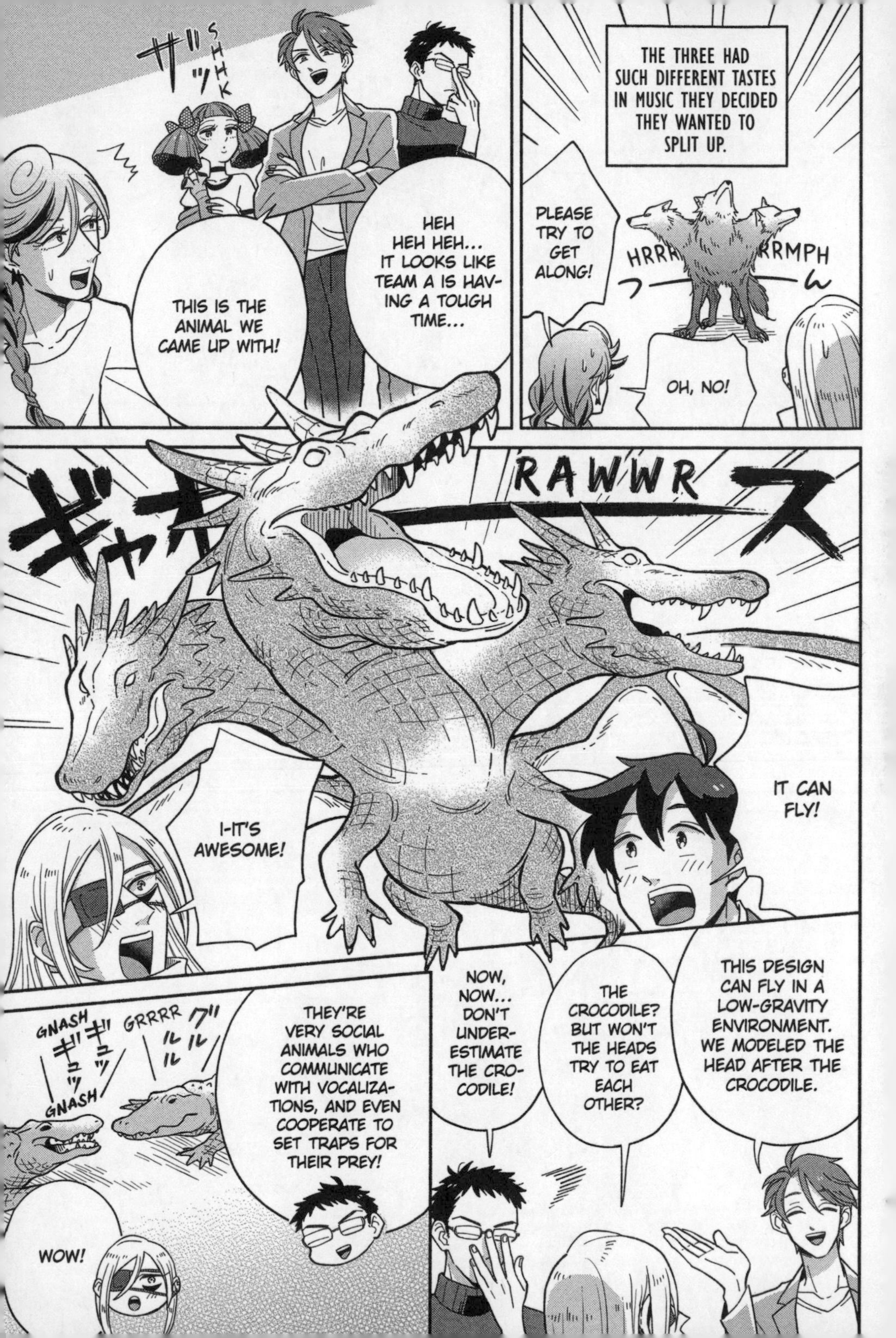
THE THREE HAD SUCH DIFFERENT TASTES IN MUSIC THEY DECIDED THEY WANTED TO SPLIT UP.
PLEASE TRY TO GET ALONG!
HRRR
RRMPH
OH, NO!
SHHK
HEH HEH HEH... IT LOOKS LIKE TEAM A IS HAVING A TOUGH TIME...
THIS IS THE ANIMAL WE CAME UP WITH!
RAWWR
IT CAN FLY!
I-IT'S AWESOME!
THIS DESIGN CAN FLY IN A LOW-GRAVITY ENVIRONMENT. WE MODELED THE HEAD AFTER THE CROCODILE.
THE CROCODILE? BUT WON'T THE HEADS TRY TO EAT EACH OTHER?
NOW, NOW... DON'T UNDERESTIMATE THE CROCODILE!
THEY'RE VERY SOCIAL ANIMALS WHO COMMUNICATE WITH VOCALIZATIONS, AND EVEN COOPERATE TO SET TRAPS FOR THEIR PREY!
GRRRR
GNASH
GNASH
WOW!

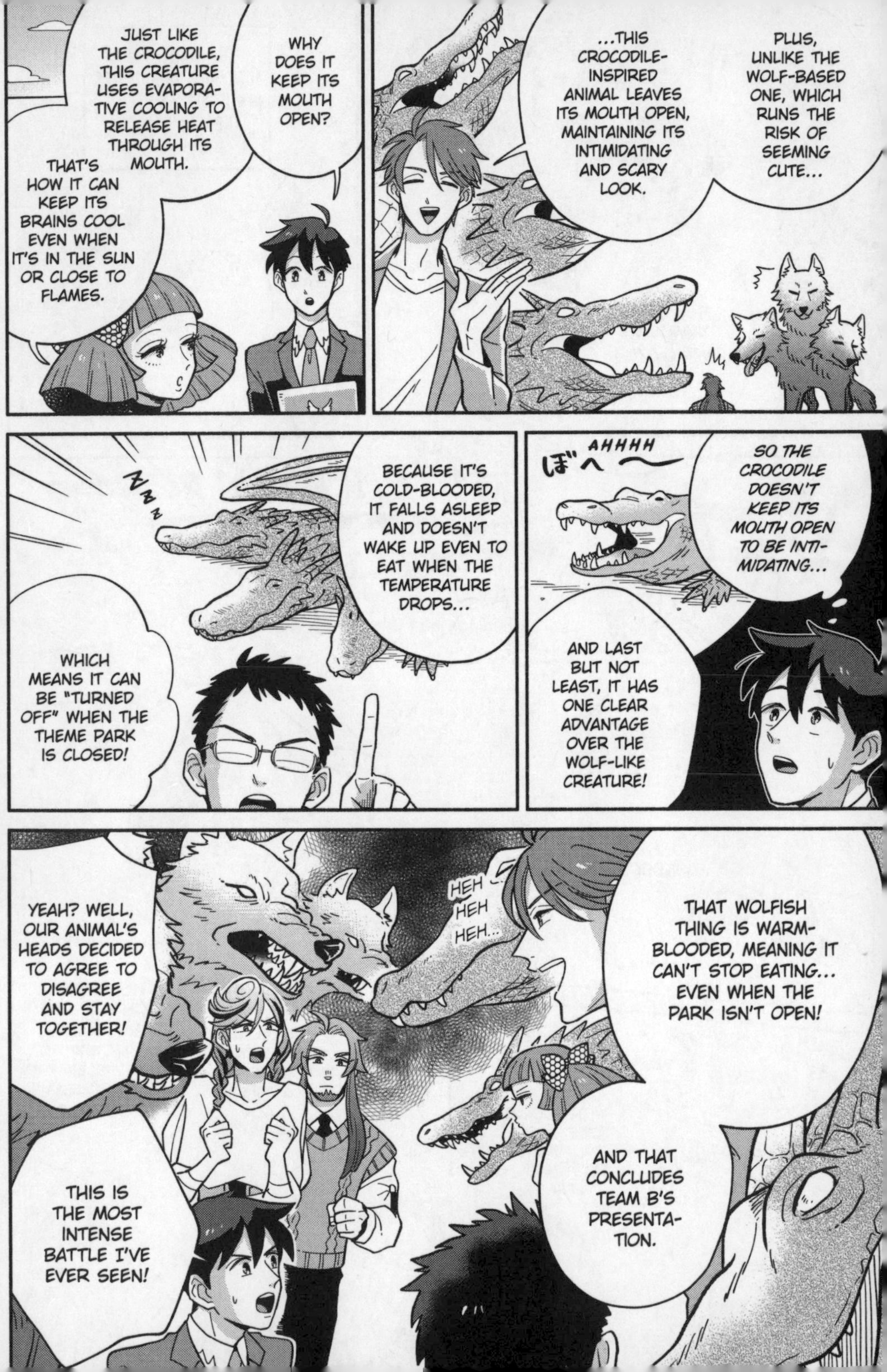
PLUS, UNLIKE THE WOLF-BASED ONE, WHICH RUNS THE RISK OF SEEMING CUTE...
...THIS CROCODILE-INSPIRED ANIMAL LEAVES ITS MOUTH OPEN, MAINTAINING ITS INTIMIDATING AND SCARY LOOK.
WHY DOES IT KEEP ITS MOUTH OPEN?
JUST LIKE THE CROCODILE, THIS CREATURE USES EVAPORATIVE COOLING TO RELEASE HEAT THROUGH ITS MOUTH.
THAT'S HOW IT CAN KEEP ITS BRAINS COOL EVEN WHEN IT'S IN THE SUN OR CLOSE TO FLAMES.
SO THE CROCODILE DOESN'T KEEP ITS MOUTH OPEN TO BE INTIMIDATING...
AHHHH
ぼへ〜
AND LAST BUT NOT LEAST, IT HAS ONE CLEAR ADVANTAGE OVER THE WOLF-LIKE CREATURE!
BECAUSE IT'S COLD-BLOODED, IT FALLS ASLEEP AND DOESN'T WAKE UP EVEN TO EAT WHEN THE TEMPERATURE DROPS...
ZZZ
WHICH MEANS IT CAN BE "TURNED OFF" WHEN THE THEME PARK IS CLOSED!
THAT WOLFISH THING IS WARM-BLOODED, MEANING IT CAN'T STOP EATING... EVEN WHEN THE PARK ISN'T OPEN!
HEH HEH HEH...
YEAH? WELL, OUR ANIMAL'S HEADS DECIDED TO AGREE TO DISAGREE AND STAY TOGETHER!
AND THAT CONCLUDES TEAM B'S PRESENTATION.
THIS IS THE MOST INTENSE BATTLE I'VE EVER SEEN!

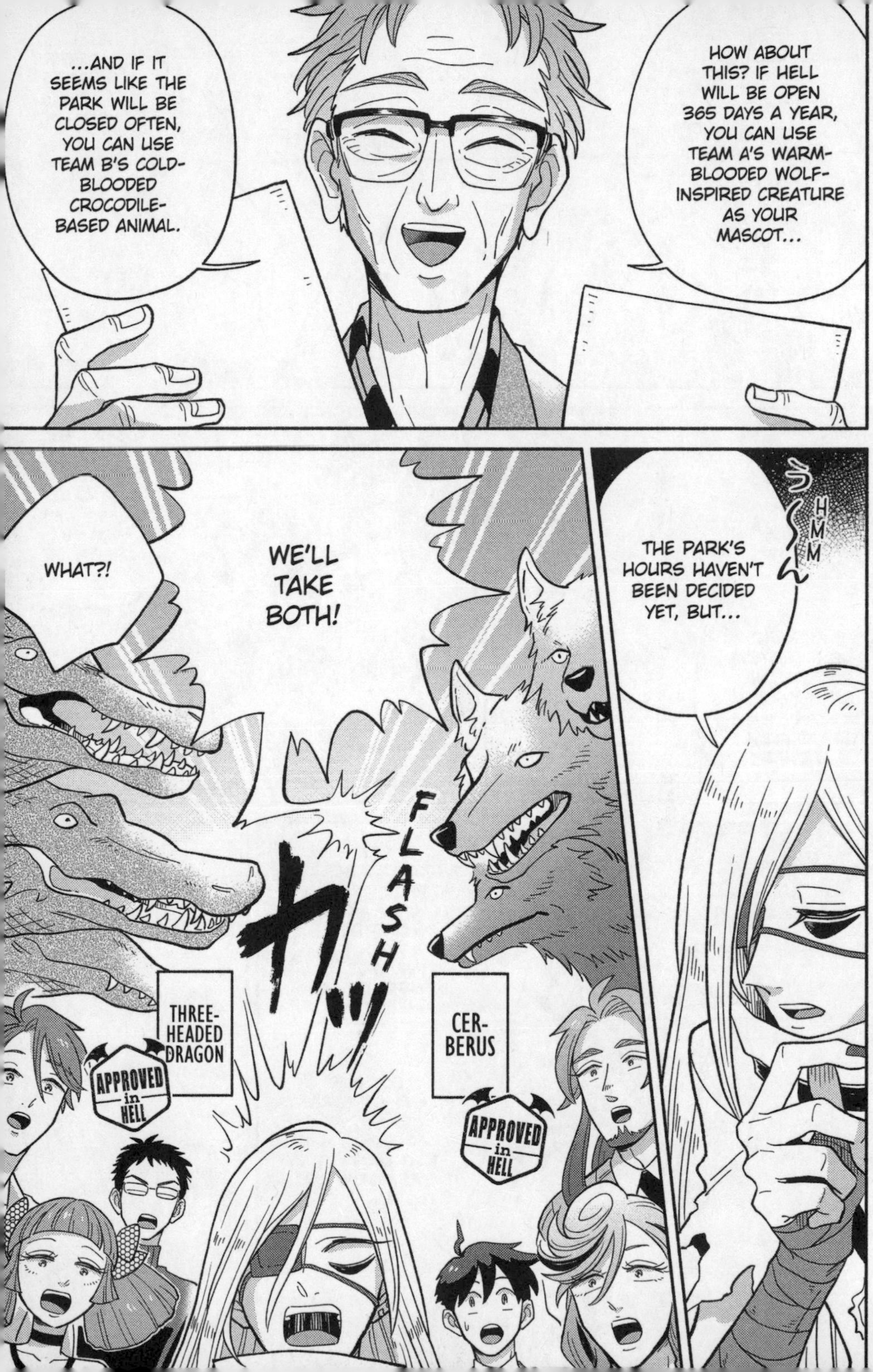
HOW ABOUT THIS? IF HELL WILL BE OPEN 365 DAYS A YEAR, YOU CAN USE TEAM A'S WARM-BLOODED WOLF-INSPIRED CREATURE AS YOUR MASCOT...
...AND IF IT SEEMS LIKE THE PARK WILL BE CLOSED OFTEN, YOU CAN USE TEAM B'S COLD-BLOODED CROCODILE-BASED ANIMAL.
う〜ん
HMM
THE PARK'S HOURS HAVEN'T BEEN DECIDED YET, BUT...
WE'LL TAKE BOTH!
WHAT?!
カッ
FLASH
CER-BERUS
APPROVED in HELL
THREE-HEADED DRAGON
APPROVED in HELL

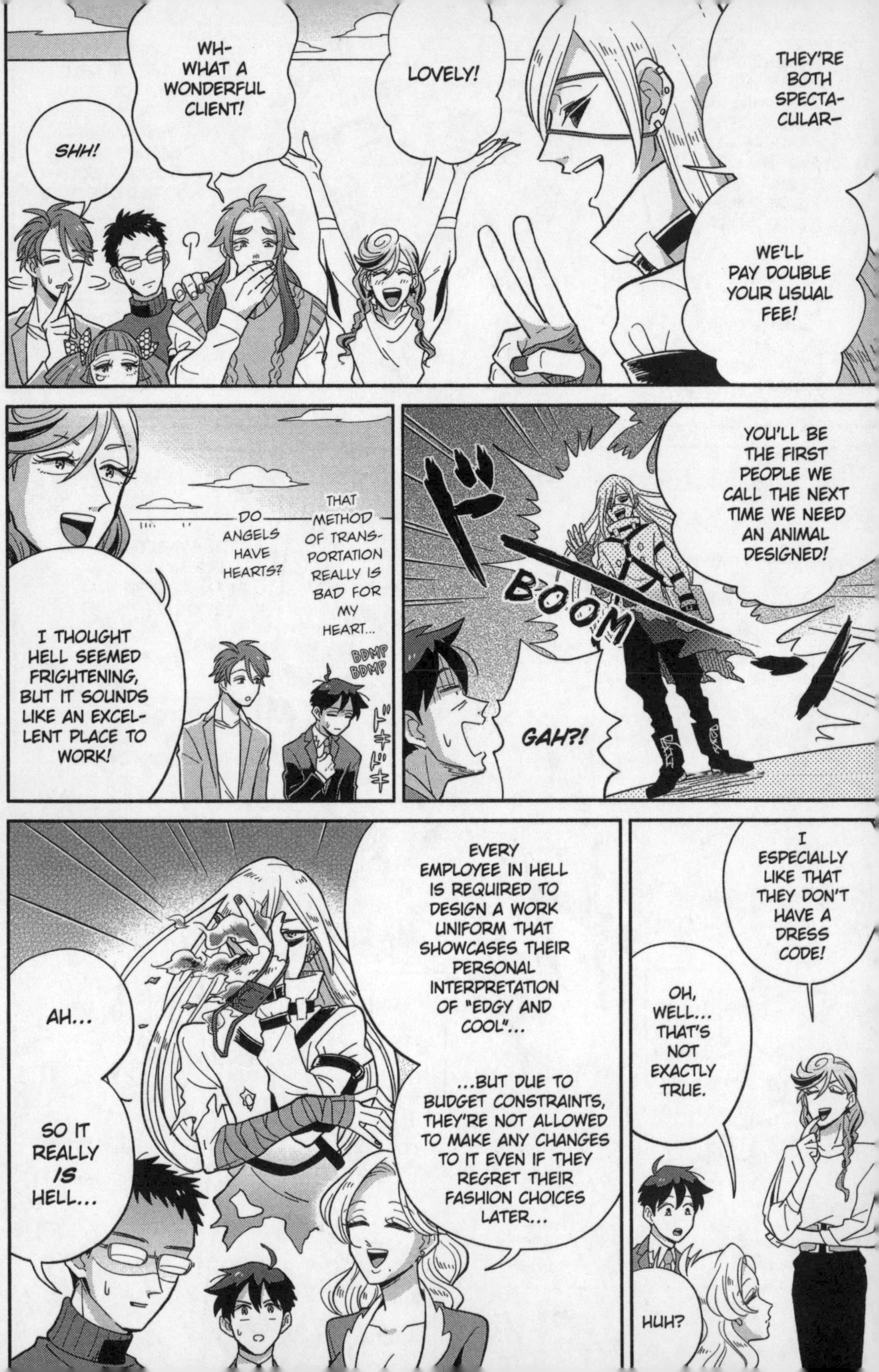
THEY'RE BOTH SPECTACULAR-
WE'LL PAY DOUBLE YOUR USUAL FEE!
LOVELY!
WH- WHAT A WONDERFUL CLIENT!
SHH!
YOU'LL BE THE FIRST PEOPLE WE CALL THE NEXT TIME WE NEED AN ANIMAL DESIGNED!
ド
BOOM
GAH?!
THAT METHOD OF TRANSPORTATION REALLY IS BAD FOR MY HEART...
BDMP BDMP
ドキドキ
DO ANGELS HAVE HEARTS?
I THOUGHT HELL SEEMED FRIGHTENING, BUT IT SOUNDS LIKE AN EXCELLENT PLACE TO WORK!
I ESPECIALLY LIKE THAT THEY DON'T HAVE A DRESS CODE!
OH, WELL... THAT'S NOT EXACTLY TRUE.
HUH?
EVERY EMPLOYEE IN HELL IS REQUIRED TO DESIGN A WORK UNIFORM THAT SHOWCASES THEIR PERSONAL INTERPRETATION OF "EDGY AND COOL"...
...BUT DUE TO BUDGET CONSTRAINTS, THEY'RE NOT ALLOWED TO MAKE ANY CHANGES TO IT EVEN IF THEY REGRET THEIR FASHION CHOICES LATER...
AH...
SO IT REALLY *IS* HELL...

THE ENCYCLOPEDIA OF
REAL ANIMALS 15

ANIMAL 42	WOLF

Three timber wolves playing in Montana, USA. (Not a Cerberus).

THE REAL THING

Photo: Minden Pictures/Aflo

Most of the animals commonly referred to as wolves are in the timber or gray wolf family. Japan was once home to subspecies like the now-extinct Ezo wolf, which inhabited Hokkaido but was killed as a livestock predator in the early 1900s, and the Japanese wolf, which inhabited Honshu and Shikoku but is also thought to have gone extinct (though some sightings are still reported today). The hierarchical relationships within a pack are clearly defined, and those at the top are the first to eat once prey is brought down. The wolves' distinct howling is used to defend the pack's territory from neighboring packs. Territories can measure up to 1000 km^2 (386 mi^2), or roughly equal to 1000 times the combined areas of the Tokyo Disneyland and Tokyo DisneySea theme parks.

[Name]	*Canis lupus*
[Classification]	Class: Mammalia
	Order: Carnivora
	Family: Canidae
	Genus: *Canis*
[Habitat]	Northern Hemisphere
[Length]	1-1.6 m (3.3-5.2 ft)

ANIMAL 43 | CROCODILE

The animals of the order Crocodilia are largely divided between crocodiles and alligators, with the former being larger and more aggressive and the latter being smaller and gentler. As cold-blooded creatures, they must frequently sun themselves to maintain their body temperature. While basking, they often open their mouths to keep the brain from overheating by releasing heat through evaporative cooling. Crocodiles feed on fish, birds, and mammals, and sometimes set up elaborate traps when hunting. The mugger crocodile, for example, hunts birds by balancing twigs on its head while keeping its body submerged in water. When the bird is lured by the potential nesting material, the mugger attacks. This behavior can only be seen during the birds' nesting season.

Crocodiles are highly social animals and have been observed to hunt in packs, with each individual being assigned a specific role. They are also very vocal, and the young communicate with their parents through a variety of calls. The order is more closely related to birds than to lizards.

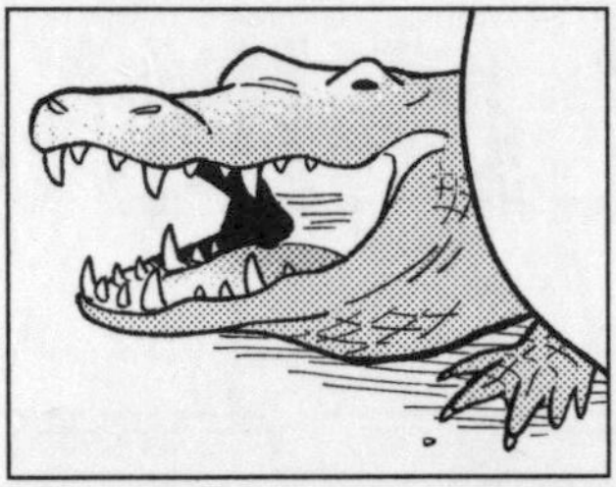

THE REAL THING

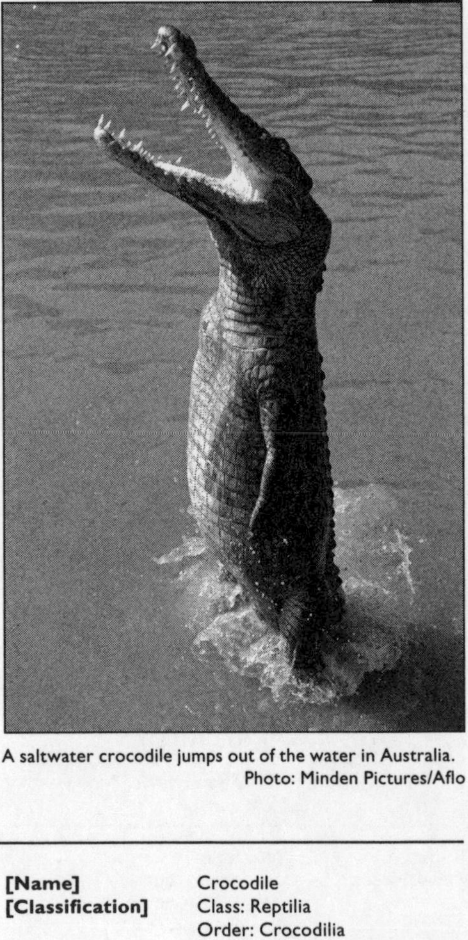

A saltwater crocodile jumps out of the water in Australia.
Photo: Minden Pictures/Aflo

[Name]	Crocodile
[Classification]	Class: Reptilia Order: Crocodilia
[Habitat]	Tropical and sub-tropical bodies of water
[Length]	1.2-7 m (6.6-23 ft)

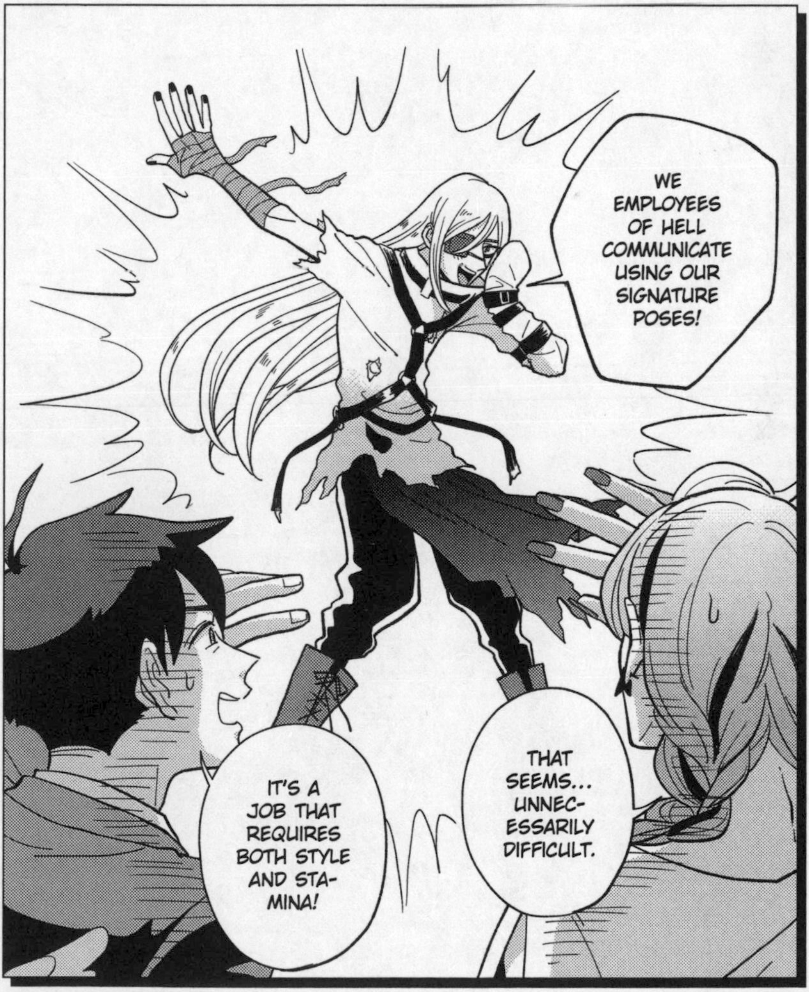
WE EMPLOYEES OF HELL COMMUNICATE USING OUR SIGNATURE POSES!
THAT SEEMS... UNNEC-ESSARILY DIFFICULT.
IT'S A JOB THAT REQUIRES BOTH STYLE AND STA-MINA!

HEAVEN'S
DESIGN TEAM

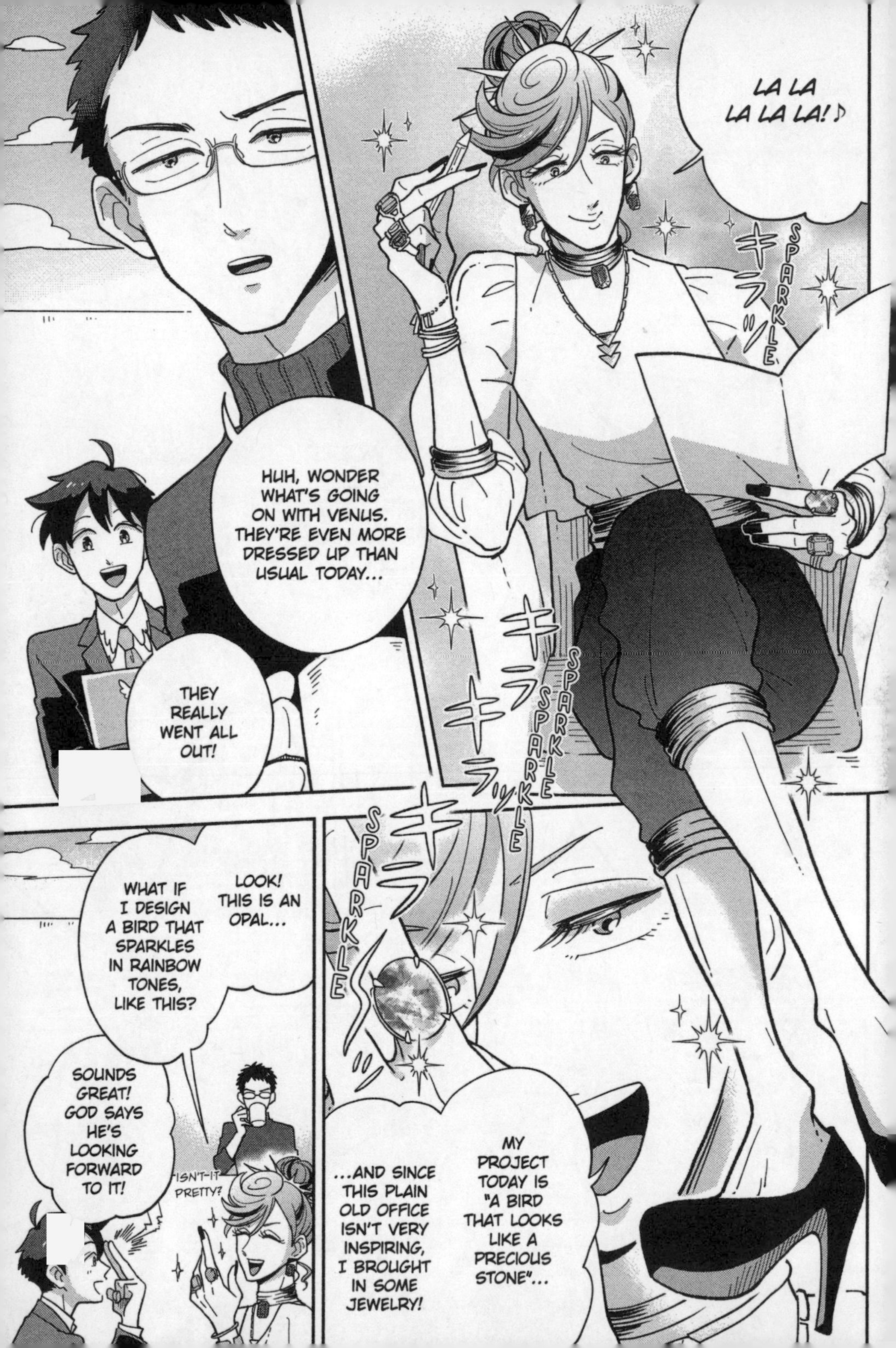
LA LA LA LA LA! ♪
SPARKLE
SPARKLE SPARKLE
HUH, WONDER WHAT'S GOING ON WITH VENUS. THEY'RE EVEN MORE DRESSED UP THAN USUAL TODAY...
THEY REALLY WENT ALL OUT!
SPARKLE SPARKLE
MY PROJECT TODAY IS "A BIRD THAT LOOKS LIKE A PRECIOUS STONE"...
...AND SINCE THIS PLAIN OLD OFFICE ISN'T VERY INSPIRING, I BROUGHT IN SOME JEWELRY!
LOOK! THIS IS AN OPAL...
WHAT IF I DESIGN A BIRD THAT SPARKLES IN RAINBOW TONES, LIKE THIS?
ISN'T IT PRETTY?
SOUNDS GREAT! GOD SAYS HE'S LOOKING FORWARD TO IT!

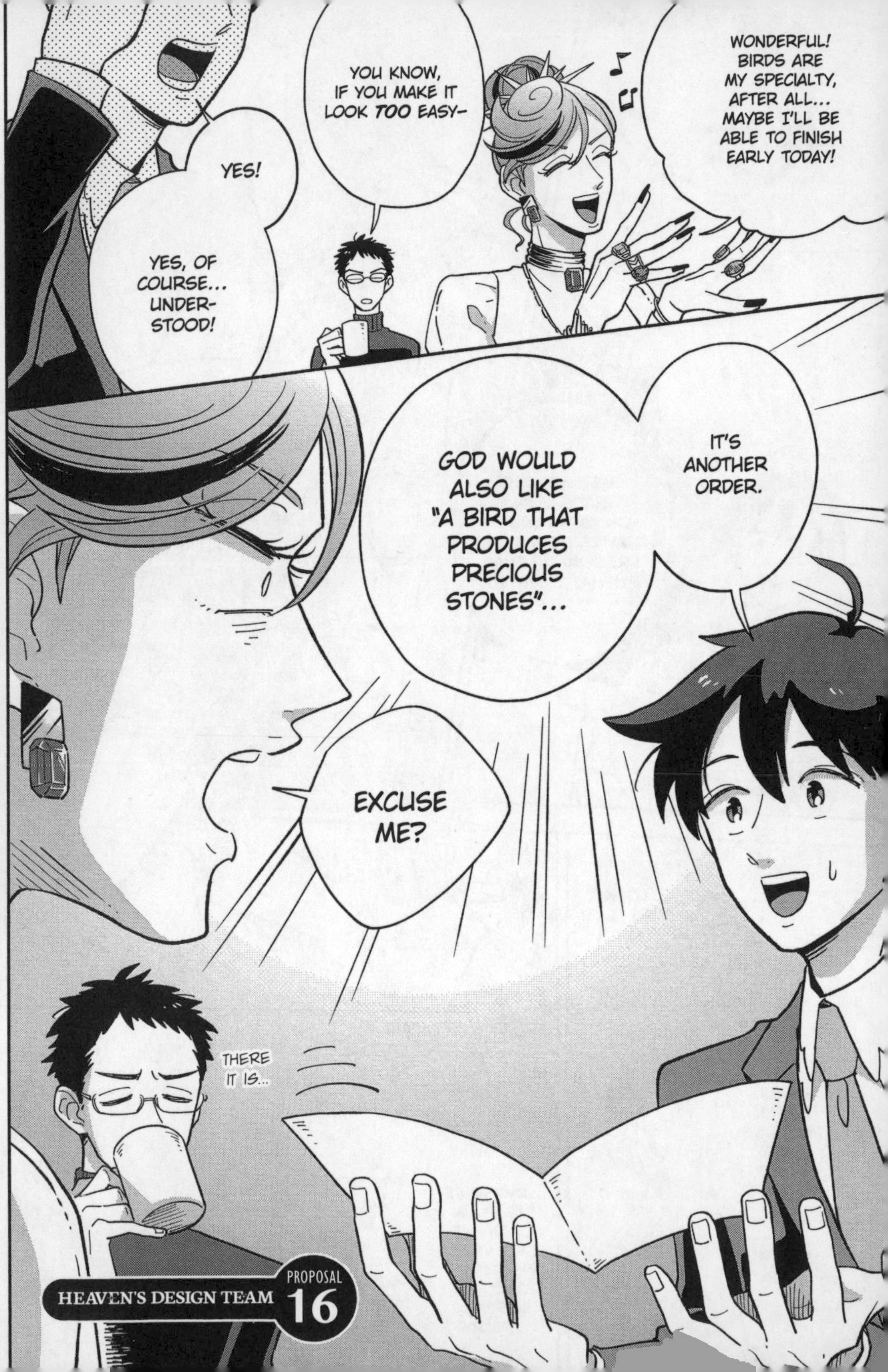
WONDERFUL! BIRDS ARE MY SPECIALTY, AFTER ALL... MAYBE I'LL BE ABLE TO FINISH EARLY TODAY!
YOU KNOW, IF YOU MAKE IT LOOK *TOO* EASY-
YES!
YES, OF COURSE... UNDER-STOOD!
IT'S ANOTHER ORDER.
GOD WOULD ALSO LIKE "A BIRD THAT PRODUCES PRECIOUS STONES"...
EXCUSE ME?
THERE IT IS...
HEAVEN'S DESIGN TEAM
PROPOSAL 16

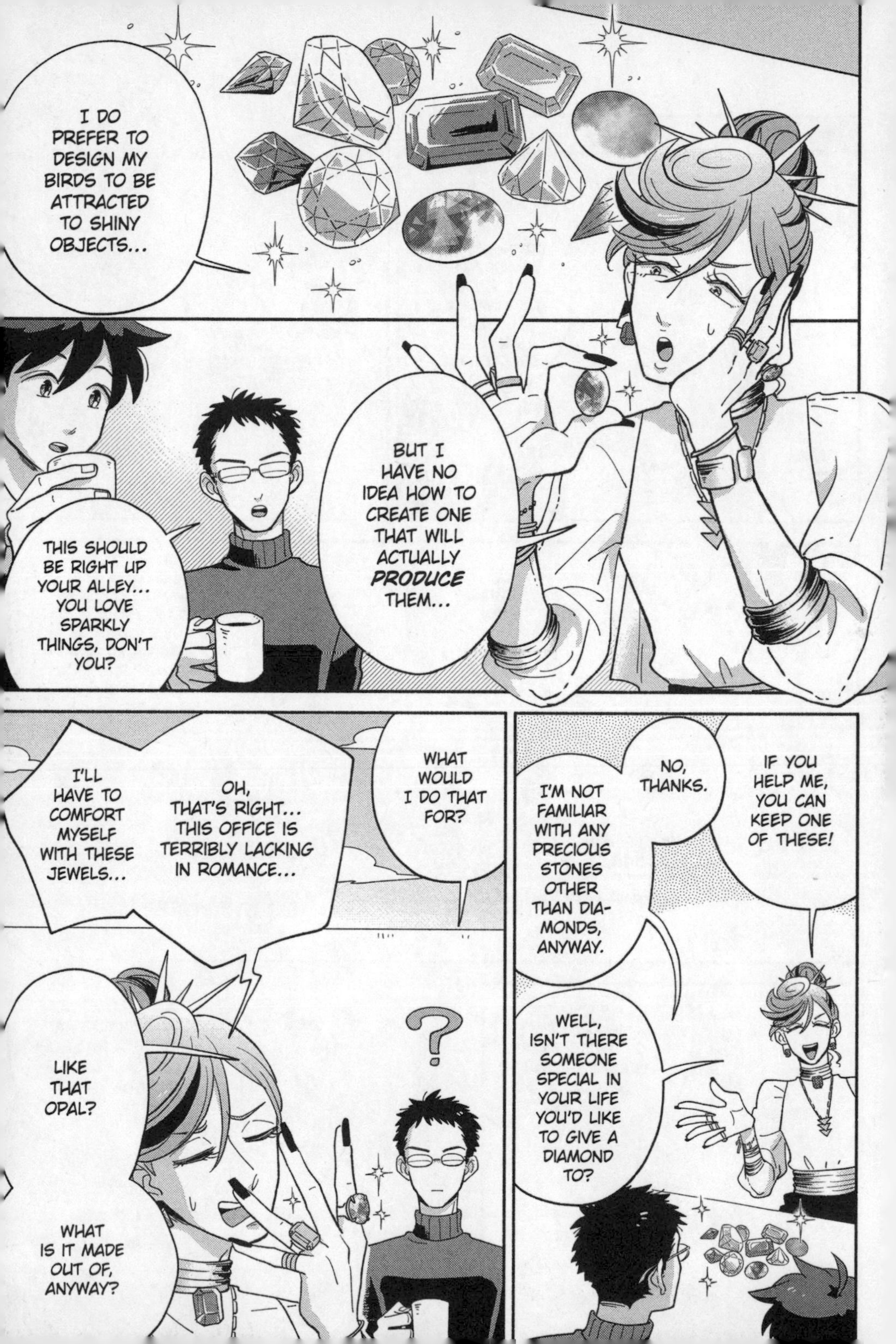
I DO PREFER TO DESIGN MY BIRDS TO BE ATTRACTED TO SHINY OBJECTS...
BUT I HAVE NO IDEA HOW TO CREATE ONE THAT WILL ACTUALLY ***PRODUCE*** THEM...
THIS SHOULD BE RIGHT UP YOUR ALLEY... YOU LOVE SPARKLY THINGS, DON'T YOU?
IF YOU HELP ME, YOU CAN KEEP ONE OF THESE!
NO, THANKS.
I'M NOT FAMILIAR WITH ANY PRECIOUS STONES OTHER THAN DIA-MONDS, ANYWAY.
WELL, ISN'T THERE SOMEONE SPECIAL IN YOUR LIFE YOU'D LIKE TO GIVE A DIAMOND TO?
WHAT WOULD I DO THAT FOR?
OH, THAT'S RIGHT... THIS OFFICE IS TERRIBLY LACKING IN ROMANCE...
I'LL HAVE TO COMFORT MYSELF WITH THESE JEWELS...
?
LIKE THAT OPAL?
WHAT IS IT MADE OUT OF, ANYWAY?

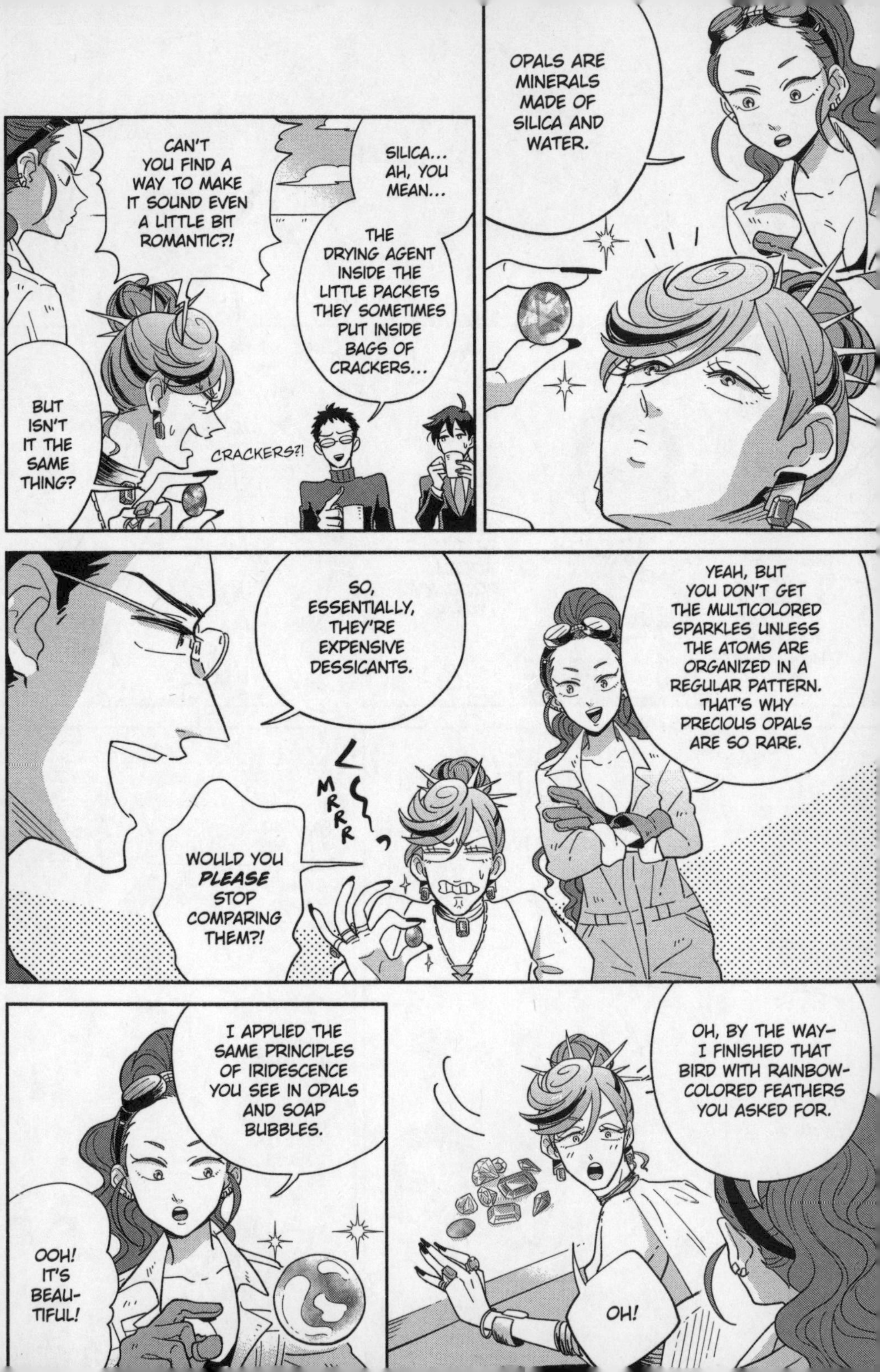
OPALS ARE MINERALS MADE OF SILICA AND WATER.
SILICA... AH, YOU MEAN...
THE DRYING AGENT INSIDE THE LITTLE PACKETS THEY SOMETIMES PUT INSIDE BAGS OF CRACKERS...
CRACKERS?!
BUT ISN'T IT THE SAME THING?
CAN'T YOU FIND A WAY TO MAKE IT SOUND EVEN A LITTLE BIT ROMANTIC?!
YEAH, BUT YOU DON'T GET THE MULTICOLORED SPARKLES UNLESS THE ATOMS ARE ORGANIZED IN A REGULAR PATTERN. THAT'S WHY PRECIOUS OPALS ARE SO RARE.
SO, ESSENTIALLY, THEY'RE EXPENSIVE DESSICANTS.
MRRR
WOULD YOU *PLEASE* STOP COMPARING THEM?!
OH, BY THE WAY— I FINISHED THAT BIRD WITH RAINBOW-COLORED FEATHERS YOU ASKED FOR.
OH!
I APPLIED THE SAME PRINCIPLES OF IRIDESCENCE YOU SEE IN OPALS AND SOAP BUBBLES.
OOH! IT'S BEAU-TIFUL!

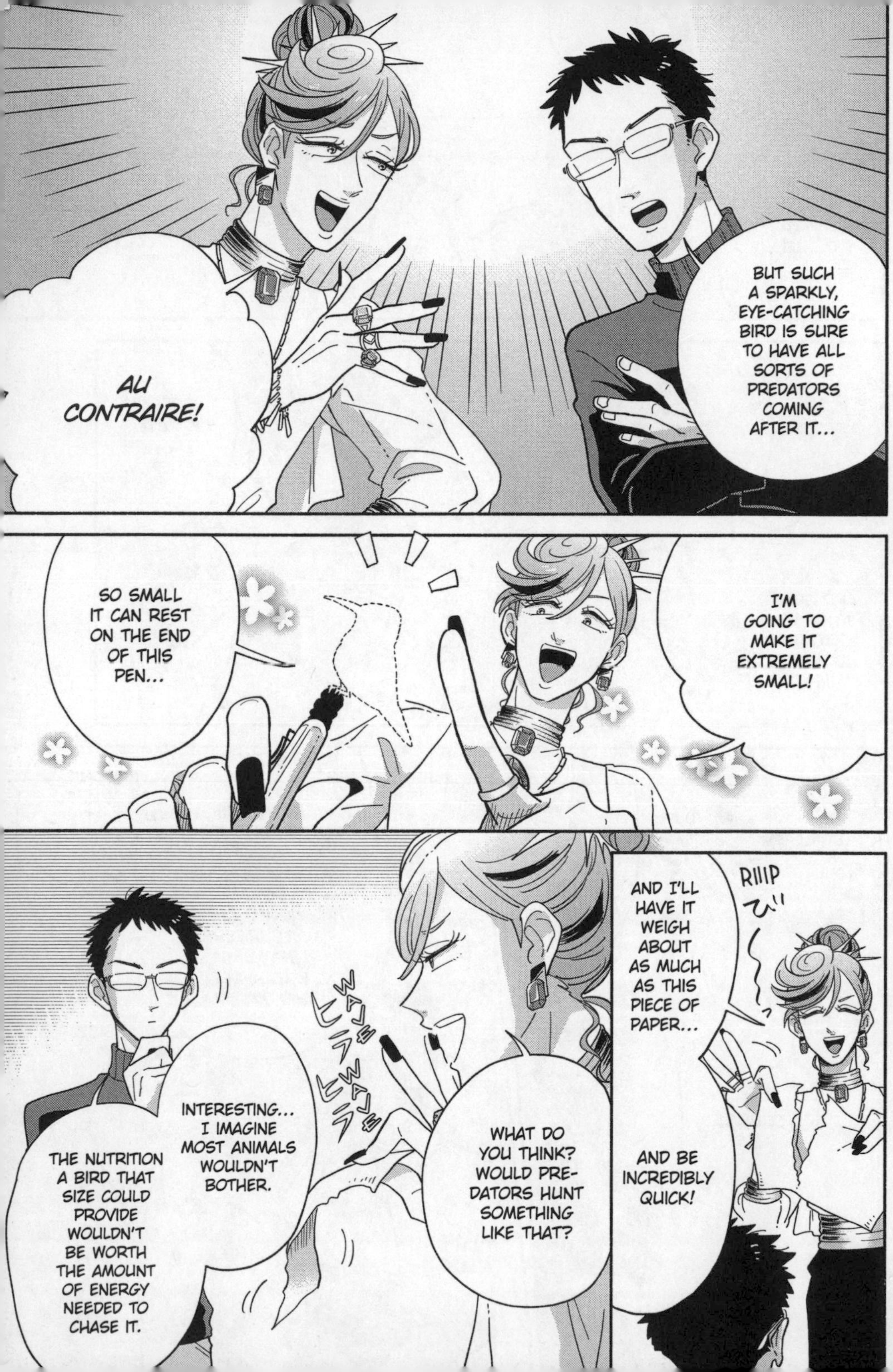
BUT SUCH A SPARKLY, EYE-CATCHING BIRD IS SURE TO HAVE ALL SORTS OF PREDATORS COMING AFTER IT...
AU CONTRAIRE!
I'M GOING TO MAKE IT EXTREMELY SMALL!
SO SMALL IT CAN REST ON THE END OF THIS PEN...
RIIIP
びッ
AND I'LL HAVE IT WEIGH ABOUT AS MUCH AS THIS PIECE OF PAPER...
AND BE INCREDIBLY QUICK!
WAVE ヒラ WAVE ヒラ
WHAT DO YOU THINK? WOULD PRE-DATORS HUNT SOMETHING LIKE THAT?
INTERESTING... I IMAGINE MOST ANIMALS WOULDN'T BOTHER.
THE NUTRITION A BIRD THAT SIZE COULD PROVIDE WOULDN'T BE WORTH THE AMOUNT OF ENERGY NEEDED TO CHASE IT.

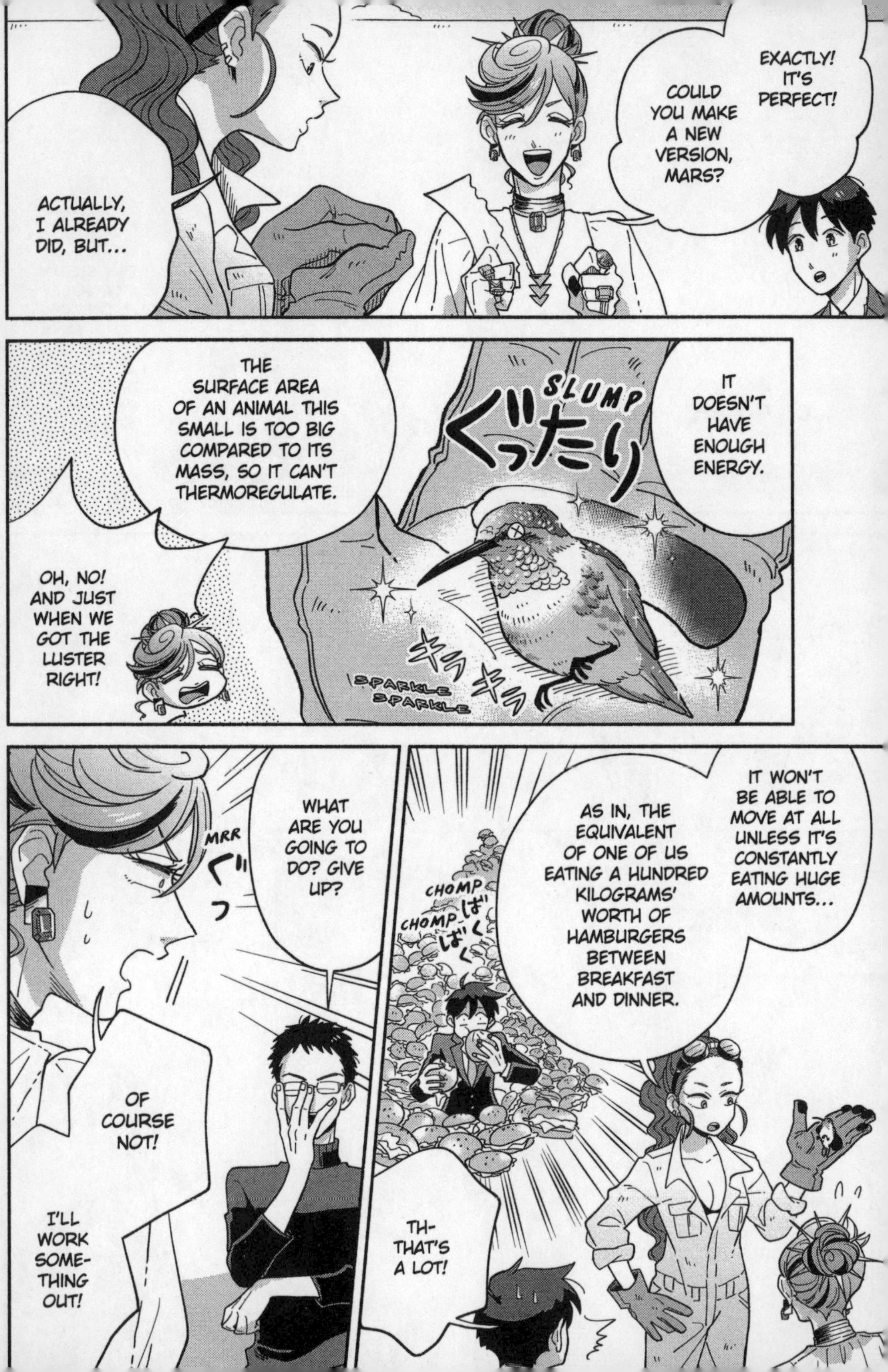
EXACTLY! IT'S PERFECT!
COULD YOU MAKE A NEW VERSION, MARS?
ACTUALLY, I ALREADY DID, BUT...
IT DOESN'T HAVE ENOUGH ENERGY.
SLUMP
ぐったり
THE SURFACE AREA OF AN ANIMAL THIS SMALL IS TOO BIG COMPARED TO ITS MASS, SO IT CAN'T THERMOREGULATE.
キラキラ
SPARKLE SPARKLE
OH, NO! AND JUST WHEN WE GOT THE LUSTER RIGHT!
IT WON'T BE ABLE TO MOVE AT ALL UNLESS IT'S CONSTANTLY EATING HUGE AMOUNTS...
AS IN, THE EQUIVALENT OF ONE OF US EATING A HUNDRED KILOGRAMS' WORTH OF HAMBURGERS BETWEEN BREAKFAST AND DINNER.
CHOMP CHOMP
ばくばく
TH- THAT'S A LOT!
WHAT ARE YOU GOING TO DO? GIVE UP?
MRR
ぐっ
OF COURSE NOT!
I'LL WORK SOMETHING OUT!

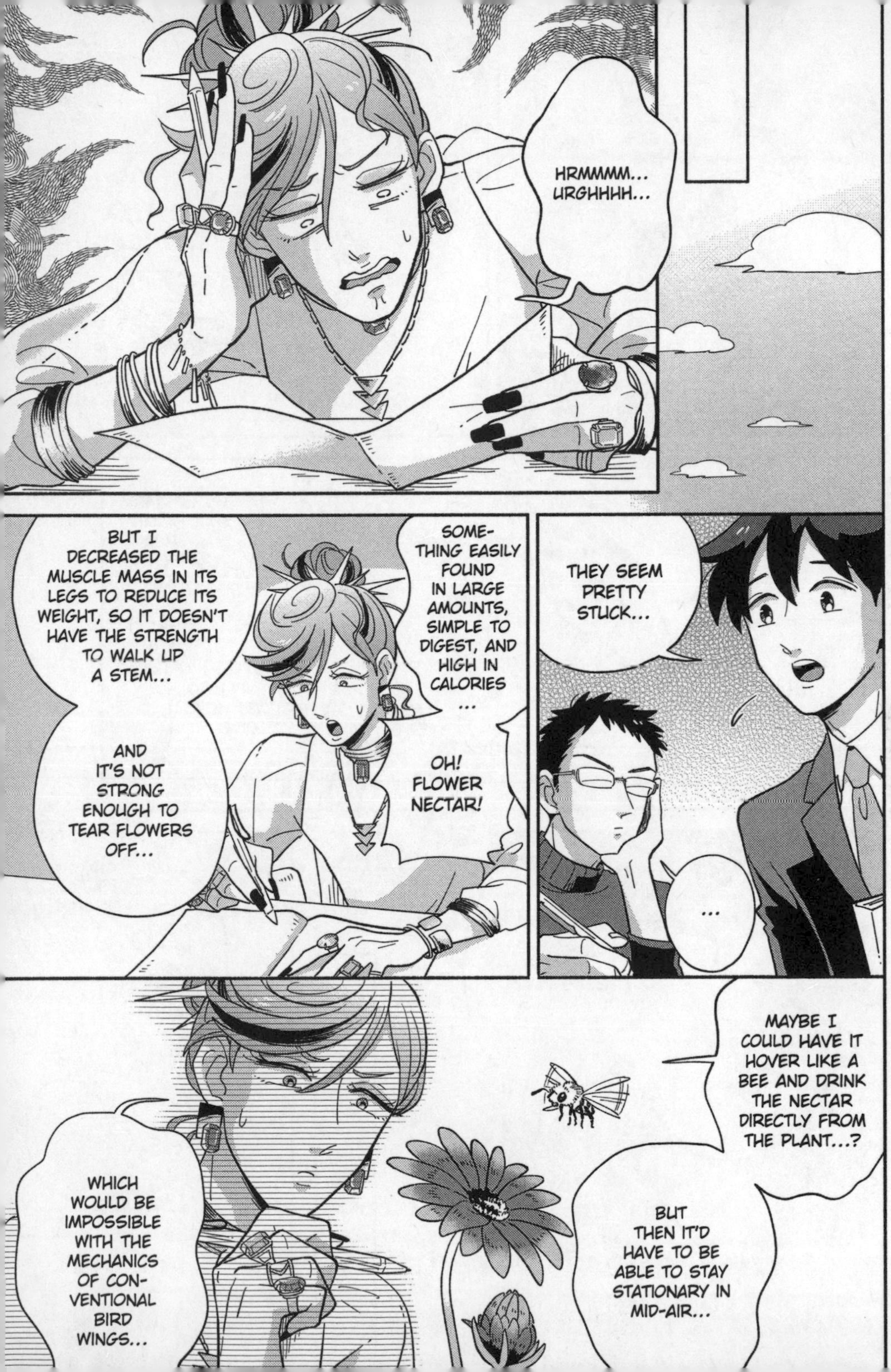
HRMMMM... URGHHHH...
THEY SEEM PRETTY STUCK...
...
SOMETHING EASILY FOUND IN LARGE AMOUNTS, SIMPLE TO DIGEST, AND HIGH IN CALORIES ...
OH! FLOWER NECTAR!
BUT I DECREASED THE MUSCLE MASS IN ITS LEGS TO REDUCE ITS WEIGHT, SO IT DOESN'T HAVE THE STRENGTH TO WALK UP A STEM...
AND IT'S NOT STRONG ENOUGH TO TEAR FLOWERS OFF...
MAYBE I COULD HAVE IT HOVER LIKE A BEE AND DRINK THE NECTAR DIRECTLY FROM THE PLANT...?
BUT THEN IT'D HAVE TO BE ABLE TO STAY STATIONARY IN MID-AIR...
WHICH WOULD BE IMPOSSIBLE WITH THE MECHANICS OF CONVENTIONAL BIRD WINGS...

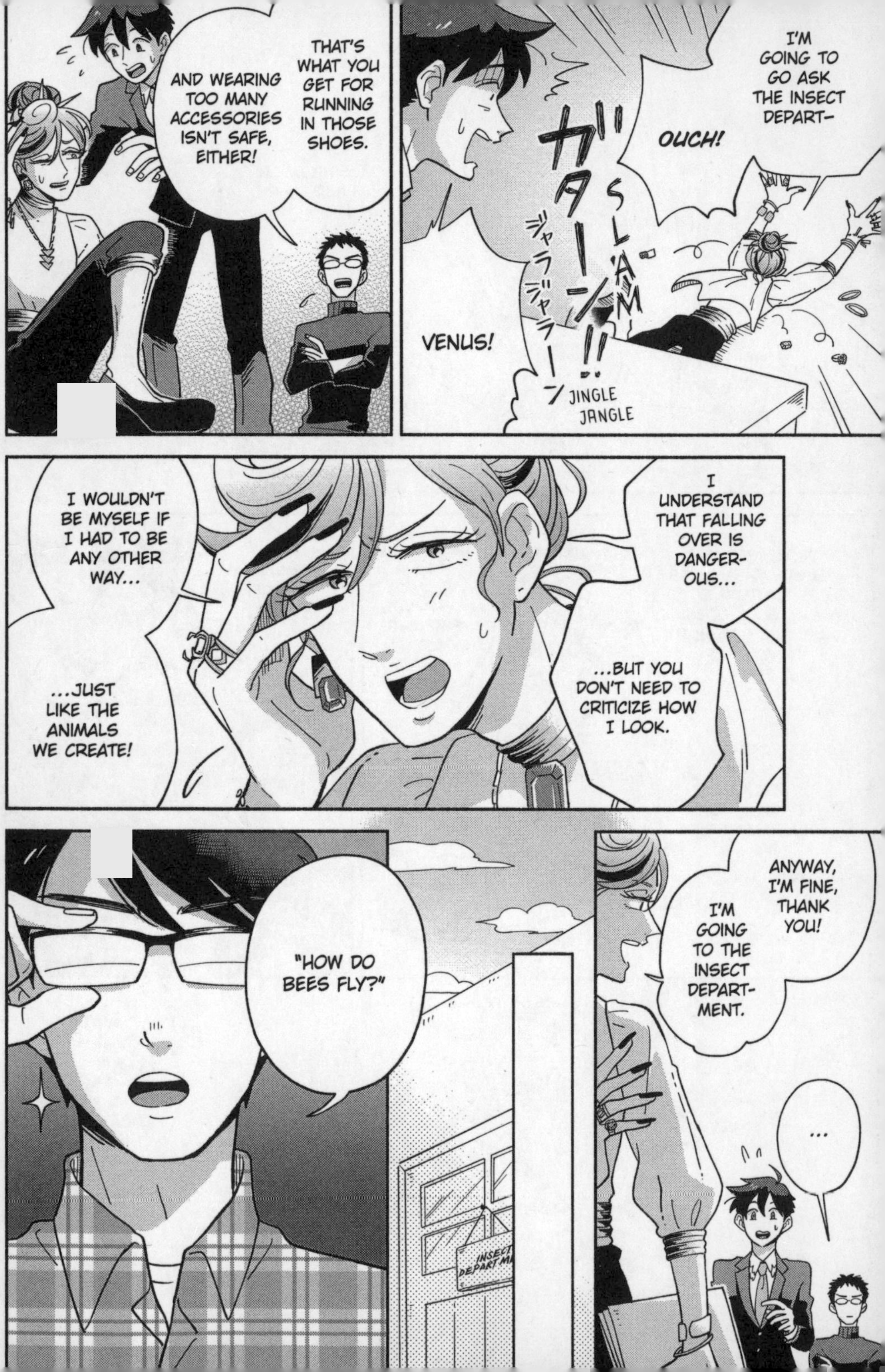
I'M GOING TO GO ASK THE INSECT DEPART-
OUCH!
ガターン!!
SLAM
ジャラジャラーン
JINGLE JANGLE
VENUS!
THAT'S WHAT YOU GET FOR RUNNING IN THOSE SHOES.
AND WEARING TOO MANY ACCESSORIES ISN'T SAFE, EITHER!
I UNDERSTAND THAT FALLING OVER IS DANGER-OUS...
...BUT YOU DON'T NEED TO CRITICIZE HOW I LOOK.
I WOULDN'T BE MYSELF IF I HAD TO BE ANY OTHER WAY...
...JUST LIKE THE ANIMALS WE CREATE!
ANYWAY, I'M FINE, THANK YOU!
I'M GOING TO THE INSECT DEPART-MENT.
...
"HOW DO BEES FLY?"

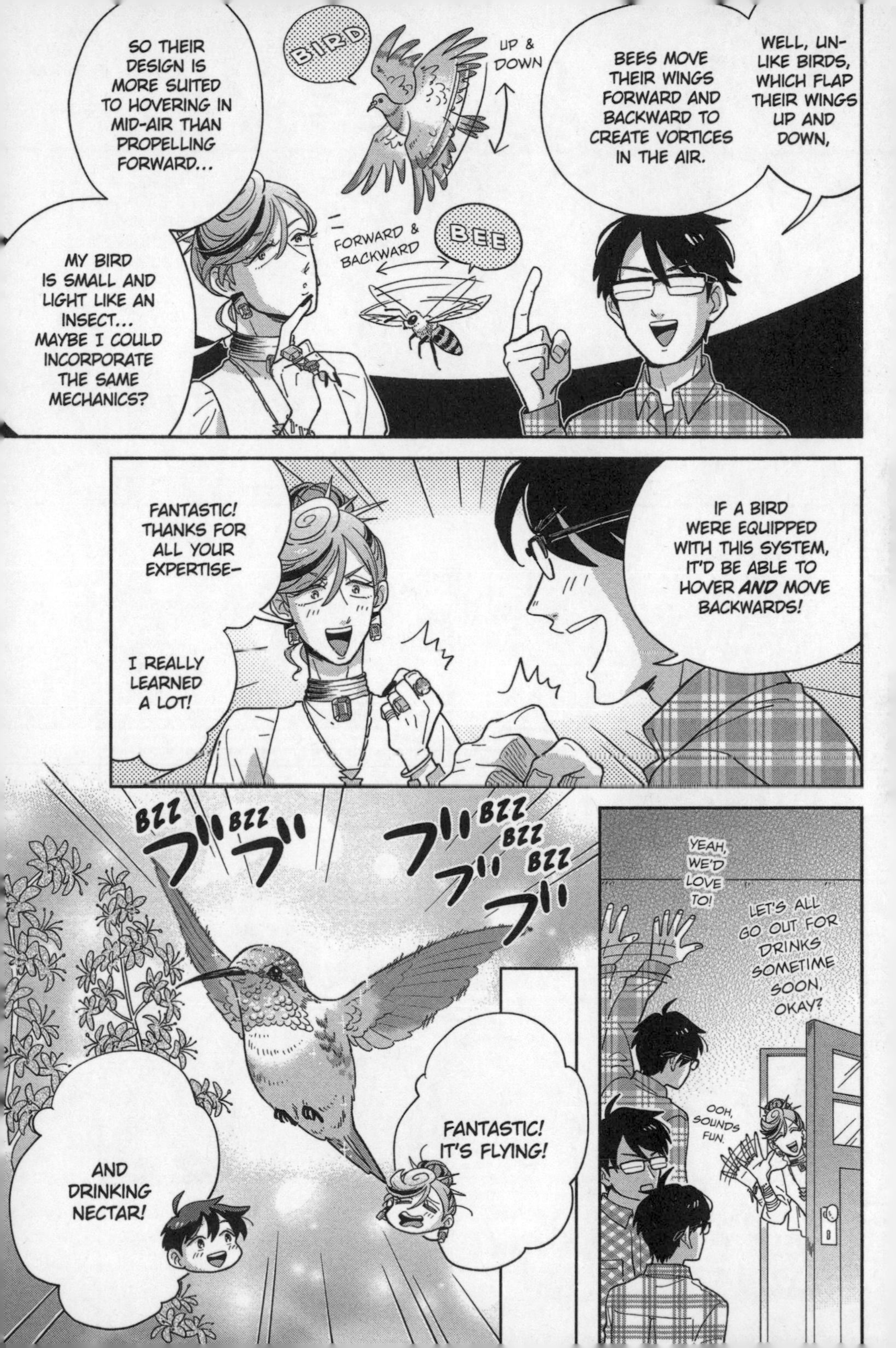
WELL, UN-LIKE BIRDS, WHICH FLAP THEIR WINGS UP AND DOWN,
BEES MOVE THEIR WINGS FORWARD AND BACKWARD TO CREATE VORTICES IN THE AIR.
UP & DOWN
BIRD
FORWARD & BACKWARD
BEE
SO THEIR DESIGN IS MORE SUITED TO HOVERING IN MID-AIR THAN PROPELLING FORWARD...
MY BIRD IS SMALL AND LIGHT LIKE AN INSECT... MAYBE I COULD INCORPORATE THE SAME MECHANICS?
IF A BIRD WERE EQUIPPED WITH THIS SYSTEM, IT'D BE ABLE TO HOVER ***AND*** MOVE BACKWARDS!
FANTASTIC! THANKS FOR ALL YOUR EXPERTISE-
I REALLY LEARNED A LOT!
LET'S ALL GO OUT FOR DRINKS SOMETIME SOON, OKAY?
YEAH, WE'D LOVE TO!
OOH, SOUNDS FUN.
ブ BZZ
ブ BZZ
ブ BZZ
ブ BZZ
ブ BZZ
ブ BZZ
FANTASTIC! IT'S FLYING!
AND DRINKING NECTAR!

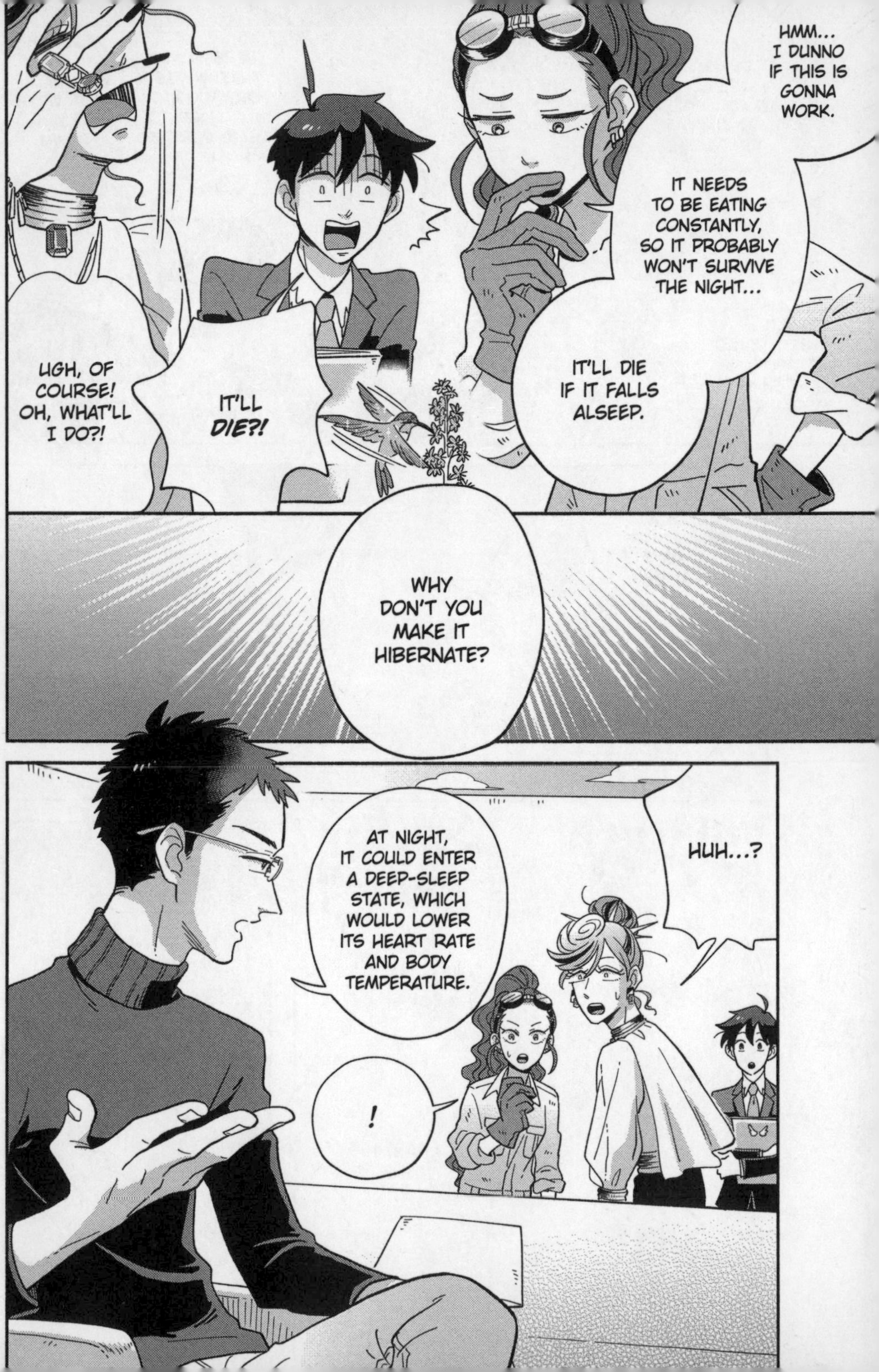
HMM... I DUNNO IF THIS IS GONNA WORK.
IT NEEDS TO BE EATING CONSTANTLY, SO IT PROBABLY WON'T SURVIVE THE NIGHT...
IT'LL DIE IF IT FALLS ALSEEP.
IT'LL *DIE?!*
UGH, OF COURSE! OH, WHAT'LL I DO?!
WHY DON'T YOU MAKE IT HIBERNATE?
HUH...?
AT NIGHT, IT COULD ENTER A DEEP-SLEEP STATE, WHICH WOULD LOWER ITS HEART RATE AND BODY TEMPERATURE.
!

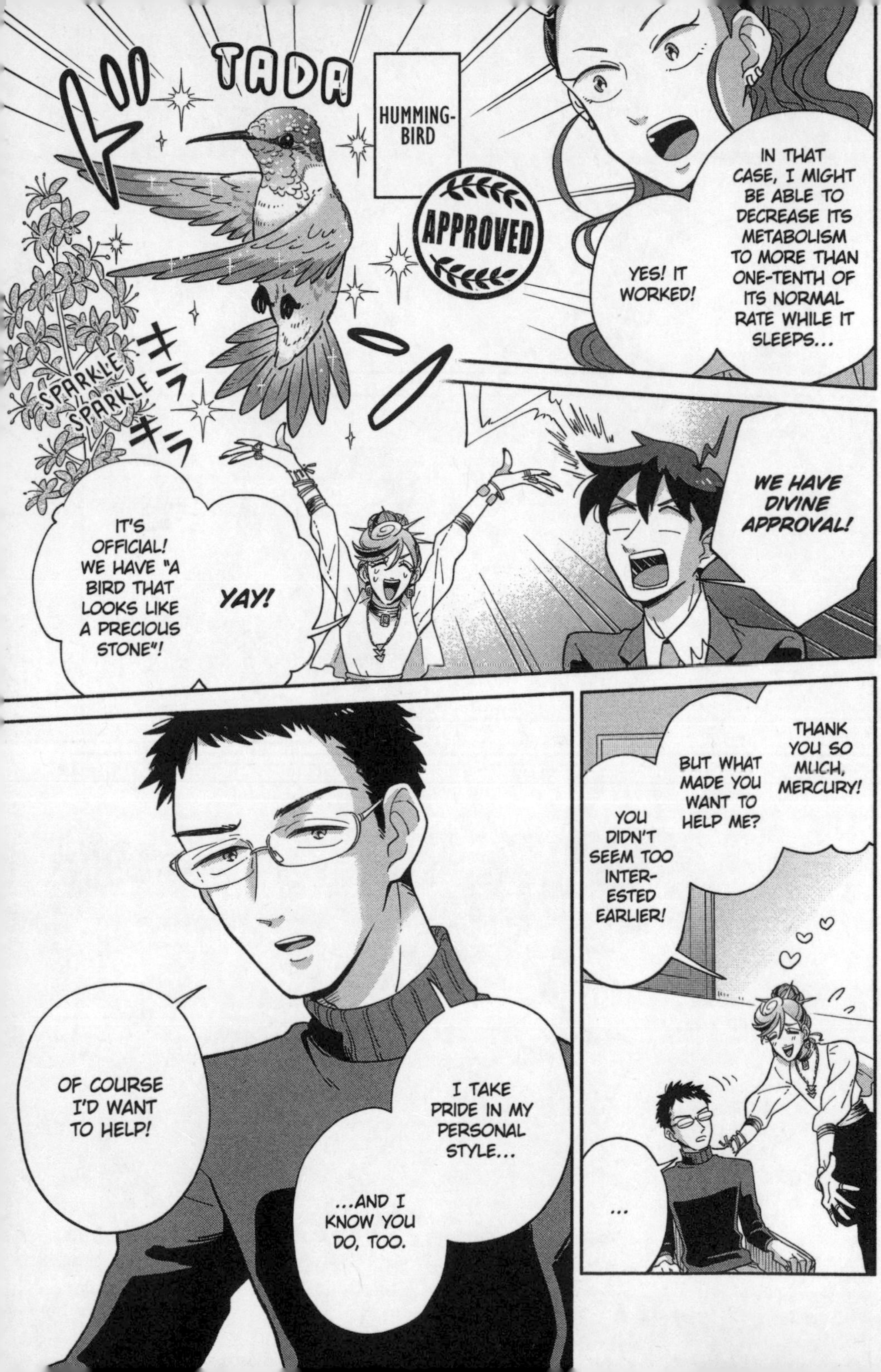
IN THAT CASE, I MIGHT BE ABLE TO DECREASE ITS METABOLISM TO MORE THAN ONE-TENTH OF ITS NORMAL RATE WHILE IT SLEEPS…
YES! IT WORKED!
TADA
HUMMING-BIRD
APPROVED
SPARKLE SPARKLE
WE HAVE DIVINE APPROVAL!
IT'S OFFICIAL! WE HAVE "A BIRD THAT LOOKS LIKE A PRECIOUS STONE"!
YAY!
THANK YOU SO MUCH, MERCURY!
BUT WHAT MADE YOU WANT TO HELP ME?
YOU DIDN'T SEEM TOO INTER-ESTED EARLIER!
…
OF COURSE I'D WANT TO HELP!
I TAKE PRIDE IN MY PERSONAL STYLE…
…AND I KNOW YOU DO, TOO.

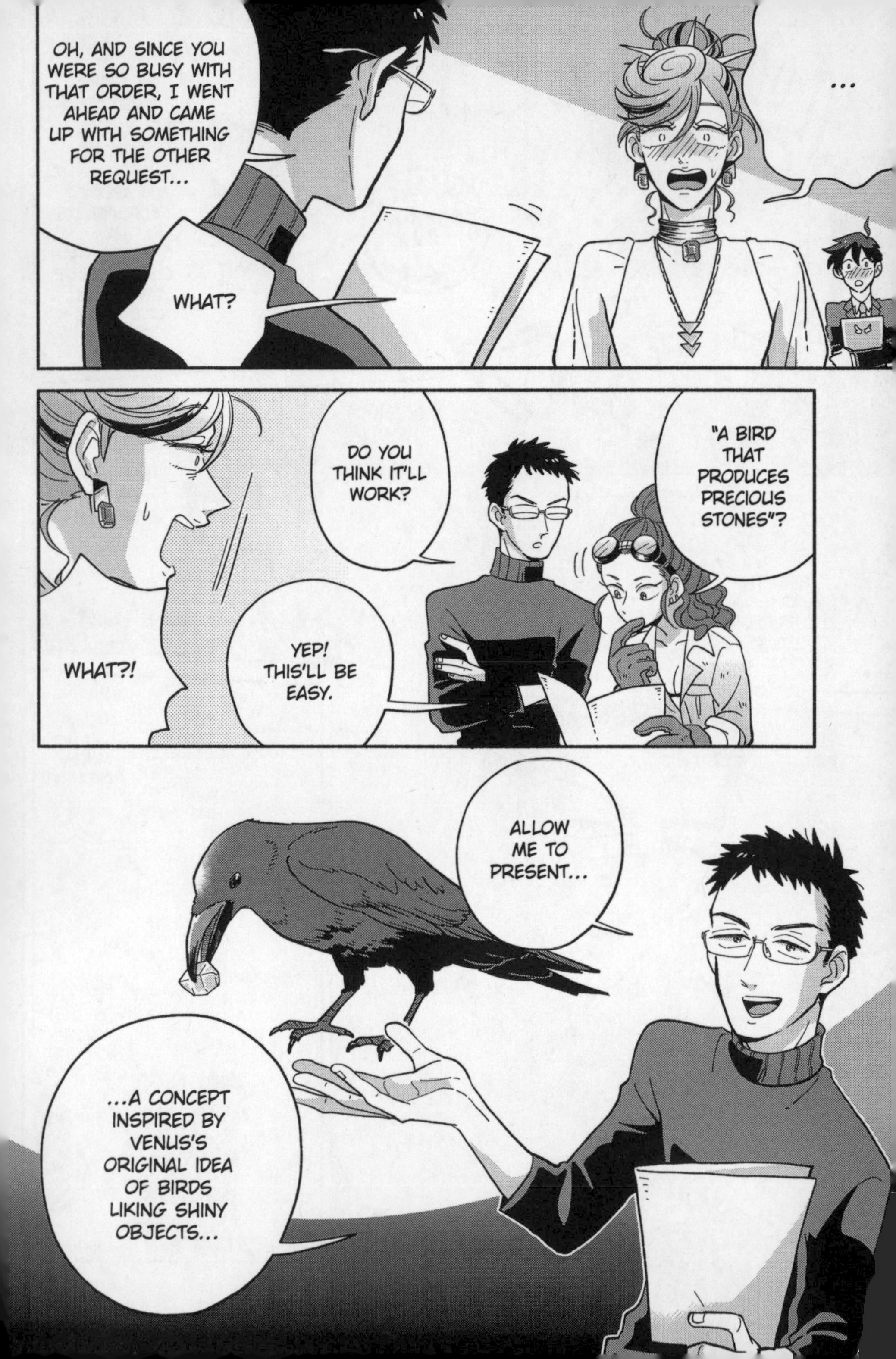
...
OH, AND SINCE YOU WERE SO BUSY WITH THAT ORDER, I WENT AHEAD AND CAME UP WITH SOMETHING FOR THE OTHER REQUEST...
WHAT?
"A BIRD THAT PRODUCES PRECIOUS STONES"?
DO YOU THINK IT'LL WORK?
YEP! THIS'LL BE EASY.
WHAT?!
ALLOW ME TO PRESENT...
...A CONCEPT INSPIRED BY VENUS'S ORIGINAL IDEA OF BIRDS LIKING SHINY OBJECTS...

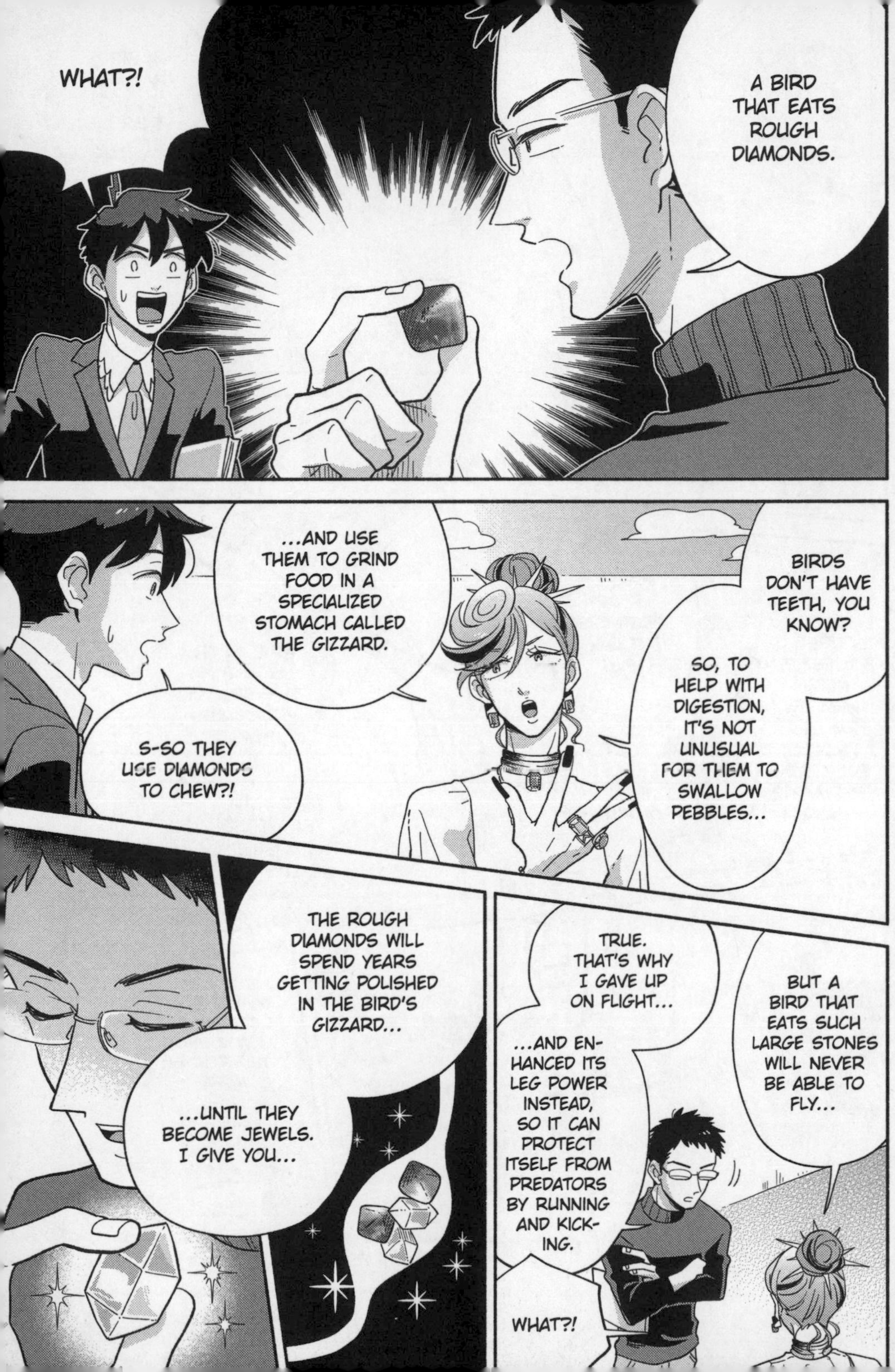
A BIRD THAT EATS ROUGH DIAMONDS.
WHAT?!
BIRDS DON'T HAVE TEETH, YOU KNOW?
SO, TO HELP WITH DIGESTION, IT'S NOT UNUSUAL FOR THEM TO SWALLOW PEBBLES...
...AND USE THEM TO GRIND FOOD IN A SPECIALIZED STOMACH CALLED THE GIZZARD.
S-SO THEY USE DIAMONDS TO CHEW?!
BUT A BIRD THAT EATS SUCH LARGE STONES WILL NEVER BE ABLE TO FLY...
TRUE. THAT'S WHY I GAVE UP ON FLIGHT...
...AND EN-HANCED ITS LEG POWER INSTEAD, SO IT CAN PROTECT ITSELF FROM PREDATORS BY RUNNING AND KICK-ING.
WHAT?!
THE ROUGH DIAMONDS WILL SPEND YEARS GETTING POLISHED IN THE BIRD'S GIZZARD...
...UNTIL THEY BECOME JEWELS. I GIVE YOU...

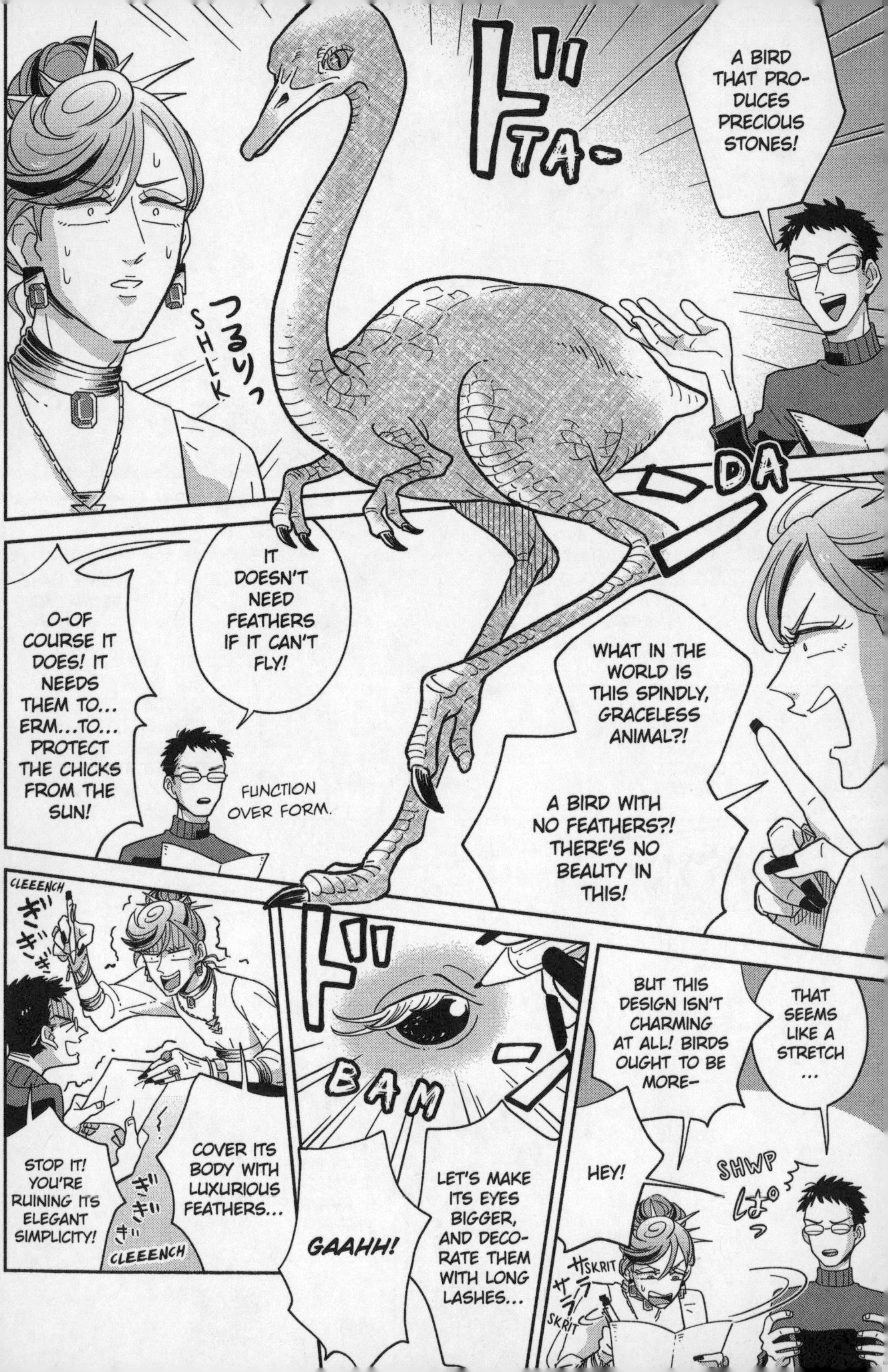
A BIRD THAT PRO-DUCES PRECIOUS STONES!
TA-
つるりっ SHLK
DA
WHAT IN THE WORLD IS THIS SPINDLY, GRACELESS ANIMAL?!
A BIRD WITH NO FEATHERS?! THERE'S NO BEAUTY IN THIS!
IT DOESN'T NEED FEATHERS IF IT CAN'T FLY!
O-OF COURSE IT DOES! IT NEEDS THEM TO... ERM...TO... PROTECT THE CHICKS FROM THE SUN!
FUNCTION OVER FORM.
THAT SEEMS LIKE A STRETCH...
BUT THIS DESIGN ISN'T CHARMING AT ALL! BIRDS OUGHT TO BE MORE–
HEY!
SHWP
SKRIT
SKRIT
BAM
LET'S MAKE ITS EYES BIGGER, AND DECO-RATE THEM WITH LONG LASHES...
GAAHH!
CLEEENCH
COVER ITS BODY WITH LUXURIOUS FEATHERS...
STOP IT! YOU'RE RUINING ITS ELEGANT SIMPLICITY!
CLEEENCH

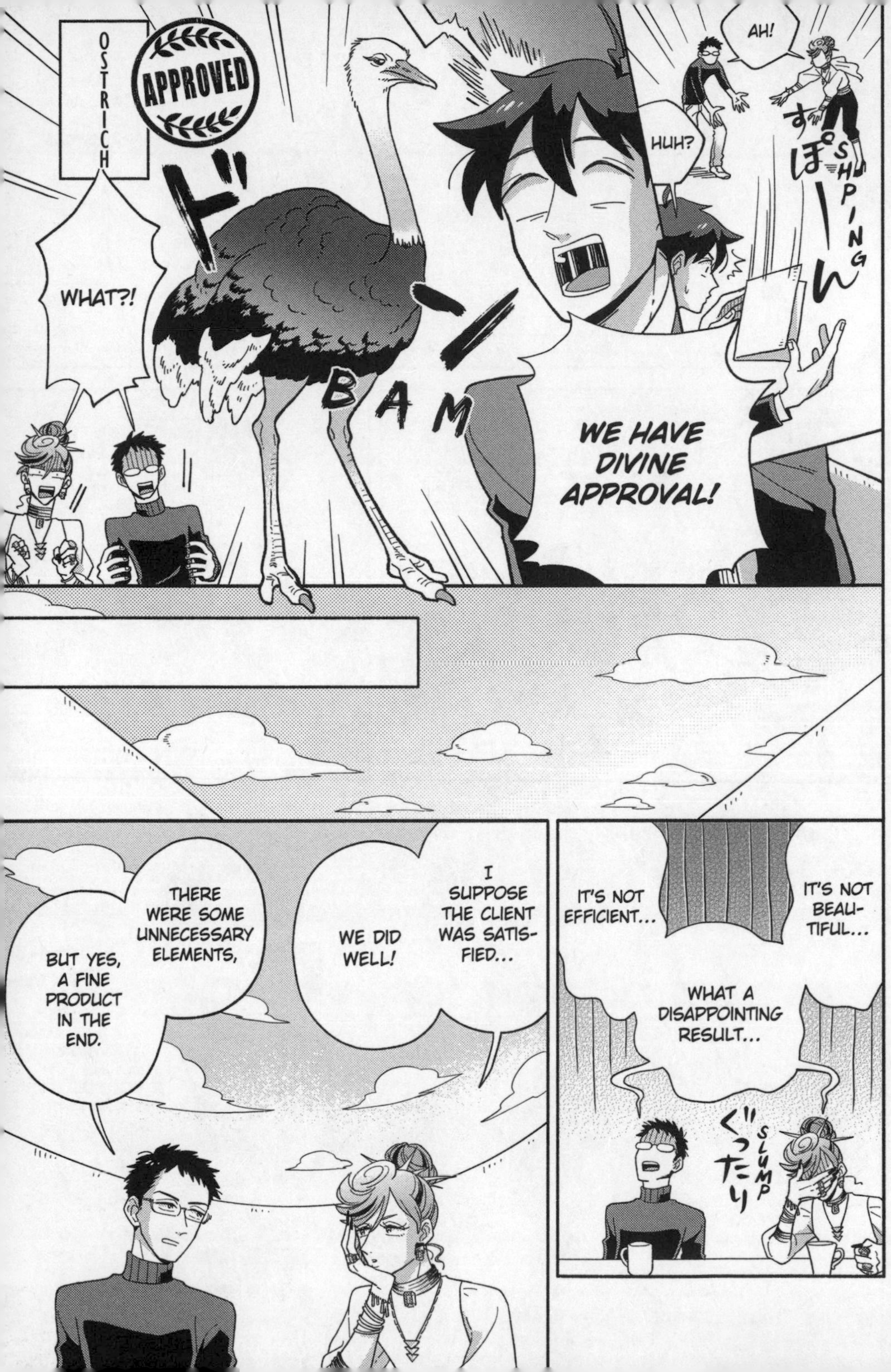
AH!
HUH?
すぽーん
SHPING
WE HAVE DIVINE APPROVAL!
ドーン
BAM
APPROVED
OSTRICH
WHAT?!
IT'S NOT BEAUTIFUL...
IT'S NOT EFFICIENT...
WHAT A DISAPPOINTING RESULT...
ぐったり
SLUMP
I SUPPOSE THE CLIENT WAS SATISFIED...
WE DID WELL!
THERE WERE SOME UNNECESSARY ELEMENTS,
BUT YES, A FINE PRODUCT IN THE END.

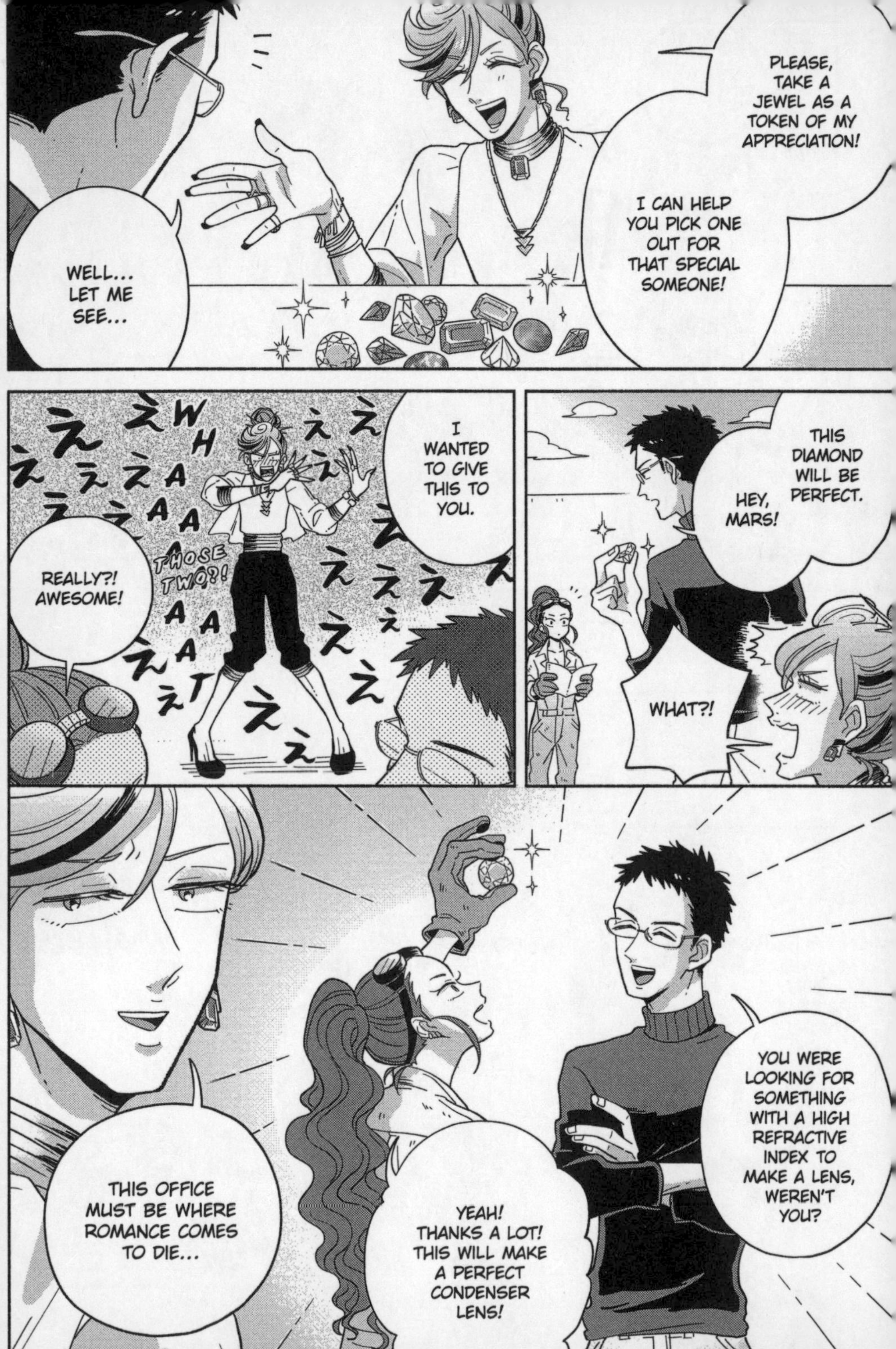
PLEASE, TAKE A JEWEL AS A TOKEN OF MY APPRECIATION!
I CAN HELP YOU PICK ONE OUT FOR THAT SPECIAL SOMEONE!
WELL... LET ME SEE...
THIS DIAMOND WILL BE PERFECT.
HEY, MARS!
WHAT?!
I WANTED TO GIVE THIS TO YOU.
WHAAAAAAAT
THOSE TWO?!
REALLY?! AWESOME!
YOU WERE LOOKING FOR SOMETHING WITH A HIGH REFRACTIVE INDEX TO MAKE A LENS, WEREN'T YOU?
YEAH! THANKS A LOT! THIS WILL MAKE A PERFECT CONDENSER LENS!
THIS OFFICE MUST BE WHERE ROMANCE COMES TO DIE...

THE ENCYCLOPEDIA OF REAL ANIMALS 16

ANIMAL 44 HUMMINGBIRD

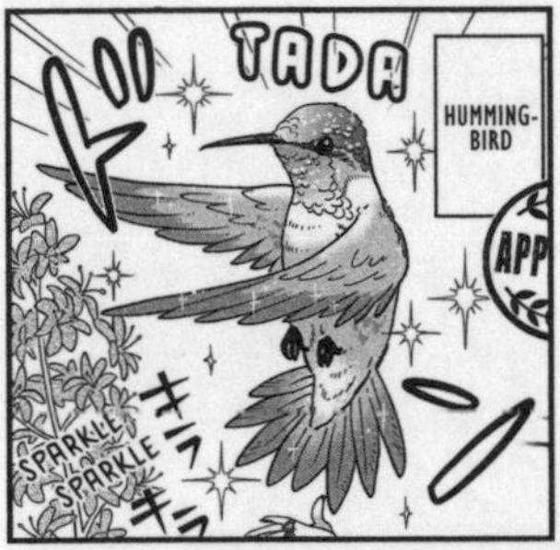
TADA
HUMMING-
BIRD
APP
キラキラ
SPARKLE SPARKLE

THE REAL THING

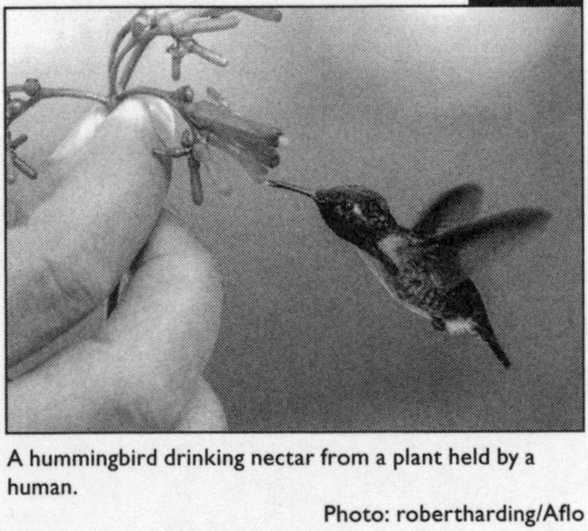

A hummingbird drinking nectar from a plant held by a human.

Photo: robertharding/Aflo

[Name] Hummingbird
[Classification] Class: Aves
Clade: Apodiformes
Family: Trochilidae
[Habitat] The Americas and the Caribbean
[Length] 5-22 cm (2-8.7 in)

The hummingbird flies more like a bee than its fellow birds, and is the only one of its kind to be able to move backwards through the air. To accomplish this, they must flap their wings extremely quickly, and their heart rate during flight can reach as high as 1,200 beats per minute. During sleep, the hummingbird enters a hibernation-like state in order to conserve as much energy as possible, decreasing its metabolism to under five percent of its normal rate.

Another unique characteristic of the hummingbird is its beautiful, brilliant plumage. Like that of precious opals or CDs, the feathers' iridescent sheen is the result of refracted light. Some species, like the Gould's jewelfront, are even named for their lustrous appearance.

The species Ven described to be able to fit on the end of a pen is known as a bee hummingbird. It is the smallest bird in the world, weighing in at only two grams (the weight of two one-yen coins, or any two US paper bills).

The ostrich can run at speeds up to 70 kilometers per hour (43.5 mph). It feeds on plants and insects, and like other birds, processes what it eats by swallowing stones and using them to grind the food in its gizzard. Because it is the largest bird in the world, the stones the ostrich swallows are also large in size, and it has even been known to swallow rough diamonds. According to one story, 53 diamonds were once found in an ostrich gizzard. However, since the animal has a penchant for shiny objects, this could be explained by the ostrich spotting a sparkling diamond in nature and trying to ingest it. The ostrich has been hunted to extinction in some areas by hunters seeking beautiful feathers and potential diamonds.

Diamond lenses, like the one mentioned in this chapter, are often used in the medical industry.

THE REAL THING

An ostrich family in South Africa.
Photo: Jeurgen & Christine Sohns/Aflo

[Name]	*Struthio camelus*
[Classification]	Class: Aves
	Order: Struthioniformes
	Family: Struthionidae
	Genus: *Struthio*
[Habitat]	Africa
[Height]	1.7-2.8 m (5.6-9.2 ft)

HEAVEN'S DESIGN TEAM

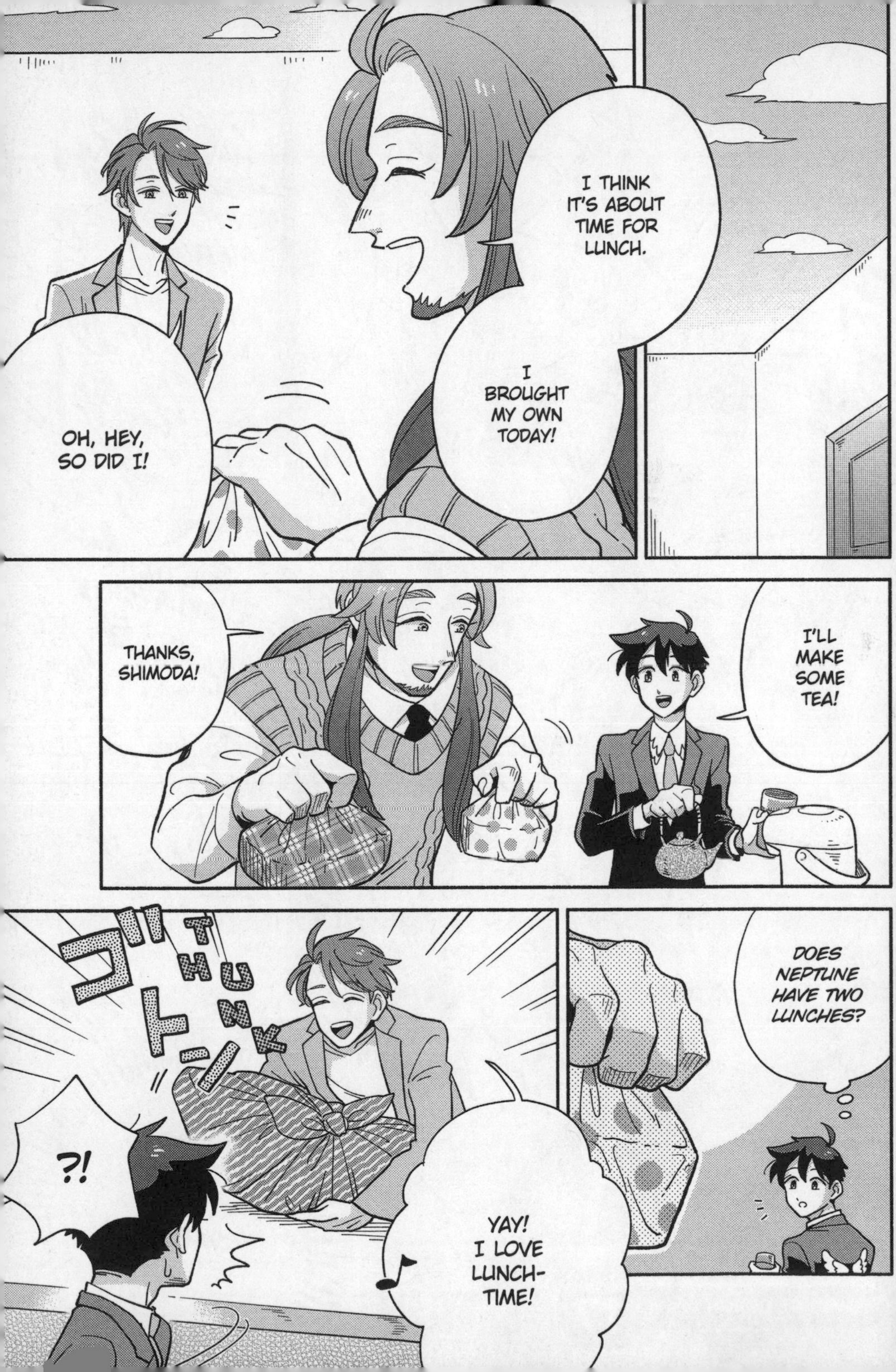
I THINK IT'S ABOUT TIME FOR LUNCH.
I BROUGHT MY OWN TODAY!
OH, HEY, SO DID I!
I'LL MAKE SOME TEA!
THANKS, SHIMODA!
DOES NEPTUNE HAVE TWO LUNCHES?
THUNK
?!
YAY! I LOVE LUNCH-TIME!

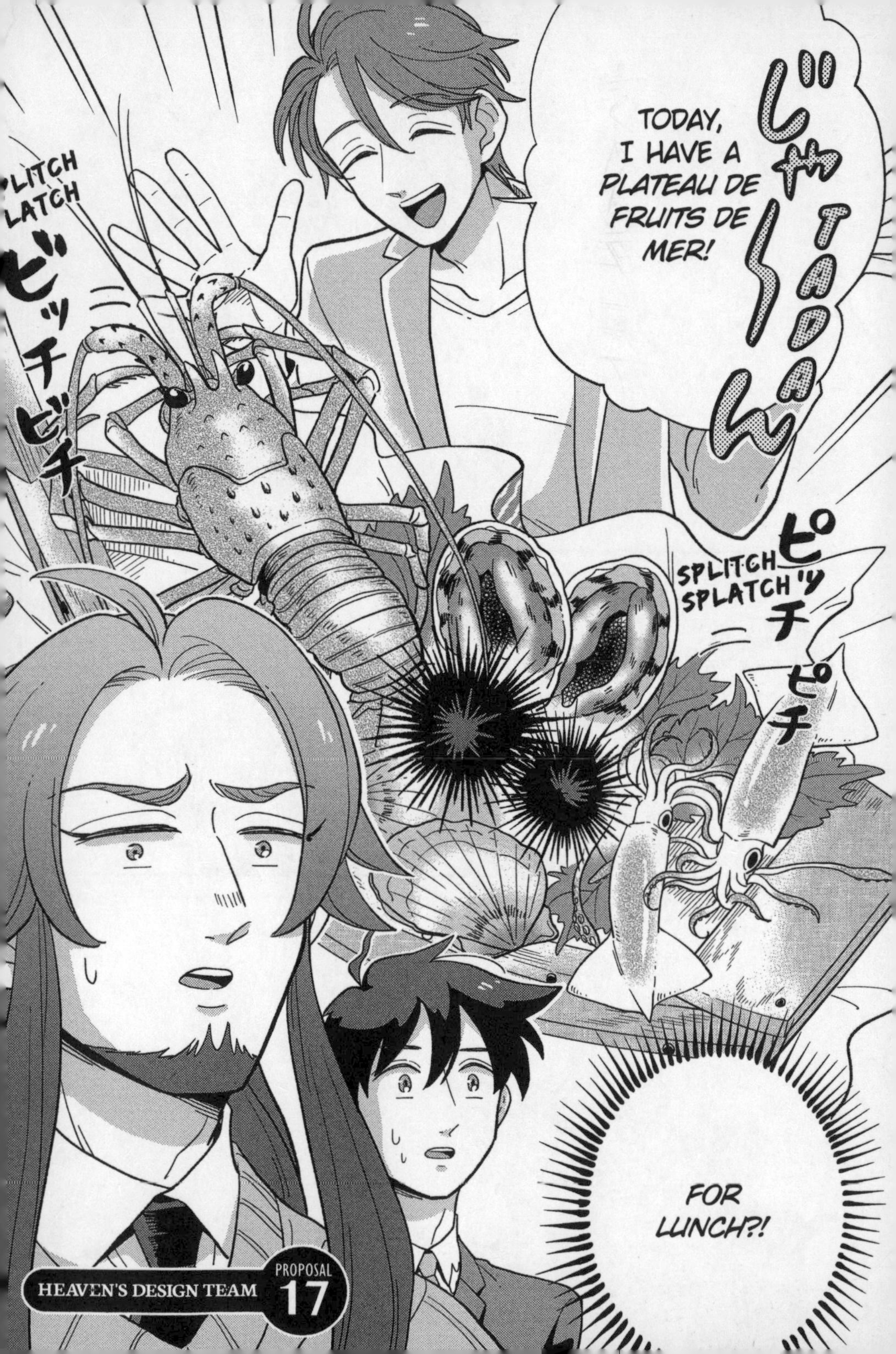
じゃ〜ん
TADAAN
TODAY, I HAVE A PLATEAU DE FRUITS DE MER!
ピッチピチ
SPLITCH SPLATCH
ビッチビチ
PLITCH LATCH
FOR LUNCH?!

HEAVEN'S DESIGN TEAM

PROPOSAL 17

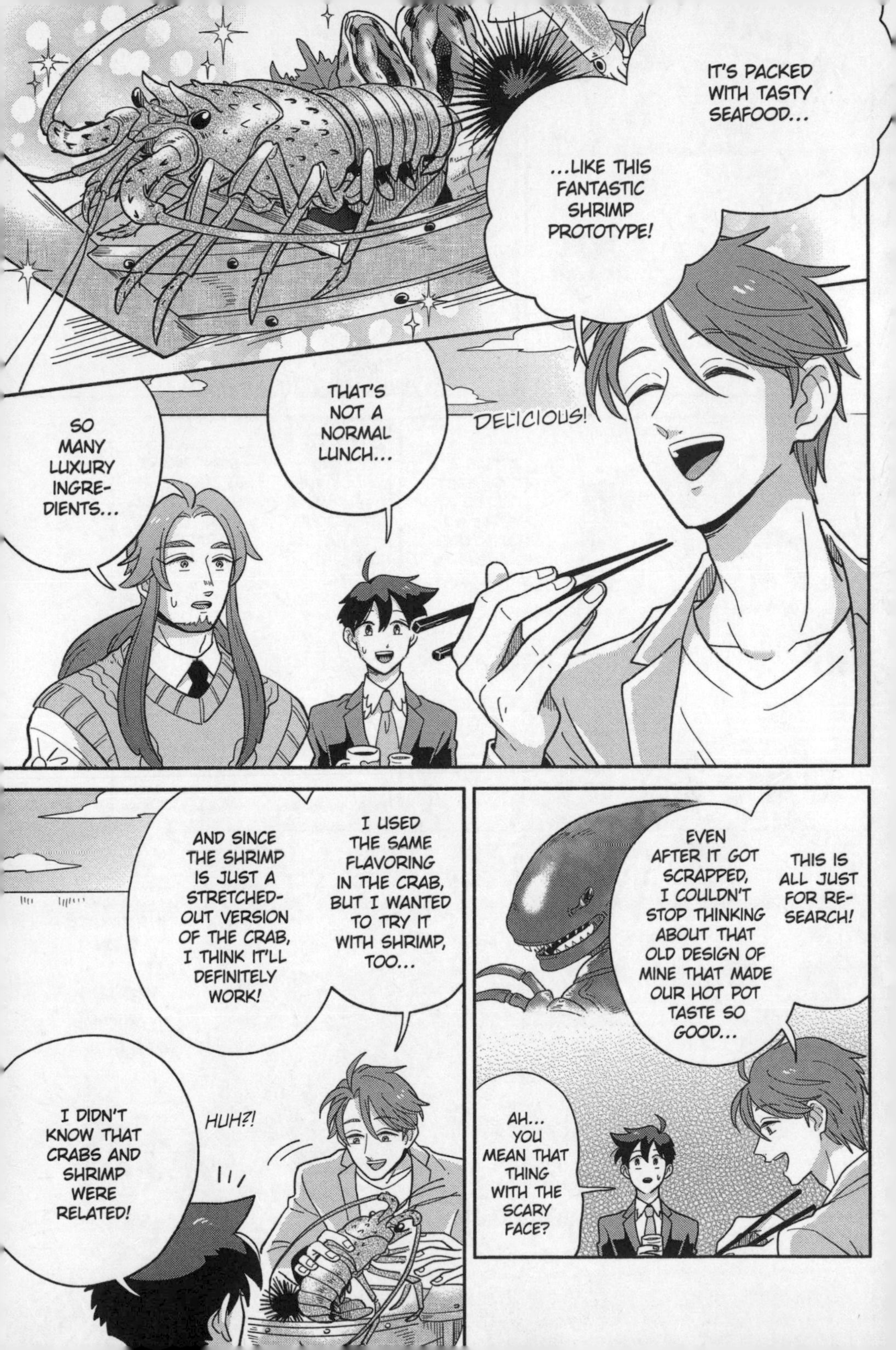
IT'S PACKED WITH TASTY SEAFOOD...
...LIKE THIS FANTASTIC SHRIMP PROTOTYPE!
DELICIOUS!
THAT'S NOT A NORMAL LUNCH...
SO MANY LUXURY INGRE-DIENTS...
THIS IS ALL JUST FOR RE-SEARCH!
EVEN AFTER IT GOT SCRAPPED, I COULDN'T STOP THINKING ABOUT THAT OLD DESIGN OF MINE THAT MADE OUR HOT POT TASTE SO GOOD...
AH... YOU MEAN THAT THING WITH THE SCARY FACE?
I USED THE SAME FLAVORING IN THE CRAB, BUT I WANTED TO TRY IT WITH SHRIMP, TOO...
AND SINCE THE SHRIMP IS JUST A STRETCHED-OUT VERSION OF THE CRAB, I THINK IT'LL DEFINITELY WORK!
HUH?!
I DIDN'T KNOW THAT CRABS AND SHRIMP WERE RELATED!

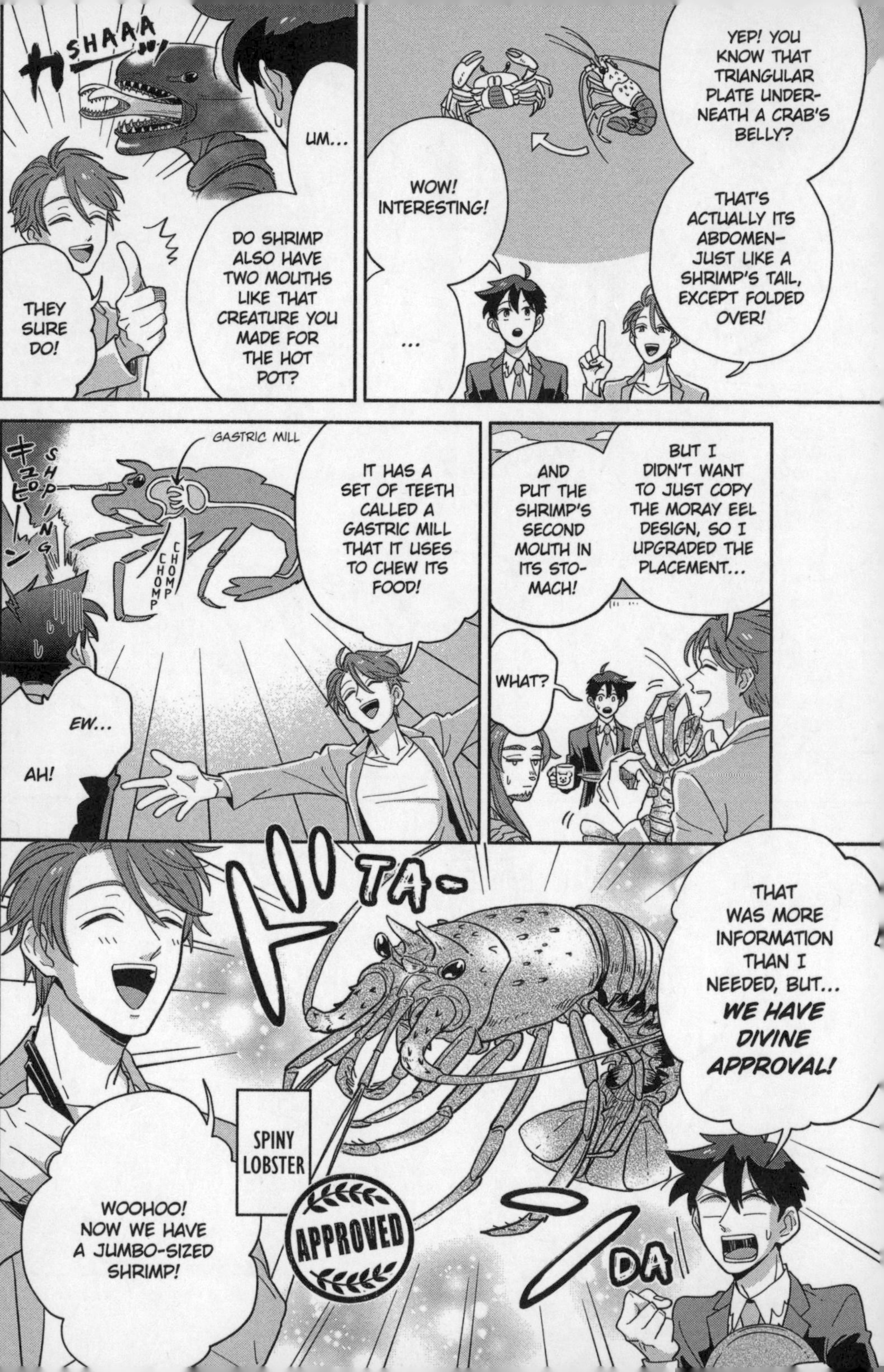
YEP! YOU KNOW THAT TRIANGULAR PLATE UNDER-NEATH A CRAB'S BELLY?
THAT'S ACTUALLY ITS ABDOMEN—JUST LIKE A SHRIMP'S TAIL, EXCEPT FOLDED OVER!
WOW! INTERESTING!
...
SHAAA
UM...
DO SHRIMP ALSO HAVE TWO MOUTHS LIKE THAT CREATURE YOU MADE FOR THE HOT POT?
THEY SURE DO!
BUT I DIDN'T WANT TO JUST COPY THE MORAY EEL DESIGN, SO I UPGRADED THE PLACEMENT...
AND PUT THE SHRIMP'S SECOND MOUTH IN ITS STO-MACH!
WHAT?
IT HAS A SET OF TEETH CALLED A GASTRIC MILL THAT IT USES TO CHEW ITS FOOD!
GASTRIC MILL
CHOMP CHOMP
SHPING
EW...
AH!
THAT WAS MORE INFORMATION THAN I NEEDED, BUT... ***WE HAVE DIVINE APPROVAL!***
TA-DA
SPINY LOBSTER
APPROVED
WOOHOO! NOW WE HAVE A JUMBO-SIZED SHRIMP!

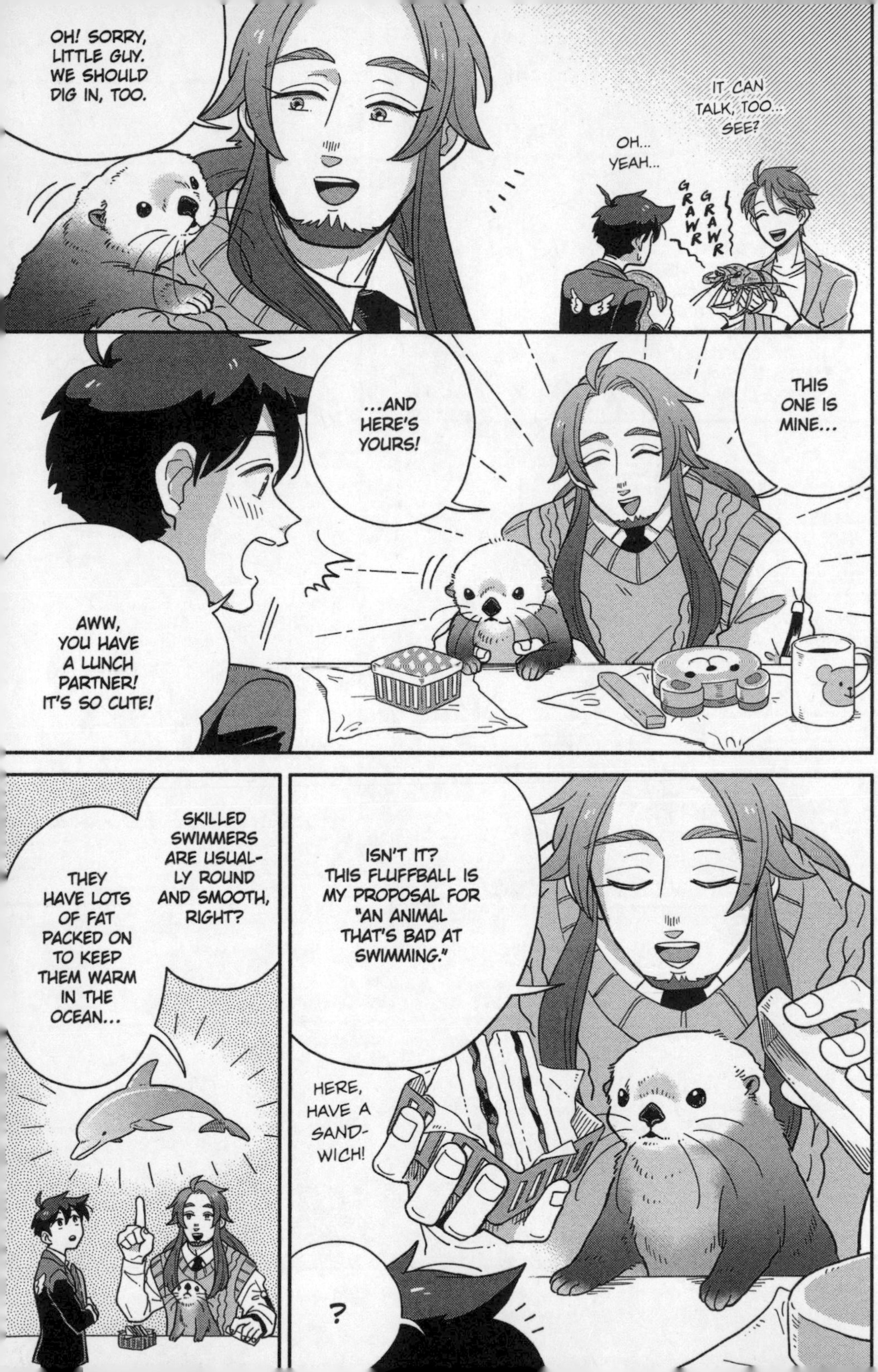
IT CAN TALK, TOO... SEE?
OH... YEAH...
GRAWR GRAWR
OH! SORRY, LITTLE GUY. WE SHOULD DIG IN, TOO.
THIS ONE IS MINE...
...AND HERE'S YOURS!
AWW, YOU HAVE A LUNCH PARTNER! IT'S SO CUTE!
ISN'T IT? THIS FLUFFBALL IS MY PROPOSAL FOR "AN ANIMAL THAT'S BAD AT SWIMMING."
HERE, HAVE A SANDWICH!
?
SKILLED SWIMMERS ARE USUALLY ROUND AND SMOOTH, RIGHT?
THEY HAVE LOTS OF FAT PACKED ON TO KEEP THEM WARM IN THE OCEAN...

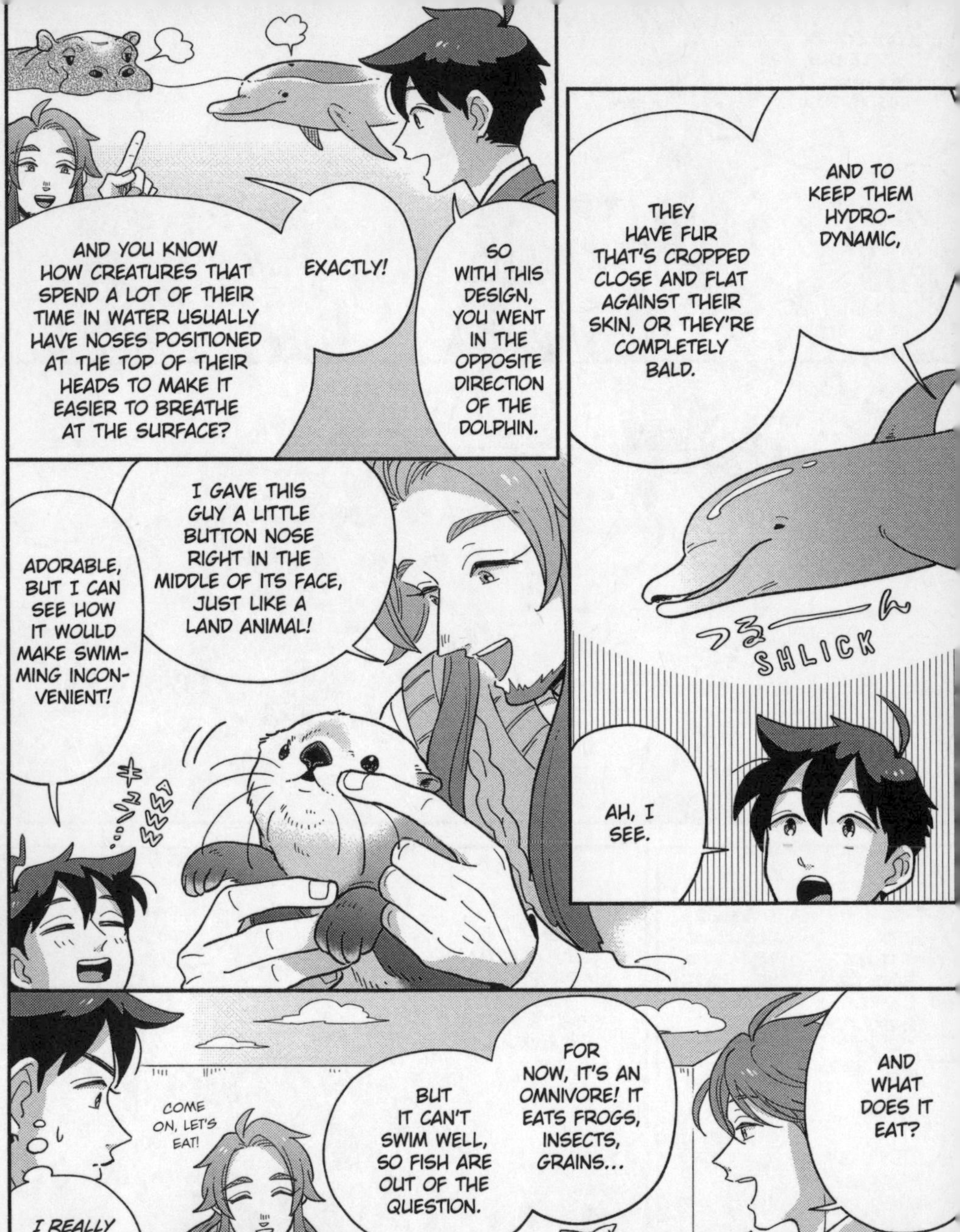
AND TO KEEP THEM HYDRO-DYNAMIC,
THEY HAVE FUR THAT'S CROPPED CLOSE AND FLAT AGAINST THEIR SKIN, OR THEY'RE COMPLETELY BALD.
つる——ん
SHLICK
AH, I SEE.
SO WITH THIS DESIGN, YOU WENT IN THE OPPOSITE DIRECTION OF THE DOLPHIN.
EXACTLY!
AND YOU KNOW HOW CREATURES THAT SPEND A LOT OF THEIR TIME IN WATER USUALLY HAVE NOSES POSITIONED AT THE TOP OF THEIR HEADS TO MAKE IT EASIER TO BREATHE AT THE SURFACE?
I GAVE THIS GUY A LITTLE BUTTON NOSE RIGHT IN THE MIDDLE OF ITS FACE, JUST LIKE A LAND ANIMAL!
ADORABLE, BUT I CAN SEE HOW IT WOULD MAKE SWIMMING INCONVENIENT!
AND WHAT DOES IT EAT?
FOR NOW, IT'S AN OMNIVORE! IT EATS FROGS, INSECTS, GRAINS...
BUT IT CAN'T SWIM WELL, SO FISH ARE OUT OF THE QUESTION.
COME ON, LET'S EAT!
I REALLY DON'T WANT TO KNOW WHAT'S IN THAT SANDWICH...

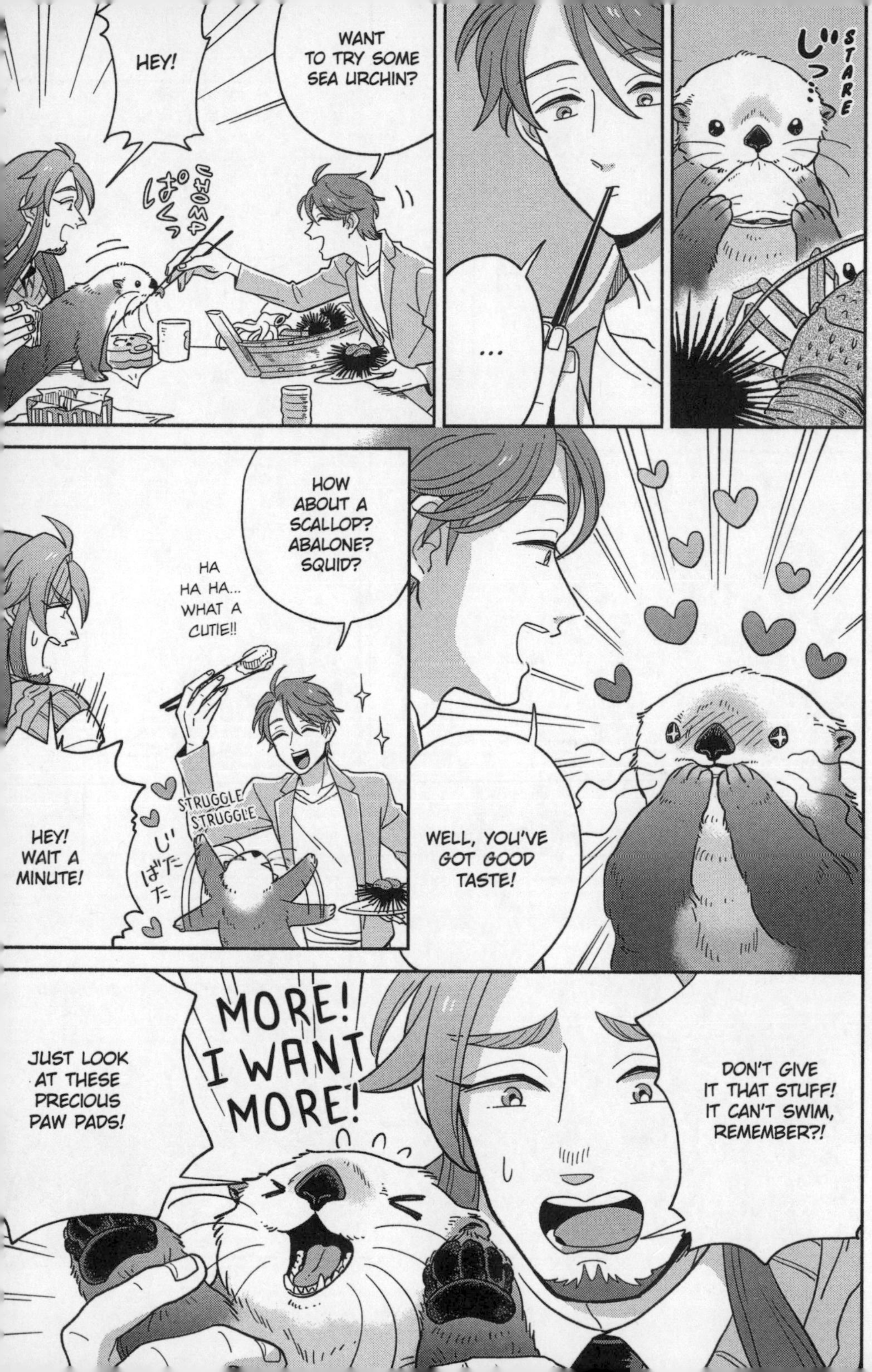

じっ
STARE
...
WANT TO TRY SOME SEA URCHIN?
HEY!
ぱくっ
CHOMP
WELL, YOU'VE GOT GOOD TASTE!
HOW ABOUT A SCALLOP? ABALONE? SQUID?
HA HA HA... WHAT A CUTIE!!
STRUGGLE STRUGGLE
じたばた
HEY! WAIT A MINUTE!
DON'T GIVE IT THAT STUFF! IT CAN'T SWIM, REMEMBER?!
MORE! I WANT MORE!
JUST LOOK AT THESE PRECIOUS PAW PADS!

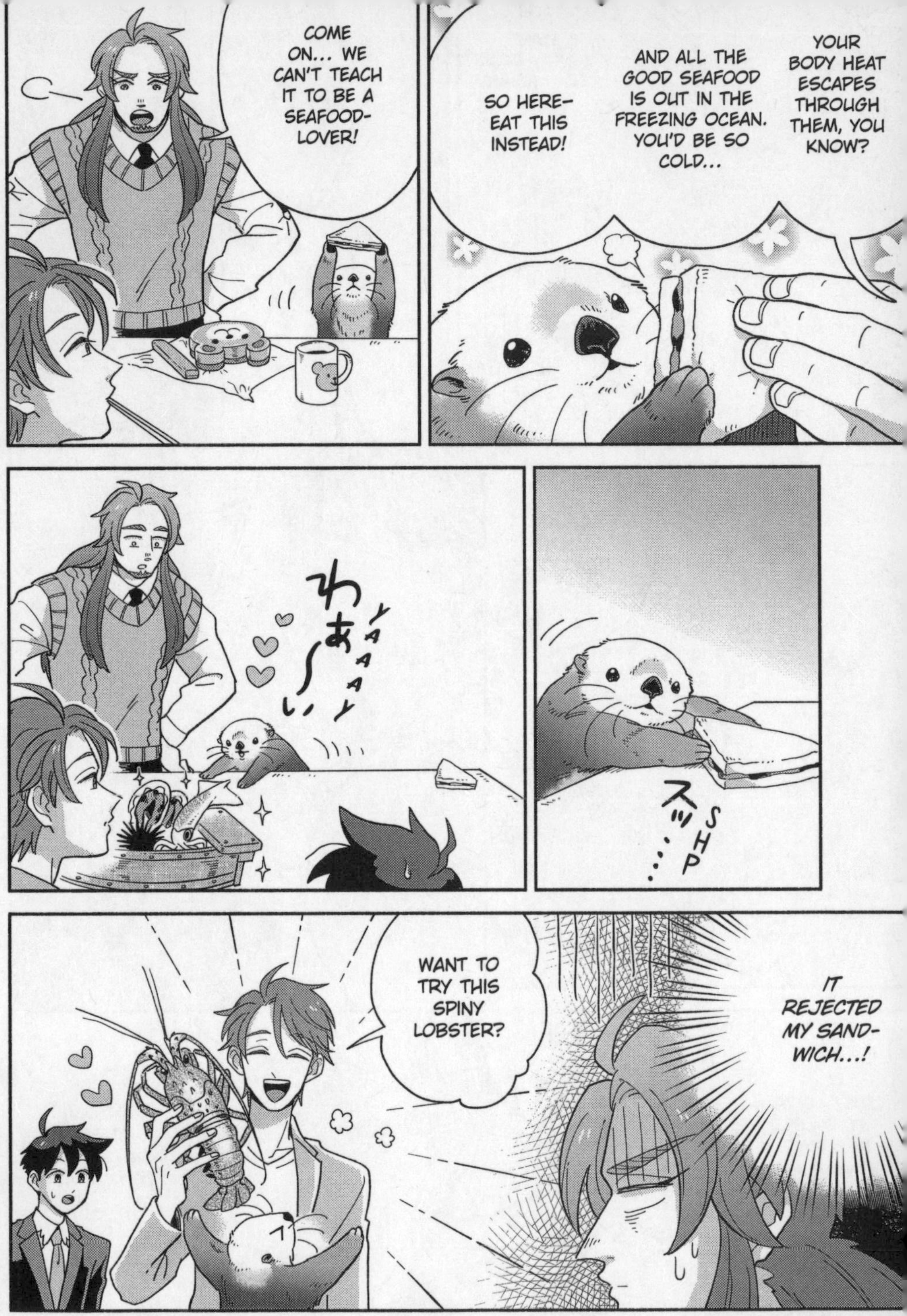
YOUR BODY HEAT ESCAPES THROUGH THEM, YOU KNOW?
AND ALL THE GOOD SEAFOOD IS OUT IN THE FREEZING OCEAN. YOU'D BE SO COLD...
SO HERE-EAT THIS INSTEAD!
COME ON... WE CAN'T TEACH IT TO BE A SEAFOOD-LOVER!
スッ
SHP...
わあ～い
YAAAAY
IT REJECTED MY SANDWICH...!
WANT TO TRY THIS SPINY LOBSTER?

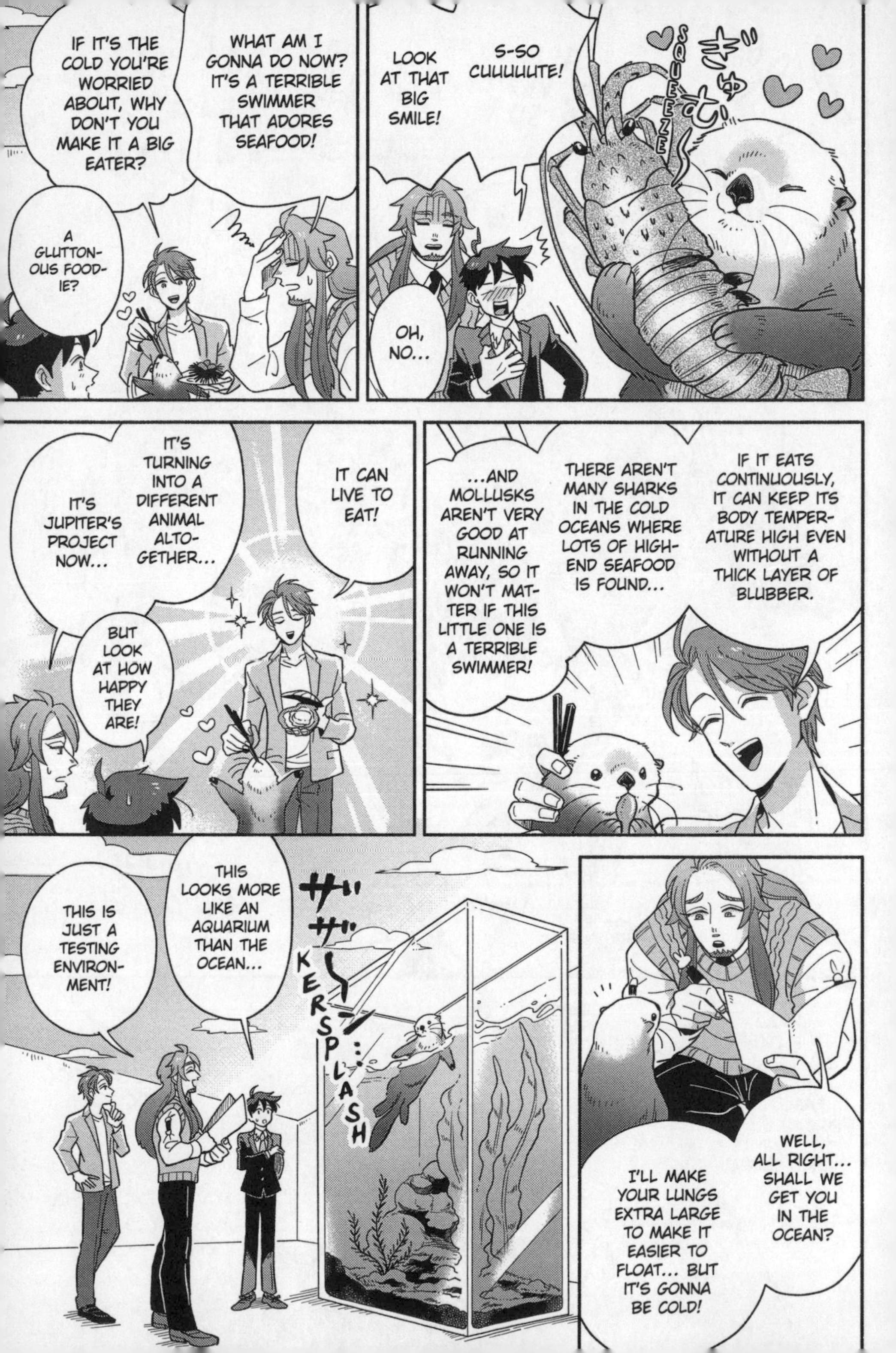
SQUEEZE
S-SO CUUUUUTE!
LOOK AT THAT BIG SMILE!
OH, NO...
WHAT AM I GONNA DO NOW? IT'S A TERRIBLE SWIMMER THAT ADORES SEAFOOD!
IF IT'S THE COLD YOU'RE WORRIED ABOUT, WHY DON'T YOU MAKE IT A BIG EATER?
A GLUTTONOUS FOODIE?
IF IT EATS CONTINUOUSLY, IT CAN KEEP ITS BODY TEMPERATURE HIGH EVEN WITHOUT A THICK LAYER OF BLUBBER.
THERE AREN'T MANY SHARKS IN THE COLD OCEANS WHERE LOTS OF HIGH-END SEAFOOD IS FOUND...
...AND MOLLUSKS AREN'T VERY GOOD AT RUNNING AWAY, SO IT WON'T MATTER IF THIS LITTLE ONE IS A TERRIBLE SWIMMER!
IT CAN LIVE TO EAT!
IT'S TURNING INTO A DIFFERENT ANIMAL ALTOGETHER...
IT'S JUPITER'S PROJECT NOW...
BUT LOOK AT HOW HAPPY THEY ARE!
WELL, ALL RIGHT... SHALL WE GET YOU IN THE OCEAN?
I'LL MAKE YOUR LUNGS EXTRA LARGE TO MAKE IT EASIER TO FLOAT... BUT IT'S GONNA BE COLD!
KERSPLASH
THIS LOOKS MORE LIKE AN AQUARIUM THAN THE OCEAN...
THIS IS JUST A TESTING ENVIRONMENT!

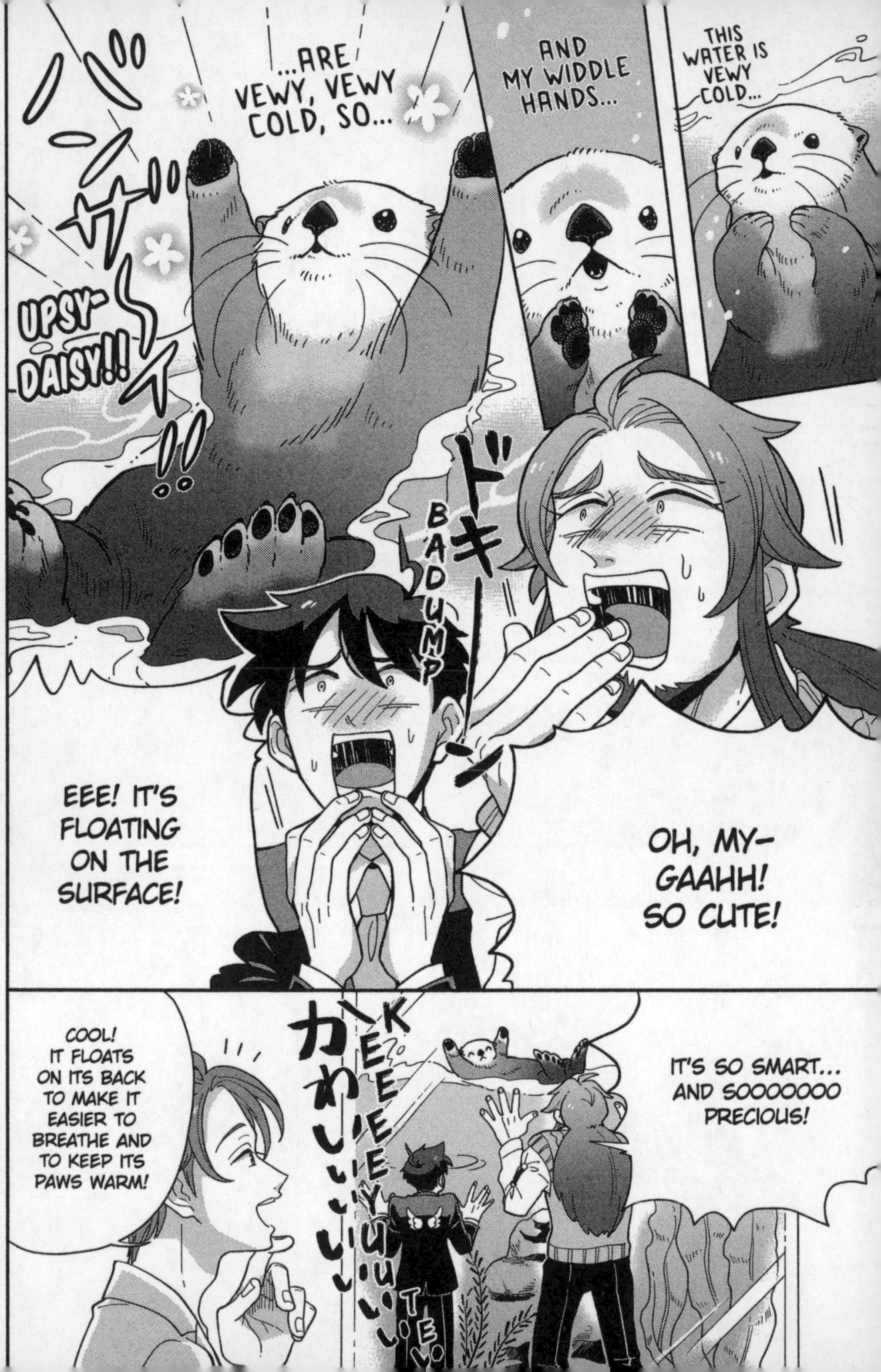
THIS WATER IS VEWY COLD...
AND MY WIDDLE HANDS...
...ARE VEWY, VEWY COLD, SO...
UPSY-DAISY!!
BADUMP
OH, MY-GAAHH! SO CUTE!
EEE! IT'S FLOATING ON THE SURFACE!
IT'S SO SMART... AND SOOOOOOO PRECIOUS!
KEEEEYUUUTE
COOL! IT FLOATS ON ITS BACK TO MAKE IT EASIER TO BREATHE AND TO KEEP ITS PAWS WARM!

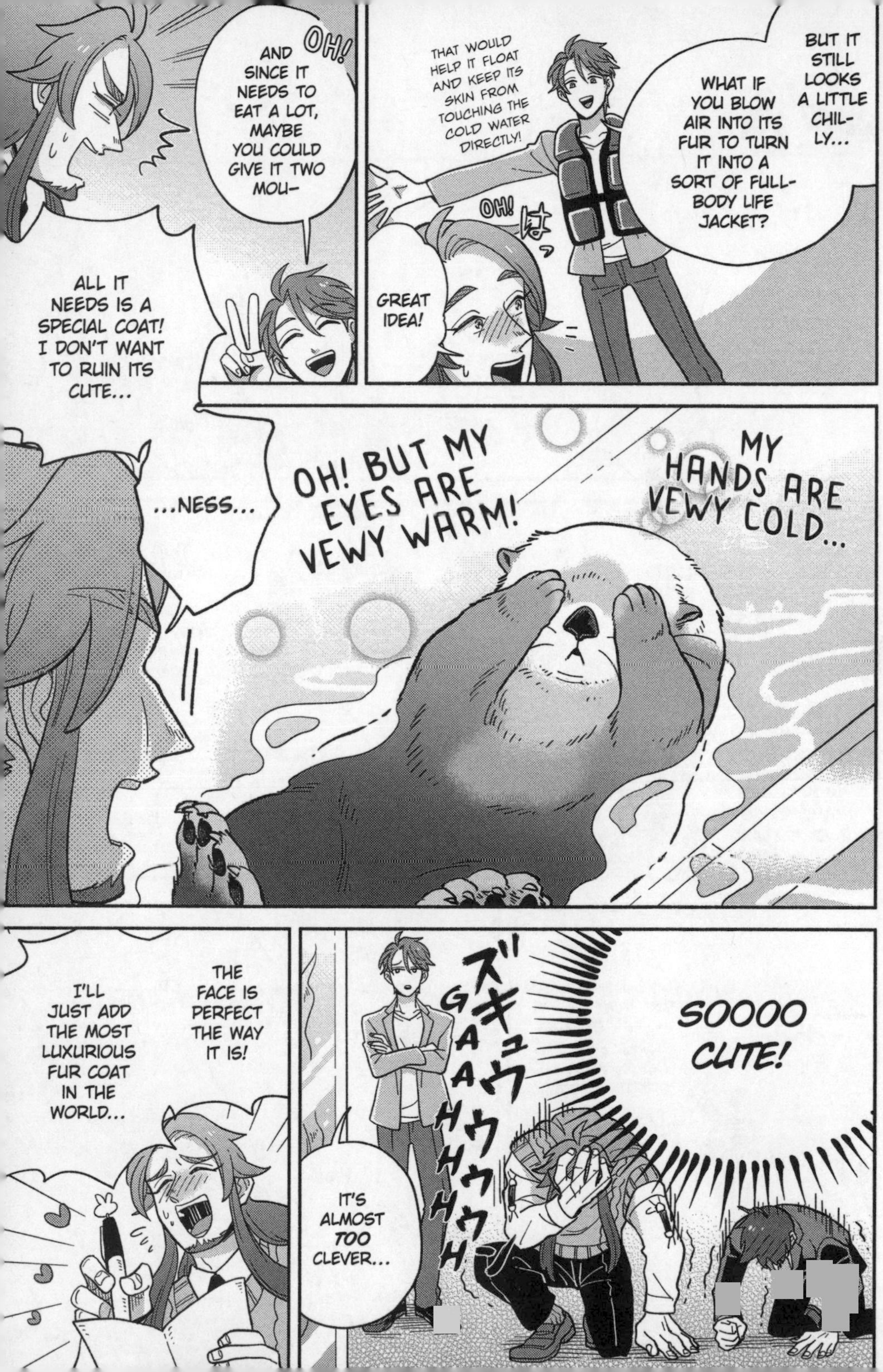
BUT IT STILL LOOKS A LITTLE CHILL-LY...
WHAT IF YOU BLOW AIR INTO ITS FUR TO TURN IT INTO A SORT OF FULL-BODY LIFE JACKET?
THAT WOULD HELP IT FLOAT AND KEEP ITS SKIN FROM TOUCHING THE COLD WATER DIRECTLY!
OH! はっ
GREAT IDEA!
OH!
AND SINCE IT NEEDS TO EAT A LOT, MAYBE YOU COULD GIVE IT TWO MOU–
ALL IT NEEDS IS A SPECIAL COAT! I DON'T WANT TO RUIN ITS CUTE...
MY HANDS ARE VEWY COLD...
OH! BUT MY EYES ARE VEWY WARM!
...NESS...
SOOOO CUTE!
ズキュウウウウ
GAAAHHHHHH
IT'S ALMOST TOO CLEVER...
THE FACE IS PERFECT THE WAY IT IS!
I'LL JUST ADD THE MOST LUXURIOUS FUR COAT IN THE WORLD...

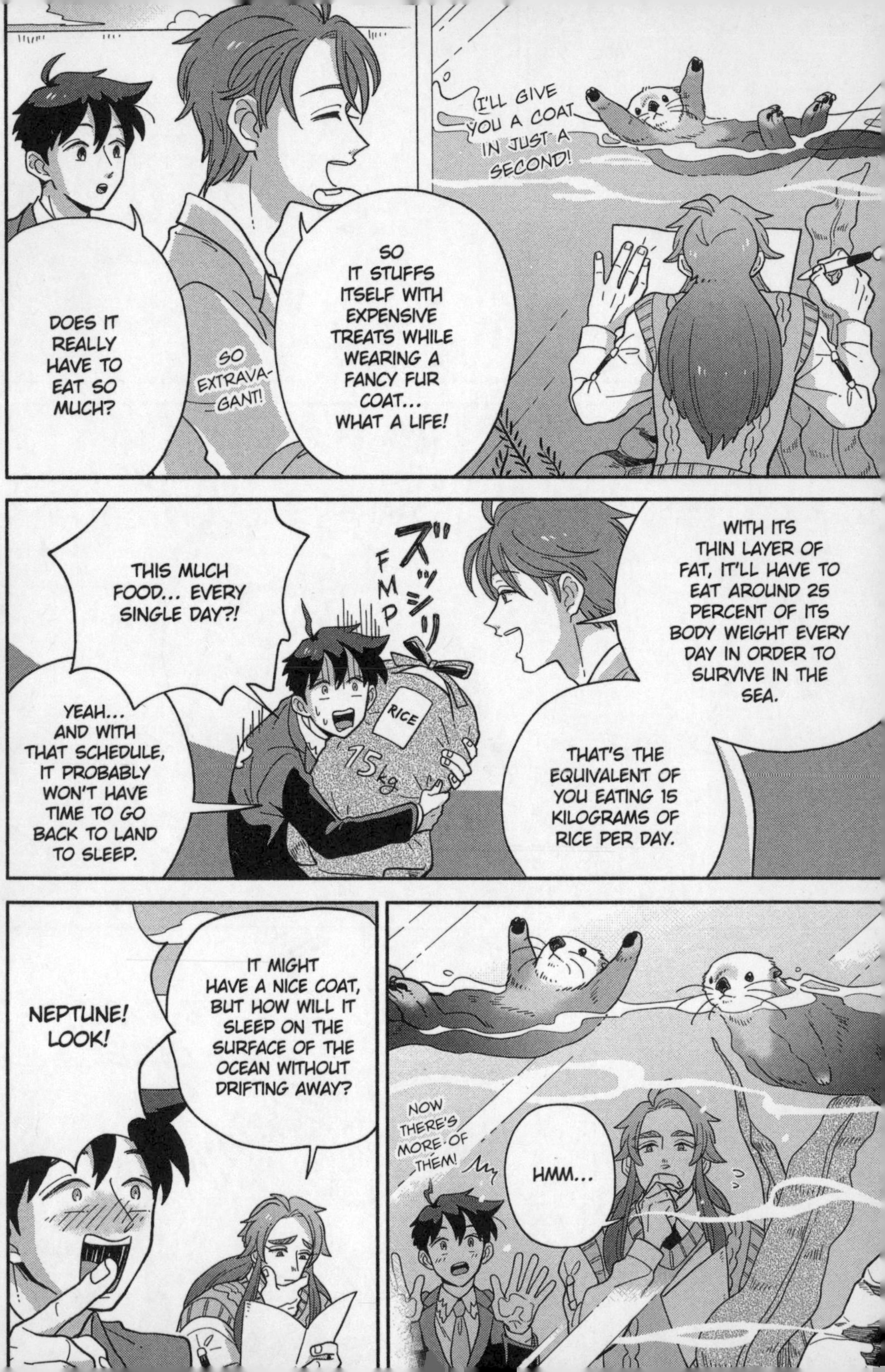
I'LL GIVE YOU A COAT IN JUST A SECOND!
SO IT STUFFS ITSELF WITH EXPENSIVE TREATS WHILE WEARING A FANCY FUR COAT... WHAT A LIFE!
SO EXTRAVAGANT!
DOES IT REALLY HAVE TO EAT SO MUCH?
WITH ITS THIN LAYER OF FAT, IT'LL HAVE TO EAT AROUND 25 PERCENT OF ITS BODY WEIGHT EVERY DAY IN ORDER TO SURVIVE IN THE SEA.
THAT'S THE EQUIVALENT OF YOU EATING 15 KILOGRAMS OF RICE PER DAY.
FMP
RICE
15kg
THIS MUCH FOOD... EVERY SINGLE DAY?!
YEAH... AND WITH THAT SCHEDULE, IT PROBABLY WON'T HAVE TIME TO GO BACK TO LAND TO SLEEP.
NOW THERE'S MORE OF THEM!
HMM...
IT MIGHT HAVE A NICE COAT, BUT HOW WILL IT SLEEP ON THE SURFACE OF THE OCEAN WITHOUT DRIFTING AWAY?
NEPTUNE! LOOK!

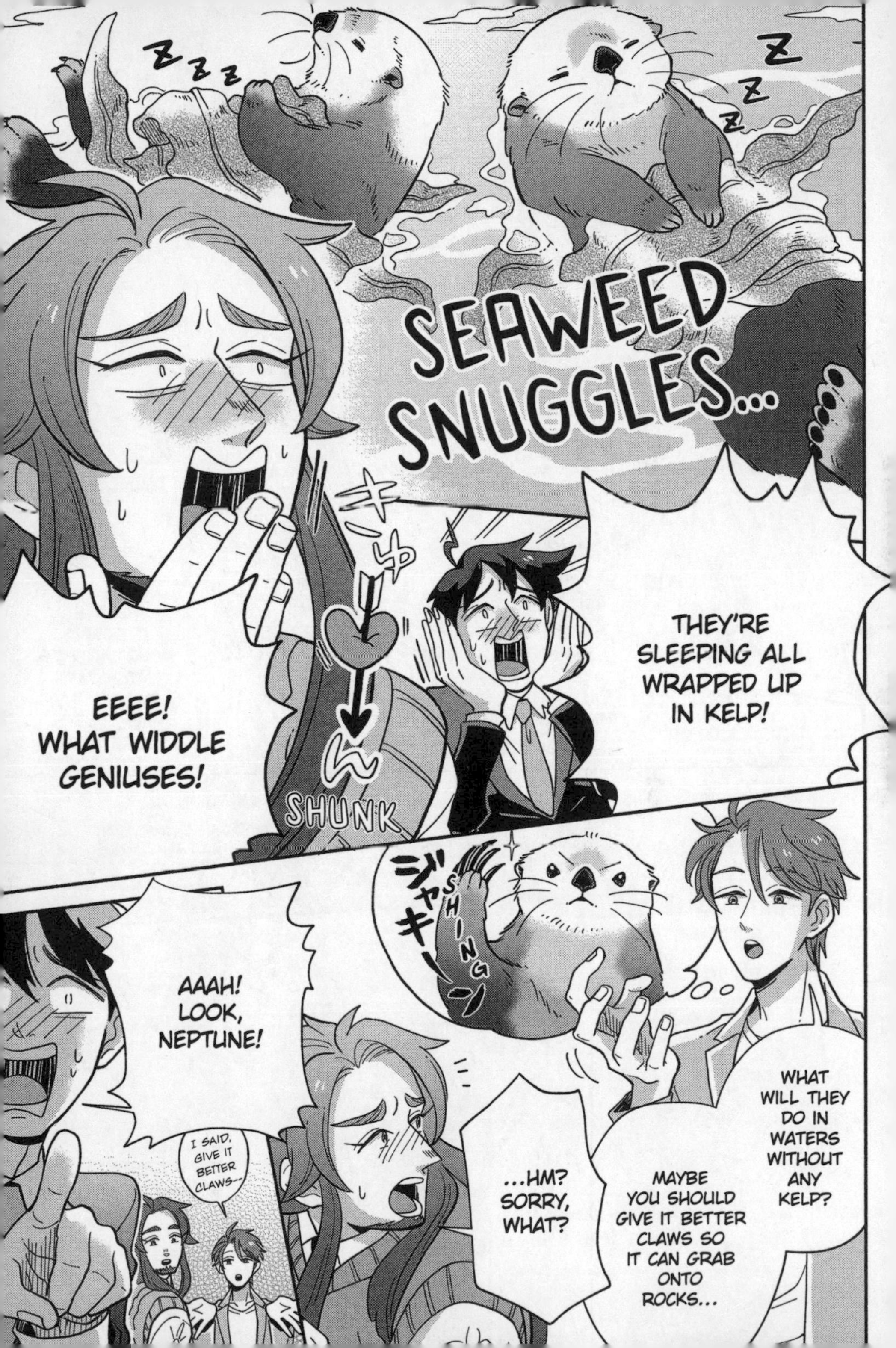
Z Z Z
Z Z Z
SEAWEED SNUGGLES...
THEY'RE SLEEPING ALL WRAPPED UP IN KELP!
EEEE! WHAT WIDDLE GENIUSES!
SHUNK
WHAT WILL THEY DO IN WATERS WITHOUT ANY KELP?
MAYBE YOU SHOULD GIVE IT BETTER CLAWS SO IT CAN GRAB ONTO ROCKS...
SHING
...HM? SORRY, WHAT?
AAAH! LOOK, NEPTUNE!
I SAID, GIVE IT BETTER CLAWS...

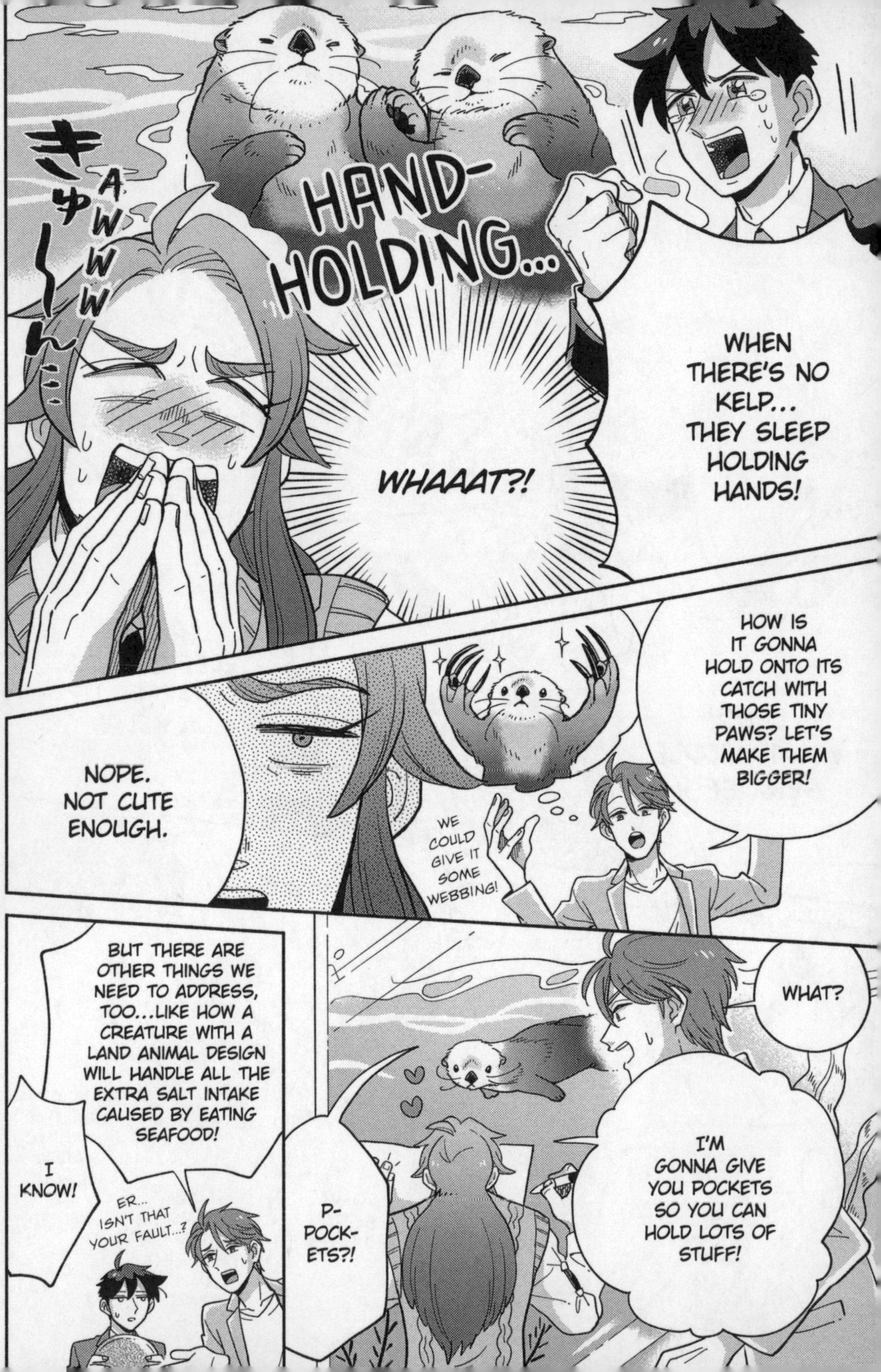
WHEN THERE'S NO KELP... THEY SLEEP HOLDING HANDS!
WHAAAT?!
HAND-HOLDING...
きゅーん
AWWWW
HOW IS IT GONNA HOLD ONTO ITS CATCH WITH THOSE TINY PAWS? LET'S MAKE THEM BIGGER!
WE COULD GIVE IT SOME WEBBING!
NOPE. NOT CUTE ENOUGH.
WHAT?
I'M GONNA GIVE YOU POCKETS SO YOU CAN HOLD LOTS OF STUFF!
P-POCK-ETS?!
BUT THERE ARE OTHER THINGS WE NEED TO ADDRESS, TOO...LIKE HOW A CREATURE WITH A LAND ANIMAL DESIGN WILL HANDLE ALL THE EXTRA SALT INTAKE CAUSED BY EATING SEAFOOD!
I KNOW!
ER... ISN'T THAT YOUR FAULT...?

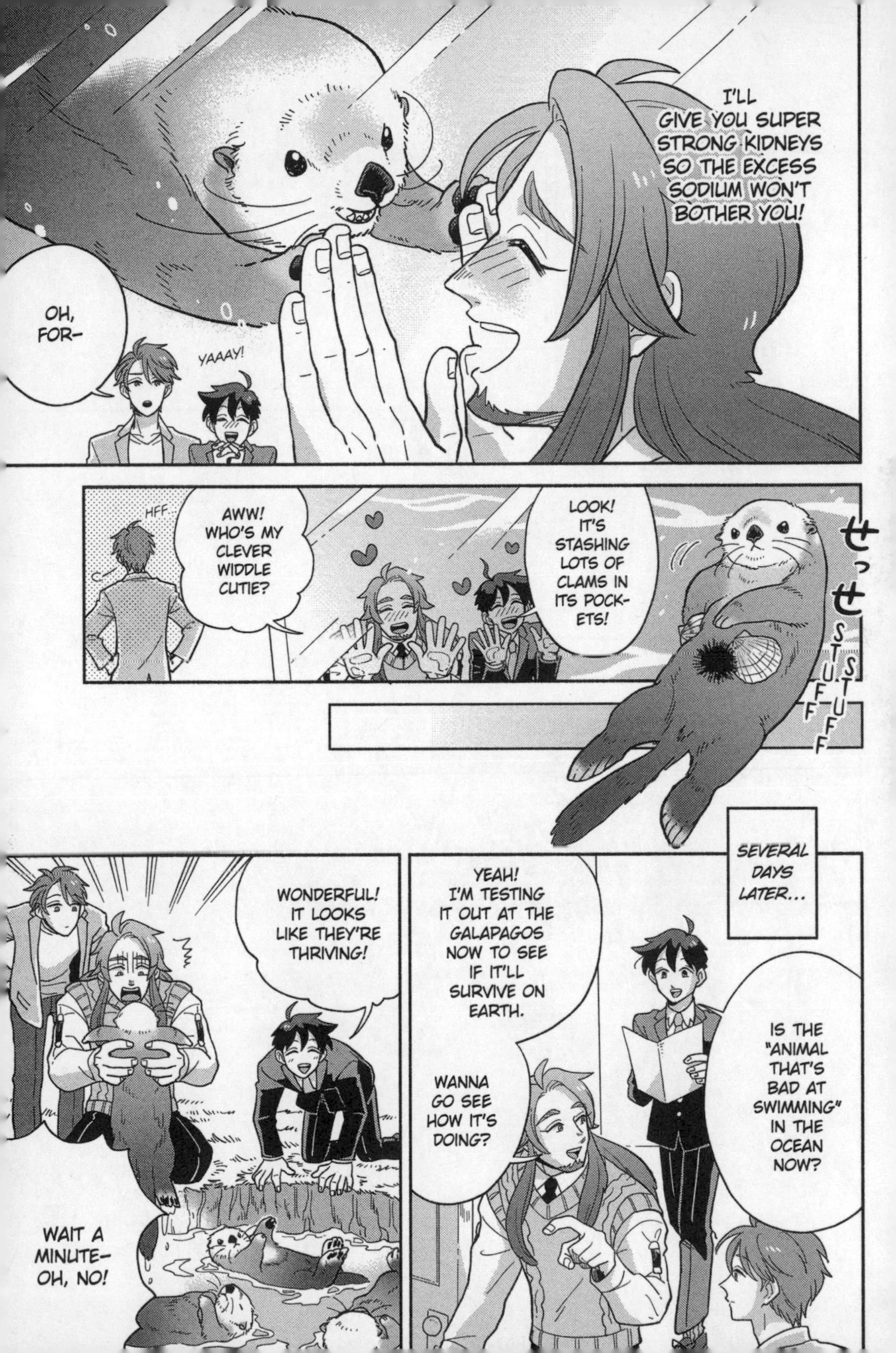
I'LL GIVE YOU SUPER STRONG KIDNEYS SO THE EXCESS SODIUM WON'T BOTHER YOU!
YAAAY!
OH, FOR-
せっせ
STUFF STUFF
LOOK! IT'S STASHING LOTS OF CLAMS IN ITS POCK-ETS!
AWW! WHO'S MY CLEVER WIDDLE CUTIE?
HFF
SEVERAL DAYS LATER...
IS THE "ANIMAL THAT'S BAD AT SWIMMING" IN THE OCEAN NOW?
YEAH! I'M TESTING IT OUT AT THE GALAPAGOS NOW TO SEE IF IT'LL SURVIVE ON EARTH.
WANNA GO SEE HOW IT'S DOING?
WONDERFUL! IT LOOKS LIKE THEY'RE THRIVING!
WAIT A MINUTE- OH, NO!

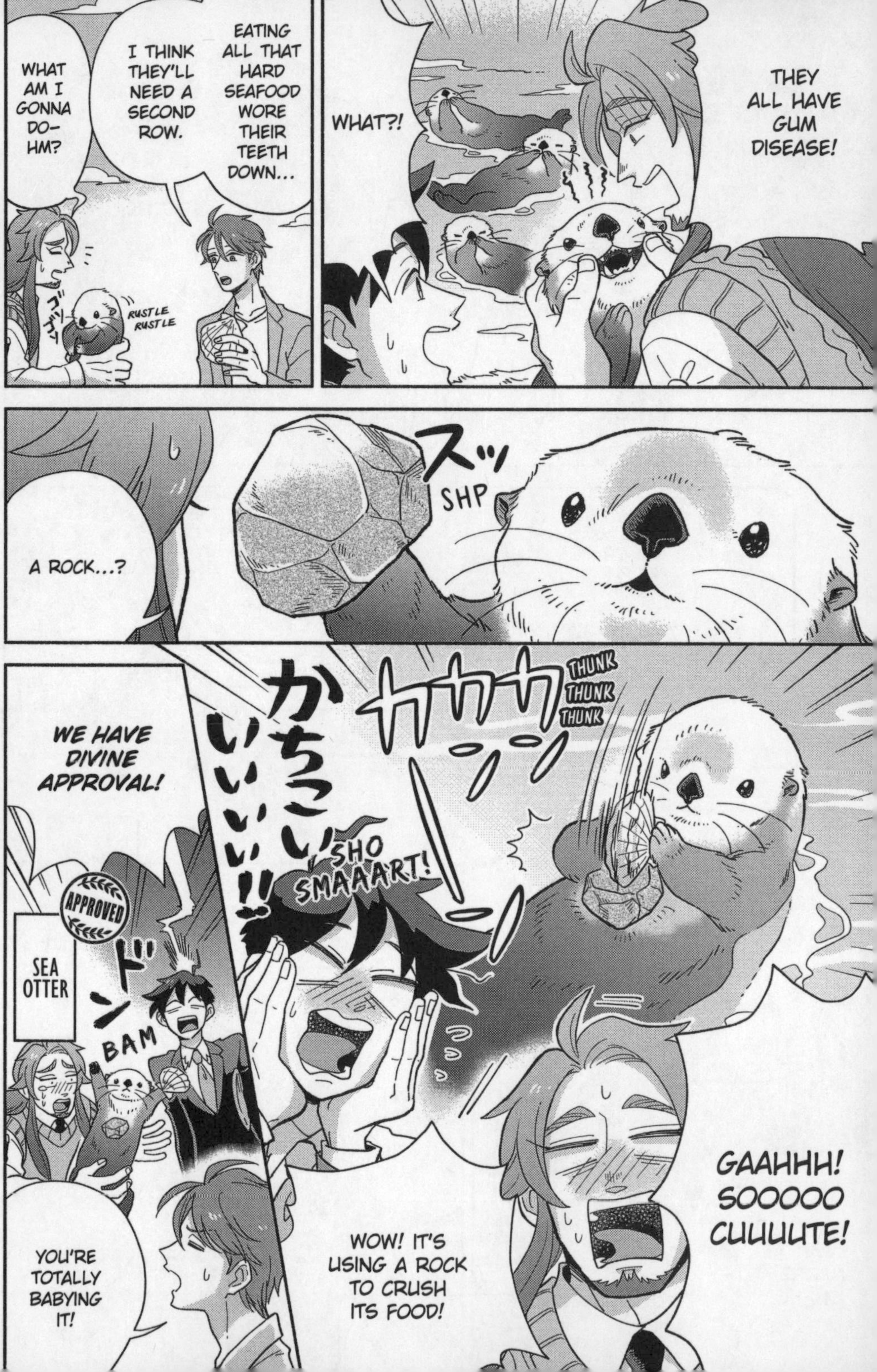
THEY ALL HAVE GUM DISEASE!
WHAT?!
EATING ALL THAT HARD SEAFOOD WORE THEIR TEETH DOWN...
I THINK THEY'LL NEED A SECOND ROW.
WHAT AM I GONNA DO—HM?
ゴソゴソ
RUSTLE RUSTLE
スッ
SHP
A ROCK...?
カカカ
THUNK THUNK THUNK
かちこいいいい!!
SHO SMAAART!
GAAHHH! SOOOOO CUUUUTE!
WOW! IT'S USING A ROCK TO CRUSH ITS FOOD!
WE HAVE DIVINE APPROVAL!
APPROVED
SEA OTTER
ドン
BAM
YOU'RE TOTALLY BABYING IT!

THE ENCYCLOPEDIA OF REAL ANIMALS 17

ANIMAL 46 | SEA OTTER

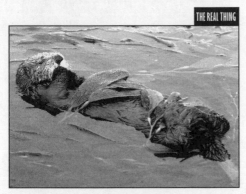

THE REAL THING

An otter wraps itself in kelp while relaxing.

Photo: Ardea/Aflo

[Name]	*Enhydra lutris*
[Classification]	Class: Mammalia Order: Carnivora Family: Mustelidae Genus: *Enhydra*
[Habitat]	Pacific Ocean from the Kuril Group (Japan) to North America
[Length]	110-150 cm (3.6-5 ft)

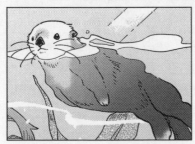

Compared to other marine mammals, the sea otter has very little blubber and is not an especially skilled swimmer. By blowing air into its fur, which has an incredible density of approximately 100,000 strands of hair per square centimeter, the sea otter can protect itself from and stay afloat on cold ocean waters. It twists its body in the water to remove any food scraps after eating, and uses its front paws to carefully groom itself. When the sea otter is tired, it wraps itself in kelp to keep from drifting out to sea. It has a loose pocket of skin under each foreleg which holds the stone it uses to crush shells and the prey it catches. According to one study, the animal can hold up to 27 clams in its pouch.

The sea otter has a high incidence of gum disease, which is believed to be caused by eating hard-shelled seafood or by ingesting gravel along with its food, causing gum damage.

| # JAPANESE SPINY LOBSTER

There are many species of spiny lobster, all of which have the two-part mastication system shared by the shrimp and the crab. When the Japanese spiny lobster eats, it first crushes its prey with the mandibles located near its mouth and then swallows. Next, the food passes through a hard protuberance known as the gastric mill, where it is ground. Then, in the pyloric portion of the stomach, located toward the stomach's exit, the food is filtered by rows of bristles which allow the smallest particles to pass through to the digestive tract. Because crabs and shrimp eat a variety of different plants and animals, each species has a specialized set of mandibles and gastric mill suited to masticating its preferred diet. When shrimp molt, they must extract all of themselves from their old shells, including their digestive lining. Upon inspecting the old shell, one can observe that it becomes thicker near the gastric mill.

THE REAL THING

The *panulirus brunneiflagellum*, which lives around the Ogasawara and Izu Groups of Japan, was recognized in 2005.

Photo: Jeurgen & Christine Sohns/Aflo

[Name]	*Panulirus japonicus*
[Classification]	Class: Malacostraca
	Order: Decapoda
	Family: Palinuridae
	Genus: *Panulirus*
[Habitat]	Pacific Ocean off the coasts of Japan, South Korea, and Taiwan
[Length]	20-40 cm (8-16 in)

HEAVEN'S
DESIGN TEAM

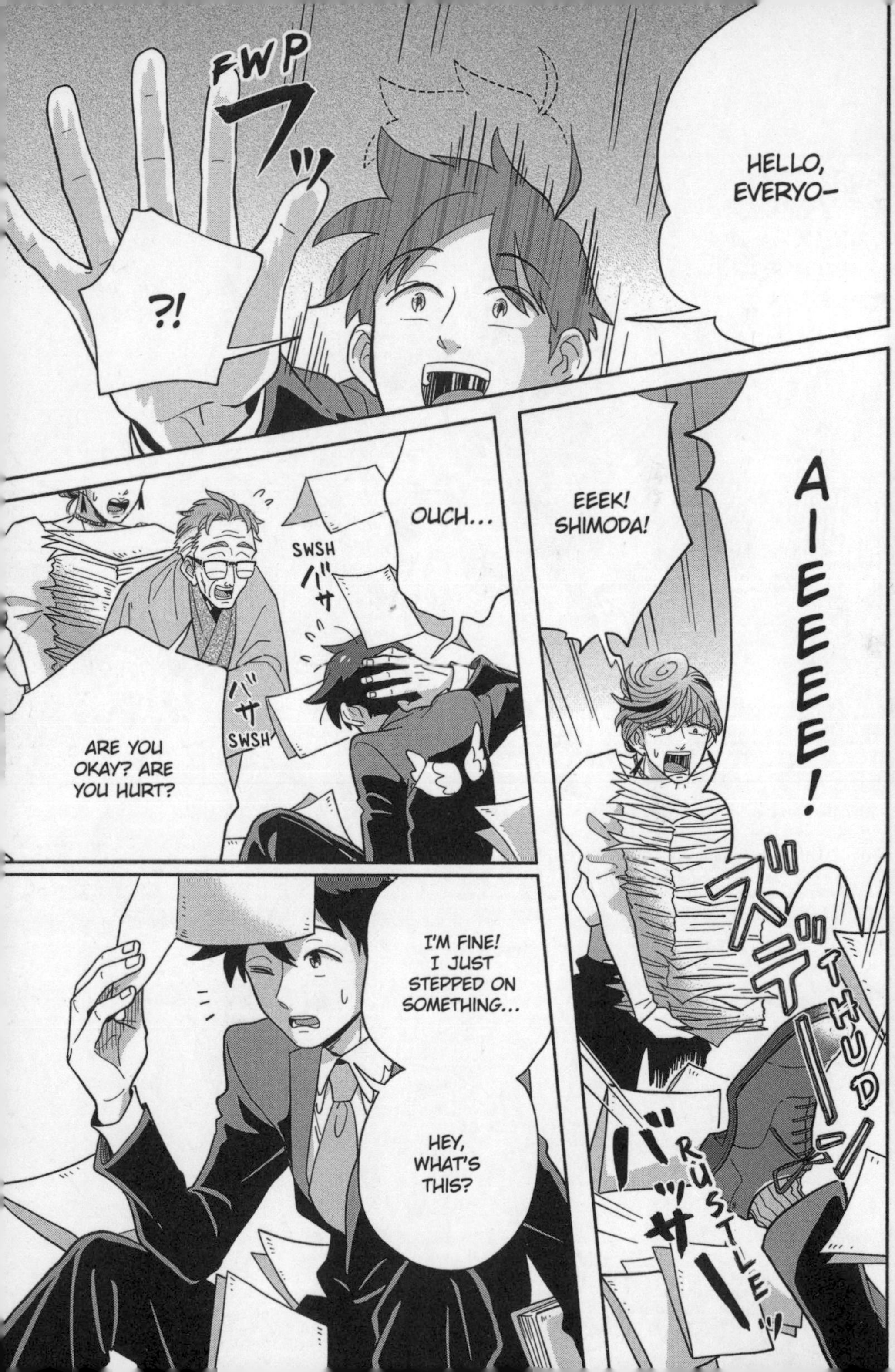
HELLO, EVERYO–
FWP
?!
EEEK! SHIMODA!
AIEEEEE!
THUD
RUSTLE
OUCH…
SWSH
SWSH
ARE YOU OKAY? ARE YOU HURT?
I'M FINE! I JUST STEPPED ON SOMETHING…
HEY, WHAT'S THIS?

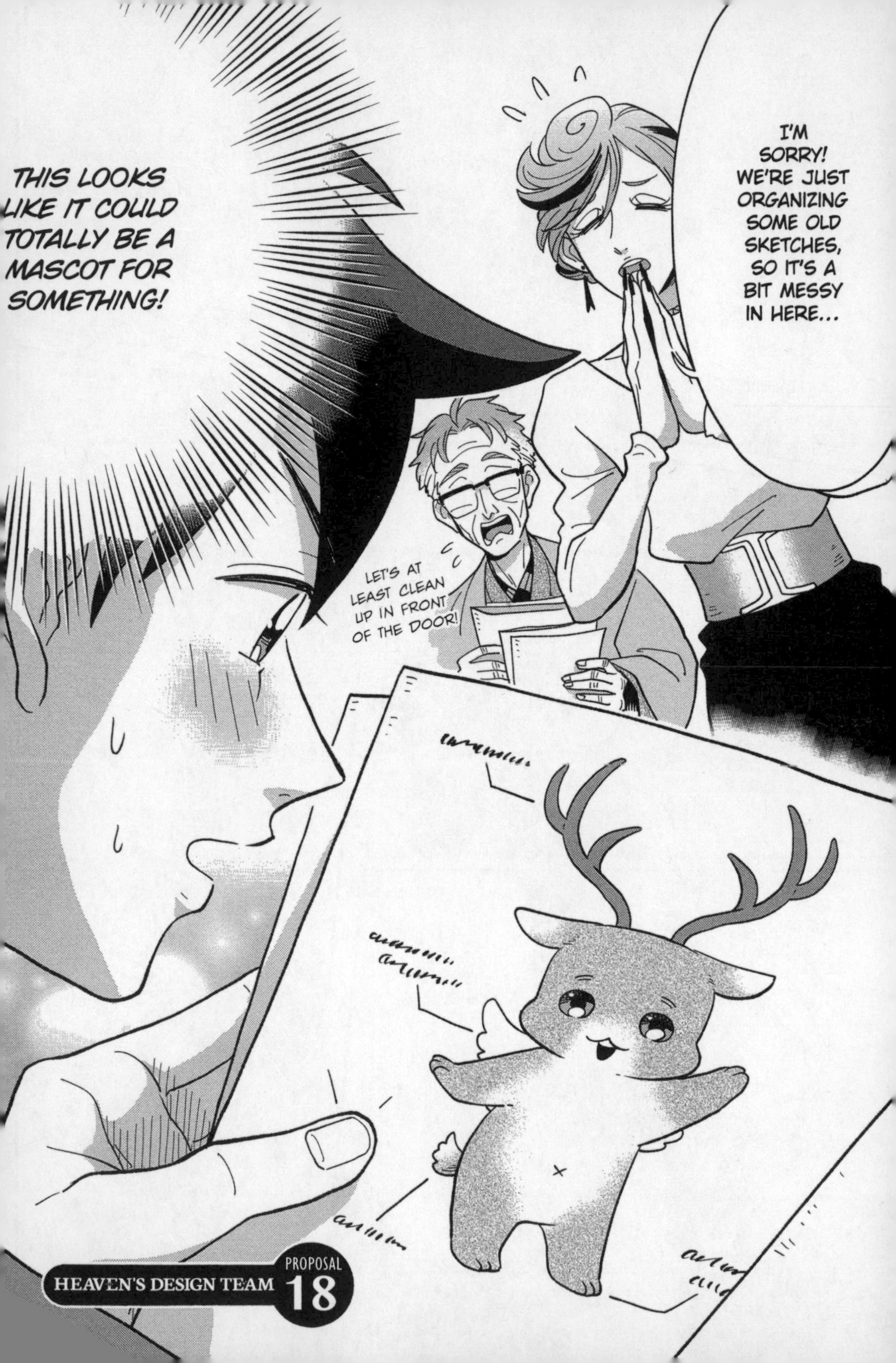
I'M SORRY! WE'RE JUST ORGANIZING SOME OLD SKETCHES, SO IT'S A BIT MESSY IN HERE...
LET'S AT LEAST CLEAN UP IN FRONT OF THE DOOR!
THIS LOOKS LIKE IT COULD TOTALLY BE A MASCOT FOR SOMETHING!
HEAVEN'S DESIGN TEAM
PROPOSAL 18

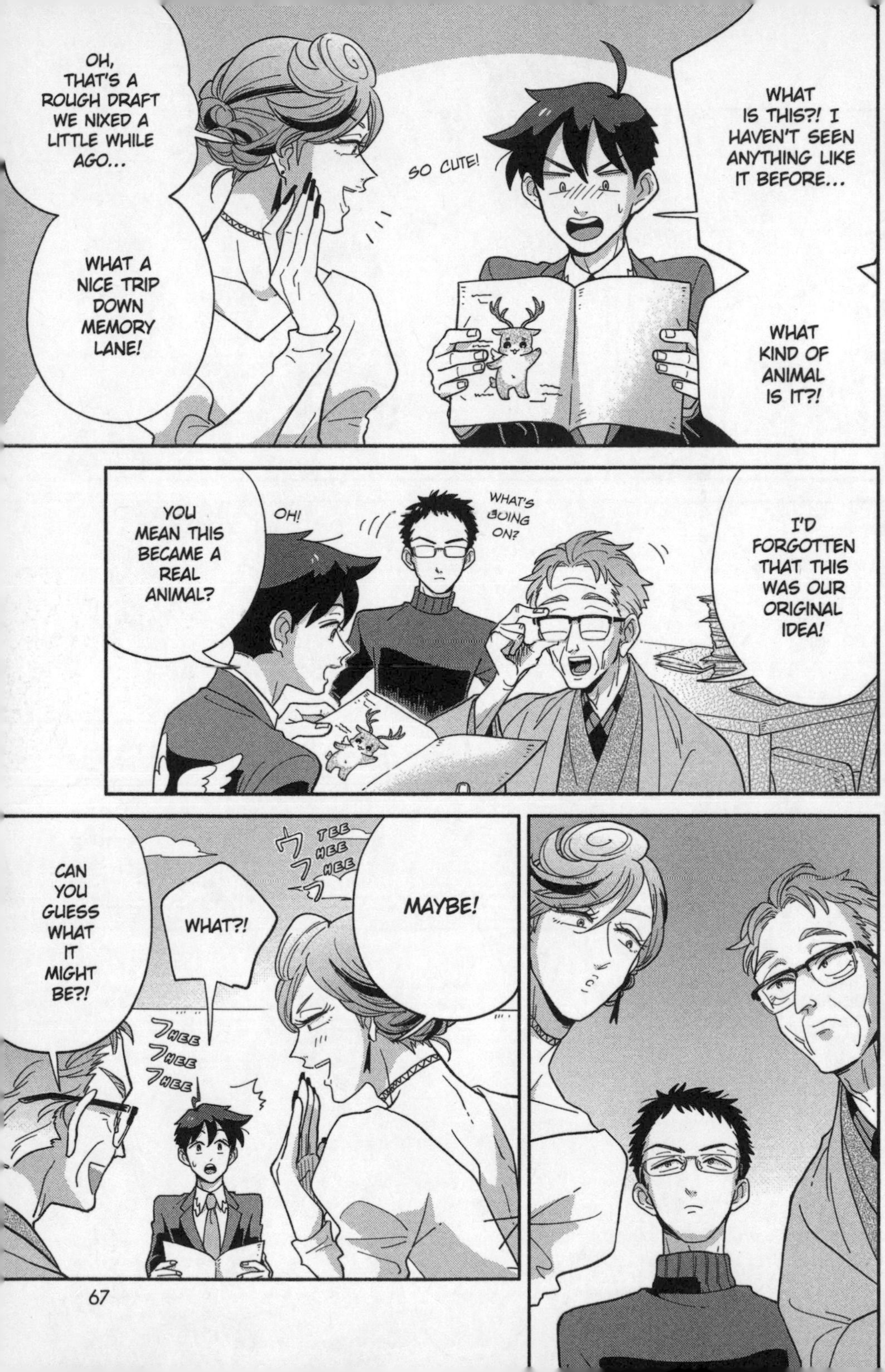
WHAT IS THIS?! I HAVEN'T SEEN ANYTHING LIKE IT BEFORE...
WHAT KIND OF ANIMAL IS IT?!
SO CUTE!
OH, THAT'S A ROUGH DRAFT WE NIXED A LITTLE WHILE AGO...
WHAT A NICE TRIP DOWN MEMORY LANE!
I'D FORGOTTEN THAT THIS WAS OUR ORIGINAL IDEA!
WHAT'S GOING ON?
OH!
YOU MEAN THIS BECAME A REAL ANIMAL?
MAYBE!
TEE HEE HEE
WHAT?!
CAN YOU GUESS WHAT IT MIGHT BE?!
HEE HEE HEE

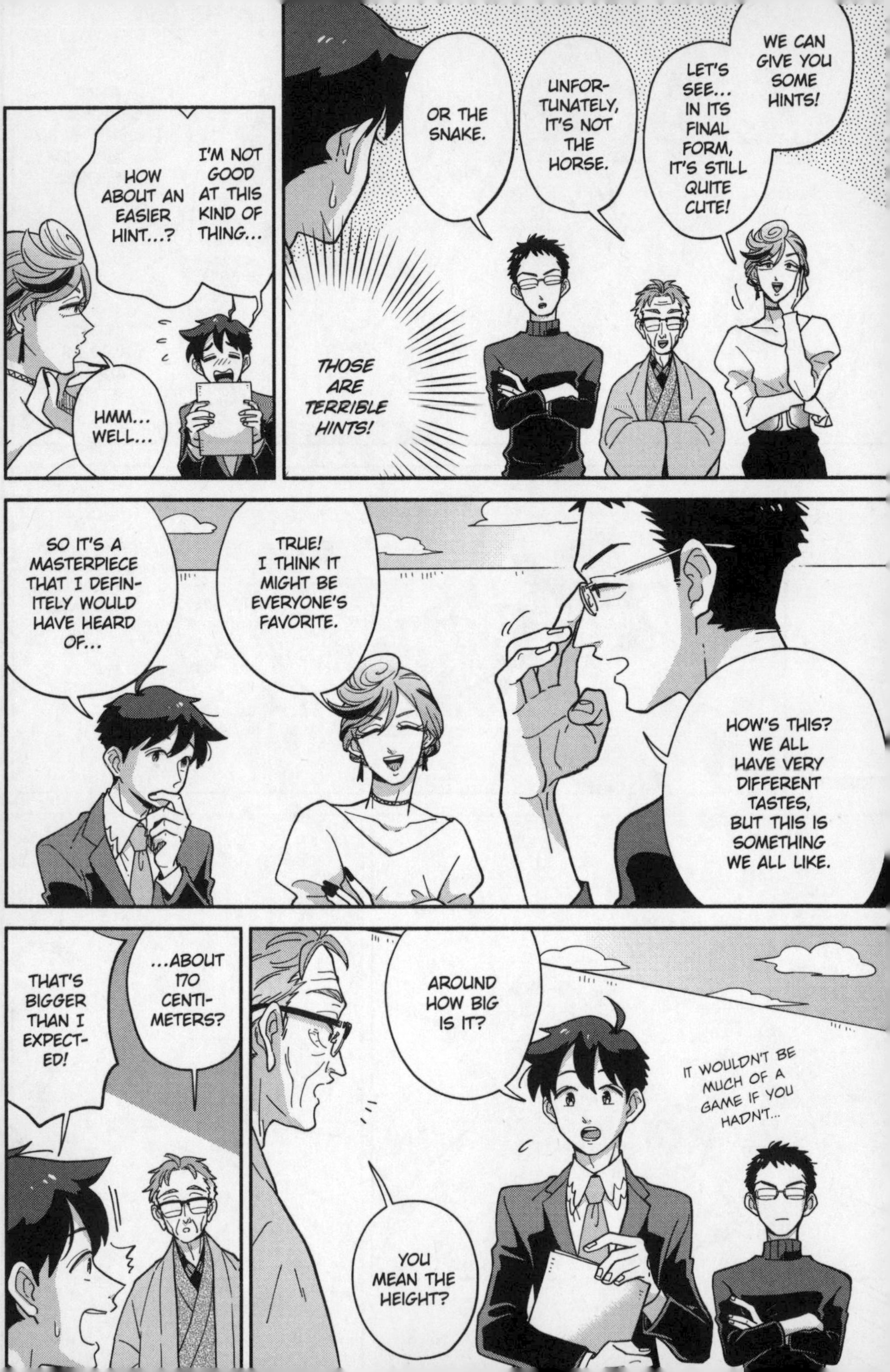
WE CAN GIVE YOU SOME HINTS!
LET'S SEE... IN ITS FINAL FORM, IT'S STILL QUITE CUTE!
UNFORTUNATELY, IT'S NOT THE HORSE.
OR THE SNAKE.
THOSE ARE TERRIBLE HINTS!
I'M NOT GOOD AT THIS KIND OF THING...
HOW ABOUT AN EASIER HINT...?
HMM... WELL...
HOW'S THIS? WE ALL HAVE VERY DIFFERENT TASTES, BUT THIS IS SOMETHING WE ALL LIKE.
TRUE! I THINK IT MIGHT BE EVERYONE'S FAVORITE.
SO IT'S A MASTERPIECE THAT I DEFINITELY WOULD HAVE HEARD OF...
IT WOULDN'T BE MUCH OF A GAME IF YOU HADN'T...
AROUND HOW BIG IS IT?
YOU MEAN THE HEIGHT?
...ABOUT 170 CENTIMETERS?
THAT'S BIGGER THAN I EXPECTED!

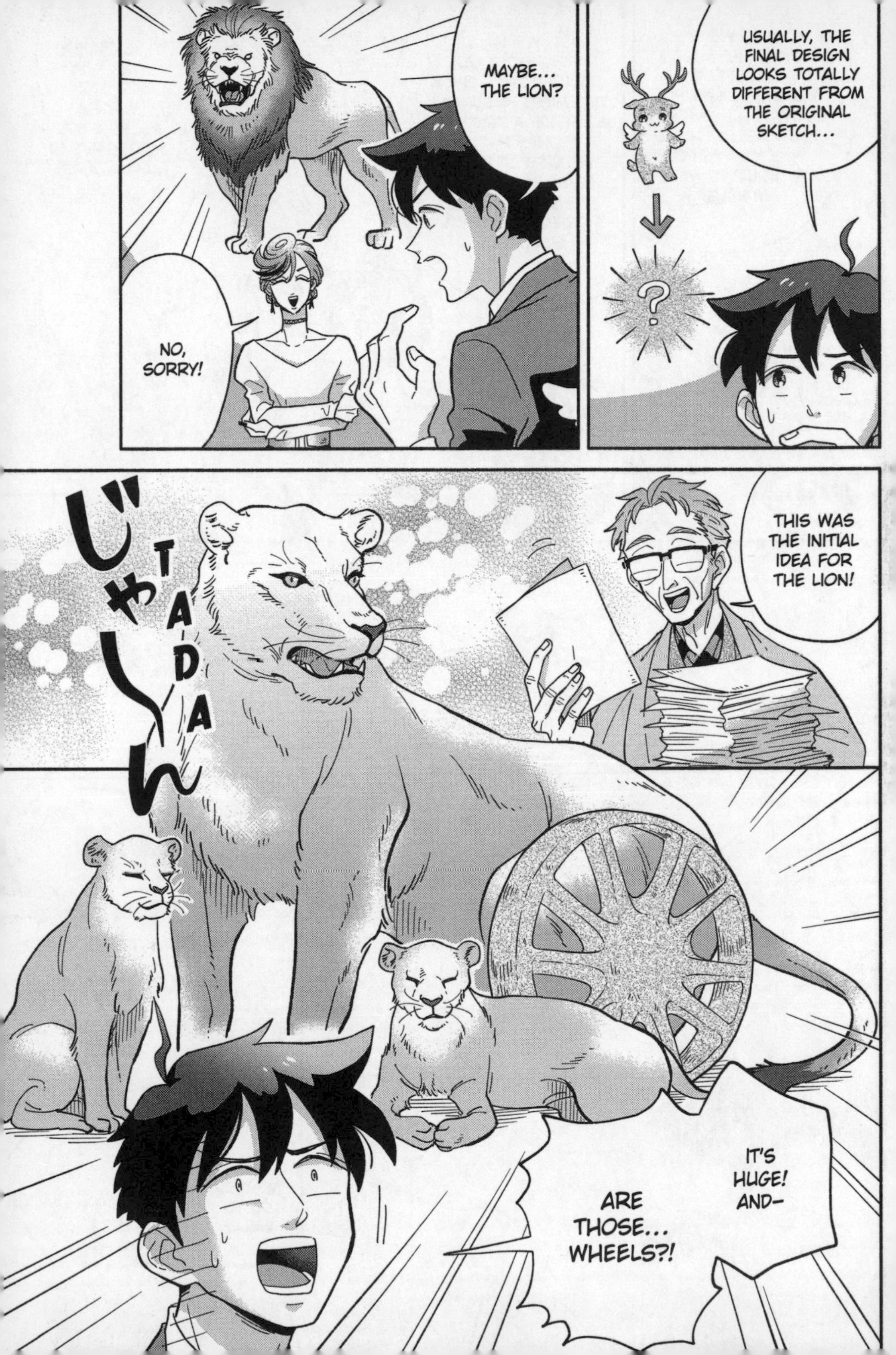
USUALLY, THE FINAL DESIGN LOOKS TOTALLY DIFFERENT FROM THE ORIGINAL SKETCH...
MAYBE... THE LION?
NO, SORRY!
THIS WAS THE INITIAL IDEA FOR THE LION!
じゃ〜ん
TADA
IT'S HUGE! AND–
ARE THOSE... WHEELS?!

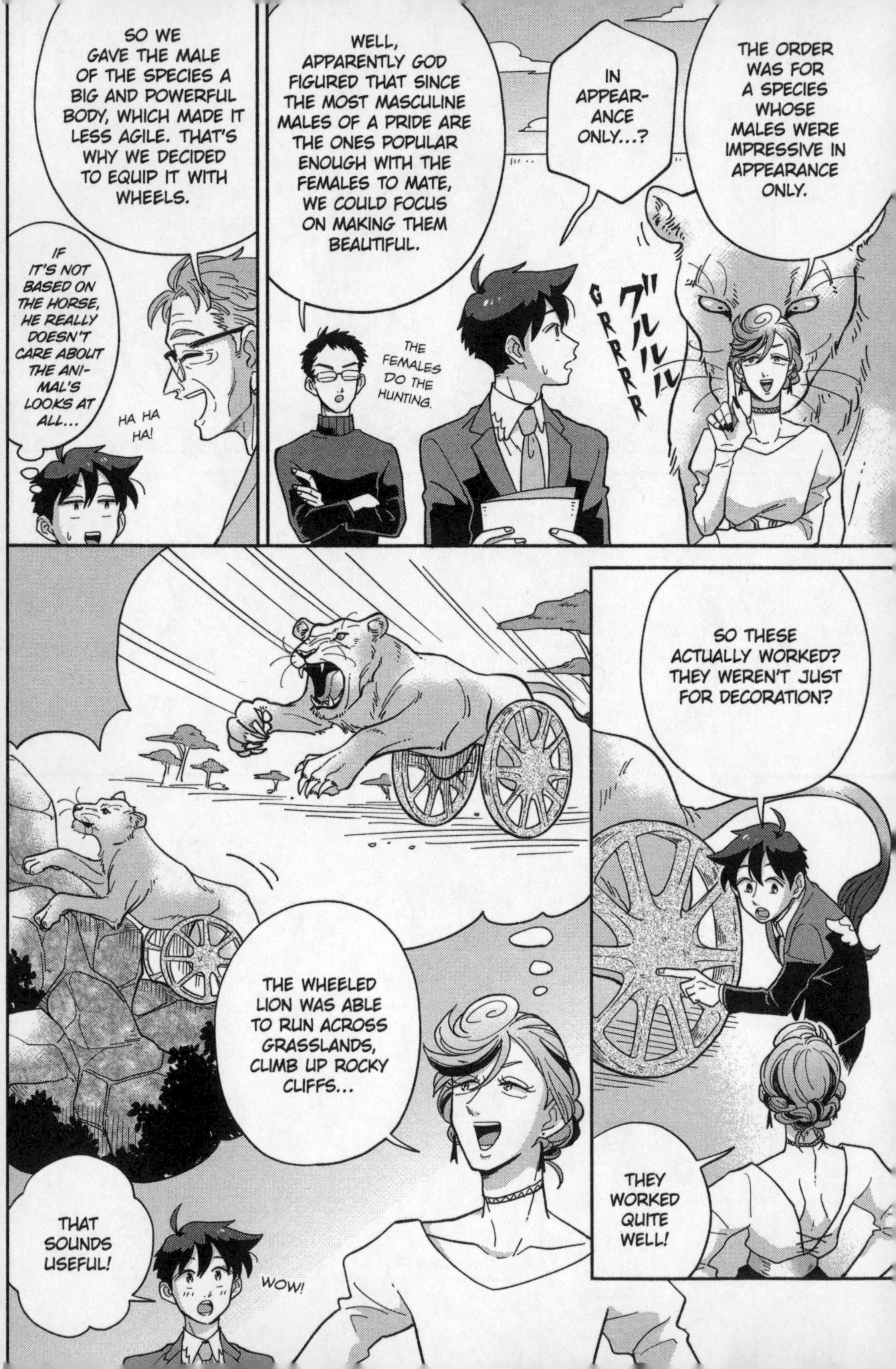
THE ORDER WAS FOR A SPECIES WHOSE MALES WERE IMPRESSIVE IN APPEARANCE ONLY.
IN APPEARANCE ONLY...?
GRRRRR
グルルル
WELL, APPARENTLY GOD FIGURED THAT SINCE THE MOST MASCULINE MALES OF A PRIDE ARE THE ONES POPULAR ENOUGH WITH THE FEMALES TO MATE, WE COULD FOCUS ON MAKING THEM BEAUTIFUL.
THE FEMALES DO THE HUNTING.
SO WE GAVE THE MALE OF THE SPECIES A BIG AND POWERFUL BODY, WHICH MADE IT LESS AGILE. THAT'S WHY WE DECIDED TO EQUIP IT WITH WHEELS.
HA HA HA!
IF IT'S NOT BASED ON THE HORSE, HE REALLY DOESN'T CARE ABOUT THE ANIMAL'S LOOKS AT ALL...
SO THESE ACTUALLY WORKED? THEY WEREN'T JUST FOR DECORATION?
THEY WORKED QUITE WELL!
THE WHEELED LION WAS ABLE TO RUN ACROSS GRASSLANDS, CLIMB UP ROCKY CLIFFS...
WOW!
THAT SOUNDS USEFUL!

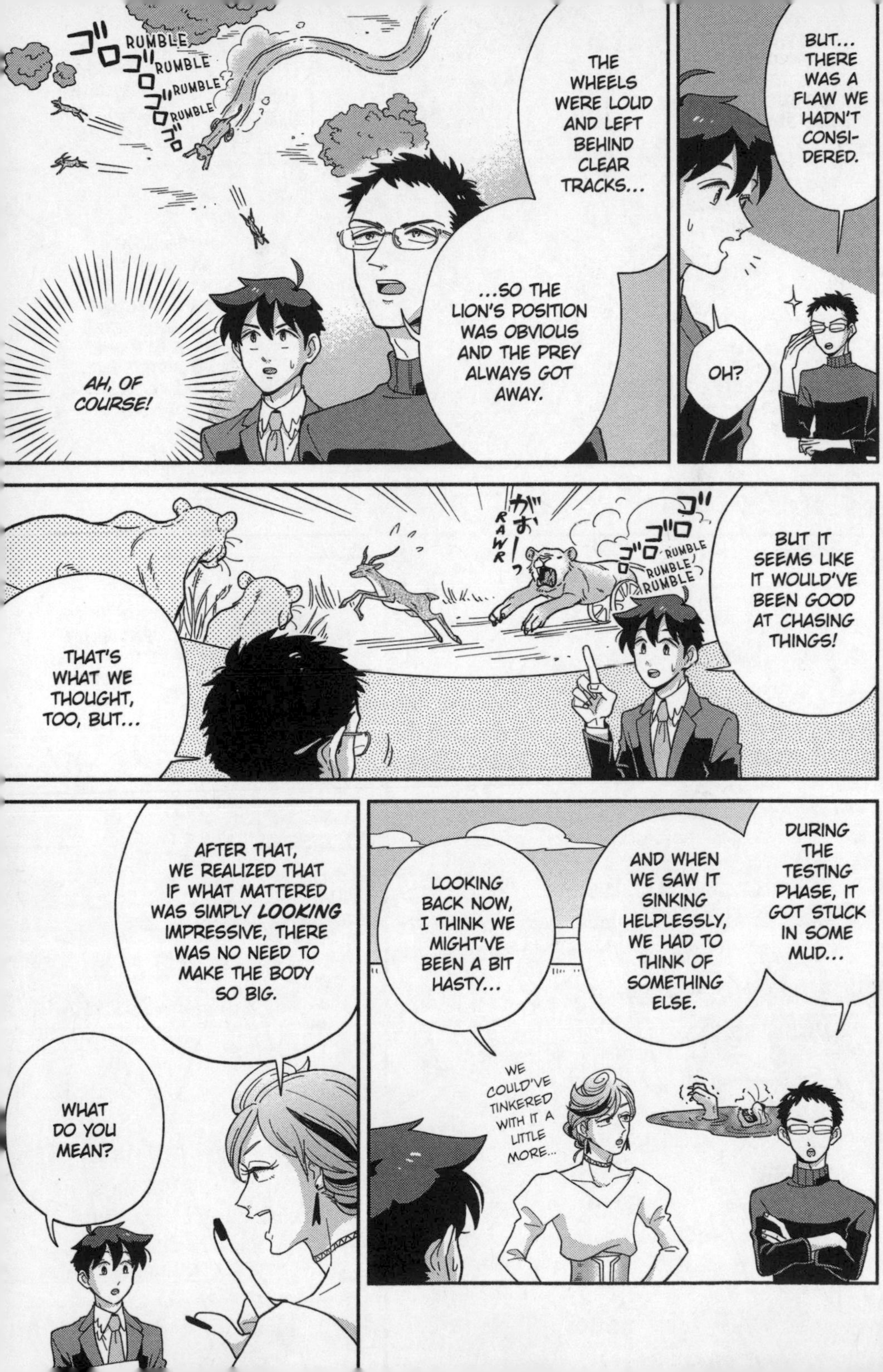
BUT... THERE WAS A FLAW WE HADN'T CONSIDERED.
OH?
ゴロゴロゴロゴロ
RUMBLE RUMBLE RUMBLE RUMBLE
THE WHEELS WERE LOUD AND LEFT BEHIND CLEAR TRACKS...
...SO THE LION'S POSITION WAS OBVIOUS AND THE PREY ALWAYS GOT AWAY.
AH, OF COURSE!
BUT IT SEEMS LIKE IT WOULD'VE BEEN GOOD AT CHASING THINGS!
ゴロゴロゴロ
RUMBLE RUMBLE RUMBLE
がおーっ
RAWR
THAT'S WHAT WE THOUGHT, TOO, BUT...
DURING THE TESTING PHASE, IT GOT STUCK IN SOME MUD...
AND WHEN WE SAW IT SINKING HELPLESSLY, WE HAD TO THINK OF SOMETHING ELSE.
LOOKING BACK NOW, I THINK WE MIGHT'VE BEEN A BIT HASTY...
WE COULD'VE TINKERED WITH IT A LITTLE MORE...
AFTER THAT, WE REALIZED THAT IF WHAT MATTERED WAS SIMPLY *LOOKING* IMPRESSIVE, THERE WAS NO NEED TO MAKE THE BODY SO BIG.
WHAT DO YOU MEAN?

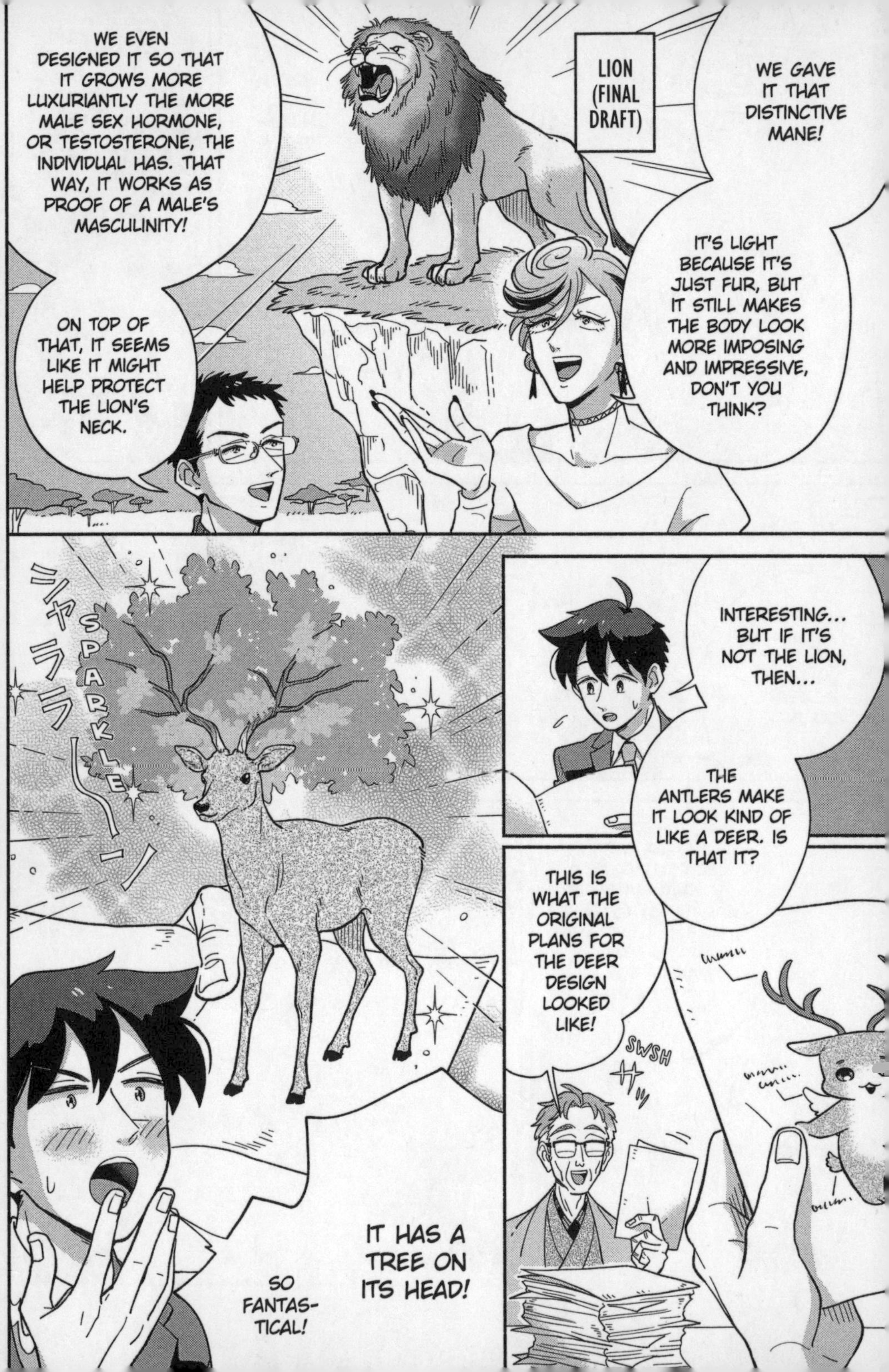

WE GAVE IT THAT DISTINCTIVE MANE!
LION (FINAL DRAFT)
WE EVEN DESIGNED IT SO THAT IT GROWS MORE LUXURIANTLY THE MORE MALE SEX HORMONE, OR TESTOSTERONE, THE INDIVIDUAL HAS. THAT WAY, IT WORKS AS PROOF OF A MALE'S MASCULINITY!
IT'S LIGHT BECAUSE IT'S JUST FUR, BUT IT STILL MAKES THE BODY LOOK MORE IMPOSING AND IMPRESSIVE, DON'T YOU THINK?
ON TOP OF THAT, IT SEEMS LIKE IT MIGHT HELP PROTECT THE LION'S NECK.
INTERESTING... BUT IF IT'S NOT THE LION, THEN...
THE ANTLERS MAKE IT LOOK KIND OF LIKE A DEER. IS THAT IT?
THIS IS WHAT THE ORIGINAL PLANS FOR THE DEER DESIGN LOOKED LIKE!
SWSH
シャララーン
SPARKLE
IT HAS A TREE ON ITS HEAD!
SO FANTASTICAL!

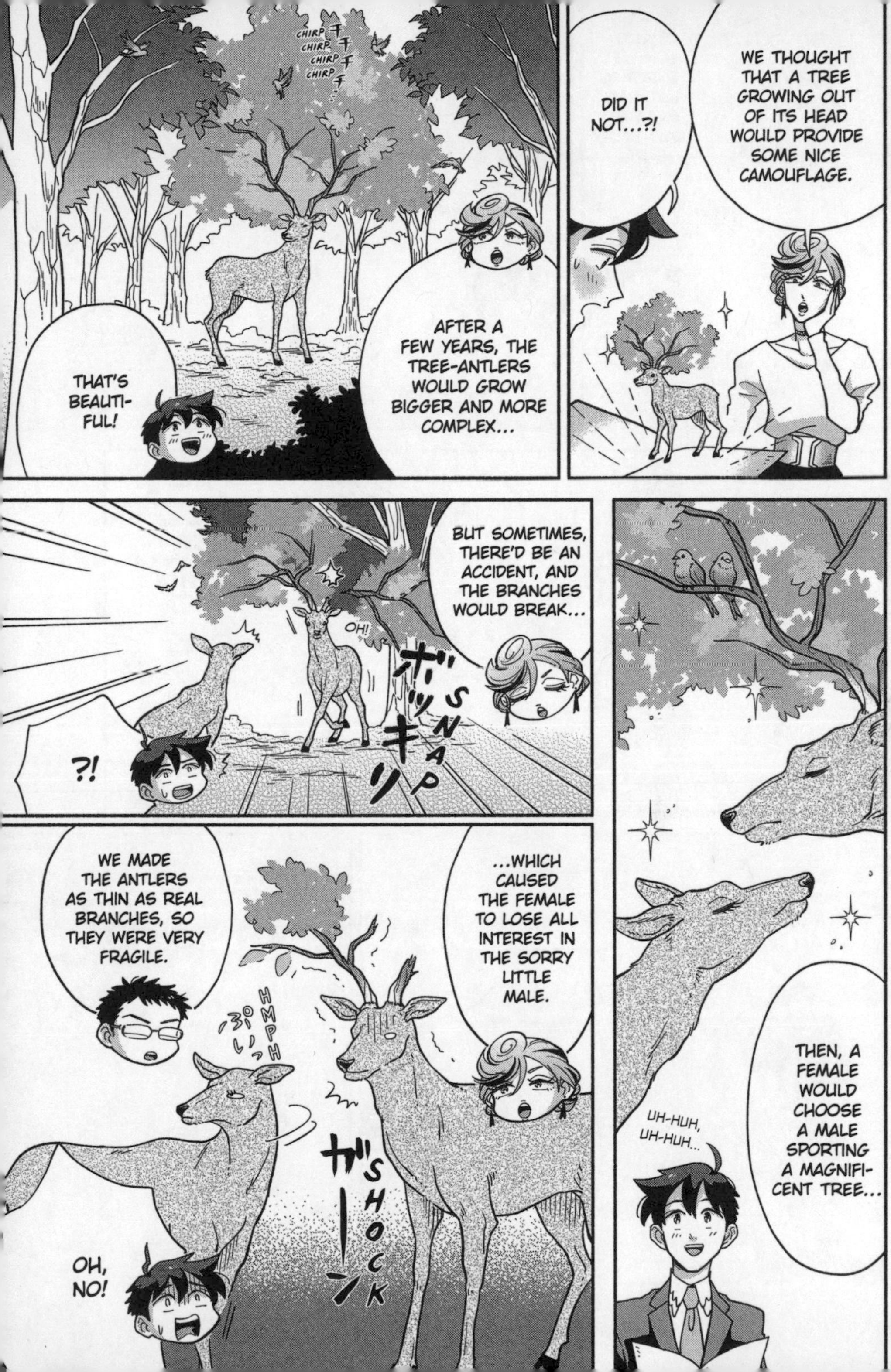

WE THOUGHT THAT A TREE GROWING OUT OF ITS HEAD WOULD PROVIDE SOME NICE CAMOUFLAGE.
DID IT NOT...?!
CHIRP CHIRP CHIRP CHIRP
AFTER A FEW YEARS, THE TREE-ANTLERS WOULD GROW BIGGER AND MORE COMPLEX...
THAT'S BEAUTI-FUL!
THEN, A FEMALE WOULD CHOOSE A MALE SPORTING A MAGNIFI-CENT TREE...
UH-HUH, UH-HUH...
BUT SOMETIMES, THERE'D BE AN ACCIDENT, AND THE BRANCHES WOULD BREAK...
OH!
SNAP
?!
...WHICH CAUSED THE FEMALE TO LOSE ALL INTEREST IN THE SORRY LITTLE MALE.
SHOCK
HMPH
WE MADE THE ANTLERS AS THIN AS REAL BRANCHES, SO THEY WERE VERY FRAGILE.
OH, NO!

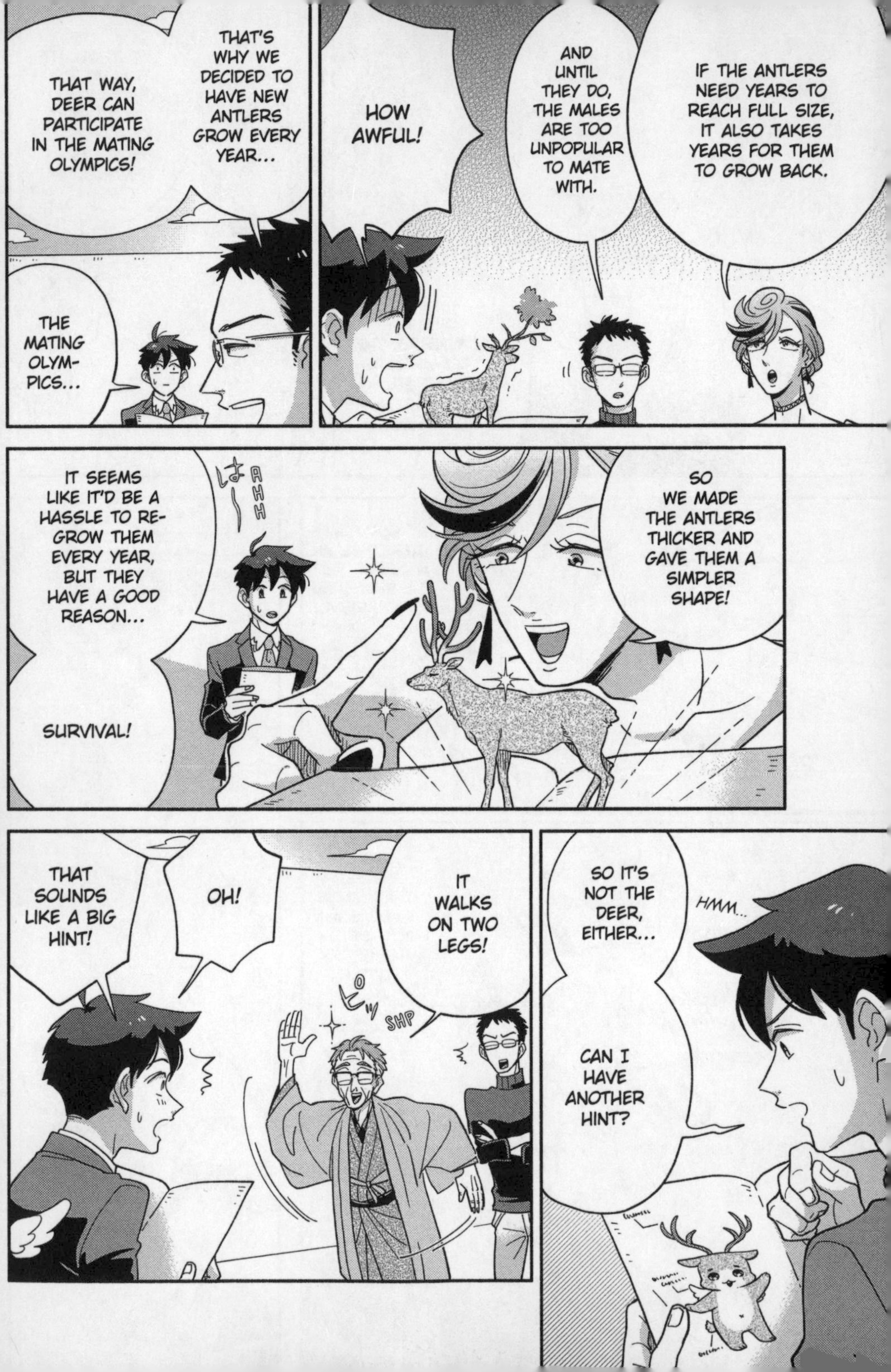
IF THE ANTLERS NEED YEARS TO REACH FULL SIZE, IT ALSO TAKES YEARS FOR THEM TO GROW BACK.
AND UNTIL THEY DO, THE MALES ARE TOO UNPOPULAR TO MATE WITH.
HOW AWFUL!
THAT'S WHY WE DECIDED TO HAVE NEW ANTLERS GROW EVERY YEAR...
THAT WAY, DEER CAN PARTICIPATE IN THE MATING OLYMPICS!
THE MATING OLYMPICS...
SO WE MADE THE ANTLERS THICKER AND GAVE THEM A SIMPLER SHAPE!
はー
AHHH
IT SEEMS LIKE IT'D BE A HASSLE TO RE-GROW THEM EVERY YEAR, BUT THEY HAVE A GOOD REASON...
SURVIVAL!
HMM...
SO IT'S NOT THE DEER, EITHER...
CAN I HAVE ANOTHER HINT?
IT WALKS ON TWO LEGS!
ピッ
SHP
OH!
THAT SOUNDS LIKE A BIG HINT!

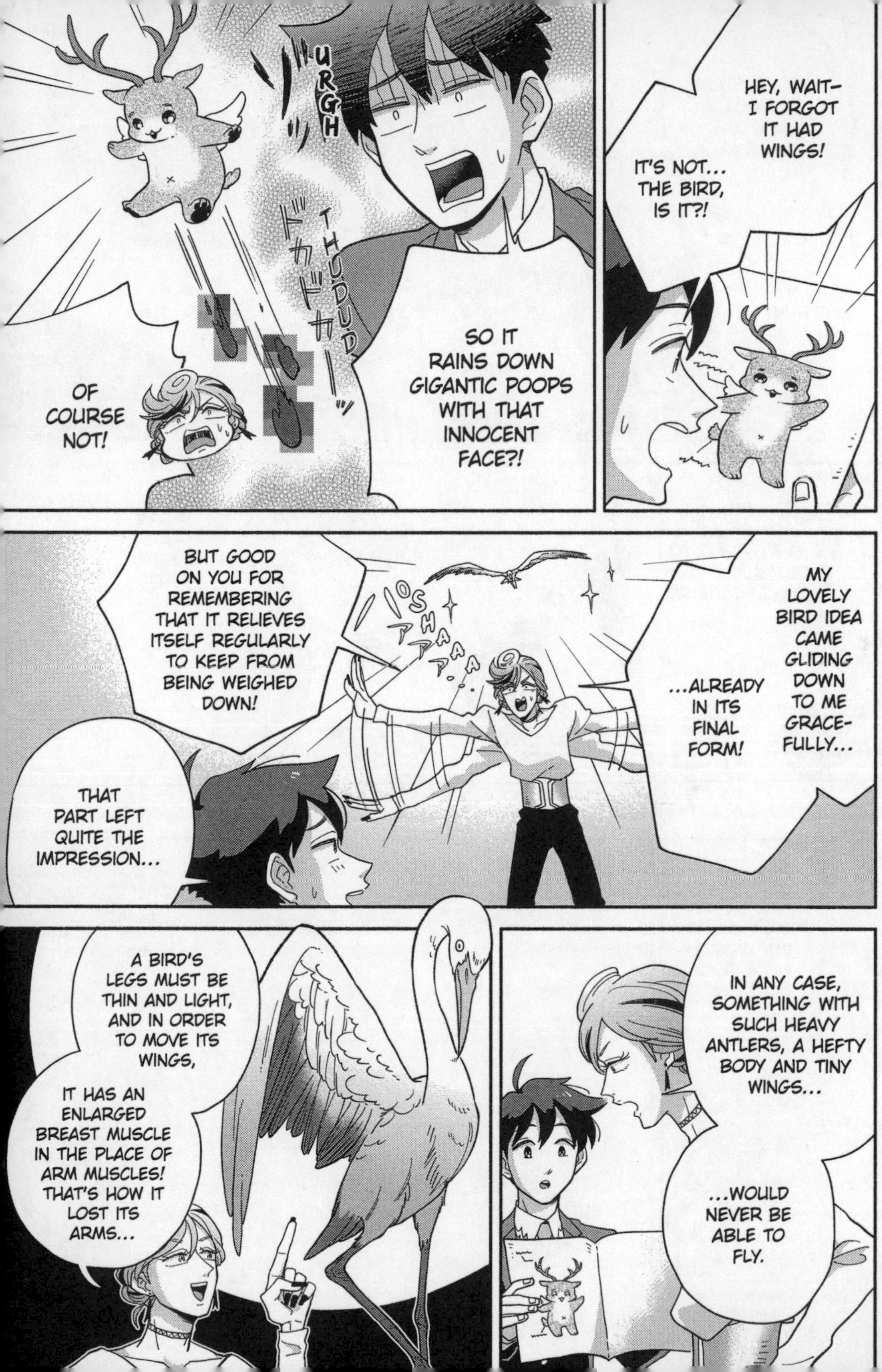

HEY, WAIT– I FORGOT IT HAD WINGS!
IT'S NOT... THE BIRD, IS IT?!
URGH
SO IT RAINS DOWN GIGANTIC POOPS WITH THAT INNOCENT FACE?!
THUDUD
OF COURSE NOT!
MY LOVELY BIRD IDEA CAME GLIDING DOWN TO ME GRACEFULLY...
...ALREADY IN ITS FINAL FORM!
SHAAAA
BUT GOOD ON YOU FOR REMEMBERING THAT IT RELIEVES ITSELF REGULARLY TO KEEP FROM BEING WEIGHED DOWN!
THAT PART LEFT QUITE THE IMPRESSION...
IN ANY CASE, SOMETHING WITH SUCH HEAVY ANTLERS, A HEFTY BODY AND TINY WINGS...
...WOULD NEVER BE ABLE TO FLY.
A BIRD'S LEGS MUST BE THIN AND LIGHT, AND IN ORDER TO MOVE ITS WINGS,
IT HAS AN ENLARGED BREAST MUSCLE IN THE PLACE OF ARM MUSCLES! THAT'S HOW IT LOST ITS ARMS...

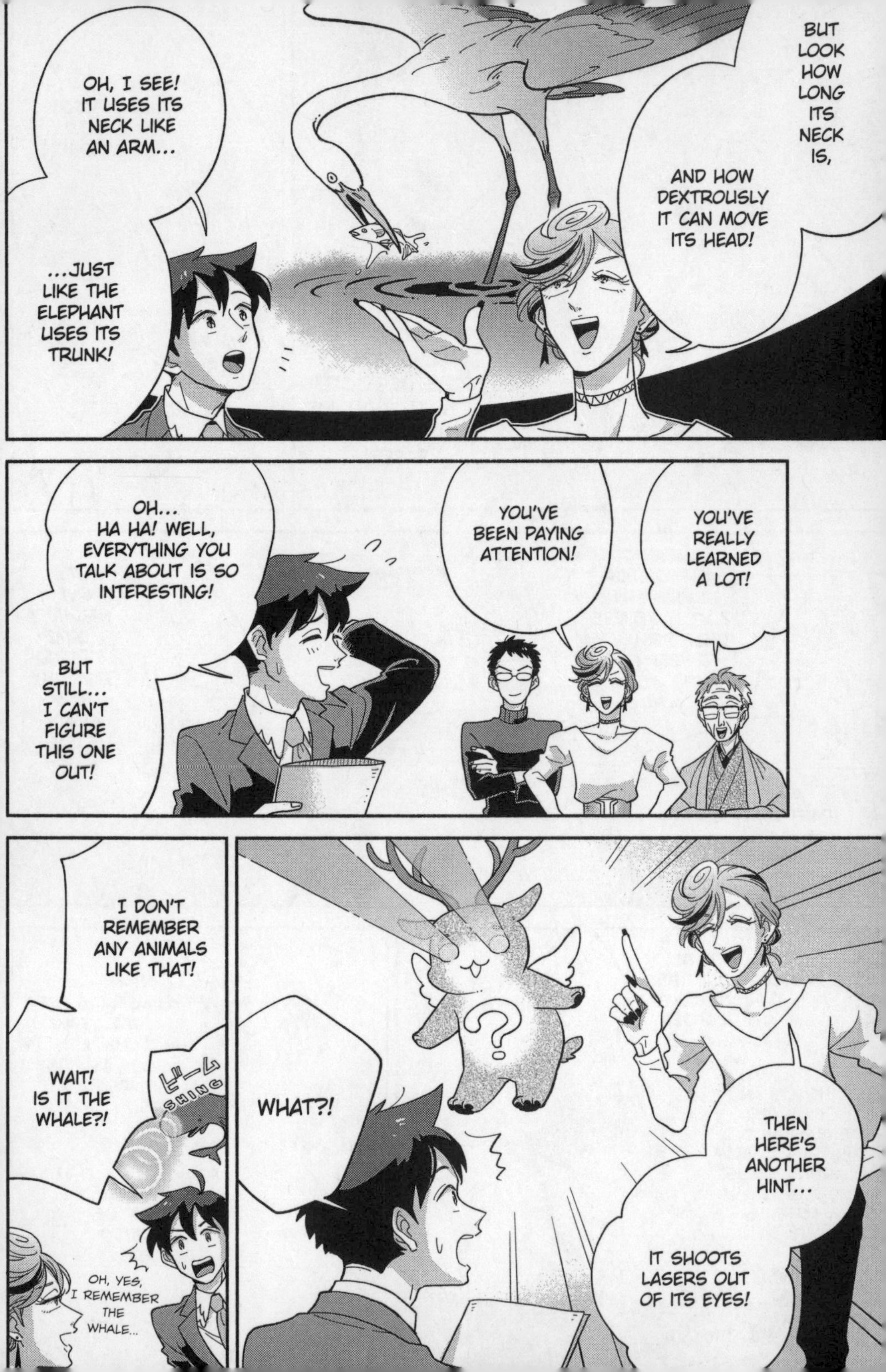
BUT LOOK HOW LONG ITS NECK IS,
AND HOW DEXTROUSLY IT CAN MOVE ITS HEAD!
OH, I SEE! IT USES ITS NECK LIKE AN ARM...
...JUST LIKE THE ELEPHANT USES ITS TRUNK!
YOU'VE REALLY LEARNED A LOT!
YOU'VE BEEN PAYING ATTENTION!
OH... HA HA! WELL, EVERYTHING YOU TALK ABOUT IS SO INTERESTING!
BUT STILL... I CAN'T FIGURE THIS ONE OUT!
THEN HERE'S ANOTHER HINT...
IT SHOOTS LASERS OUT OF ITS EYES!
WHAT?!
I DON'T REMEMBER ANY ANIMALS LIKE THAT!
WAIT! IS IT THE WHALE?!
ビーム
SHING
OH, YES, I REMEMBER THE WHALE...

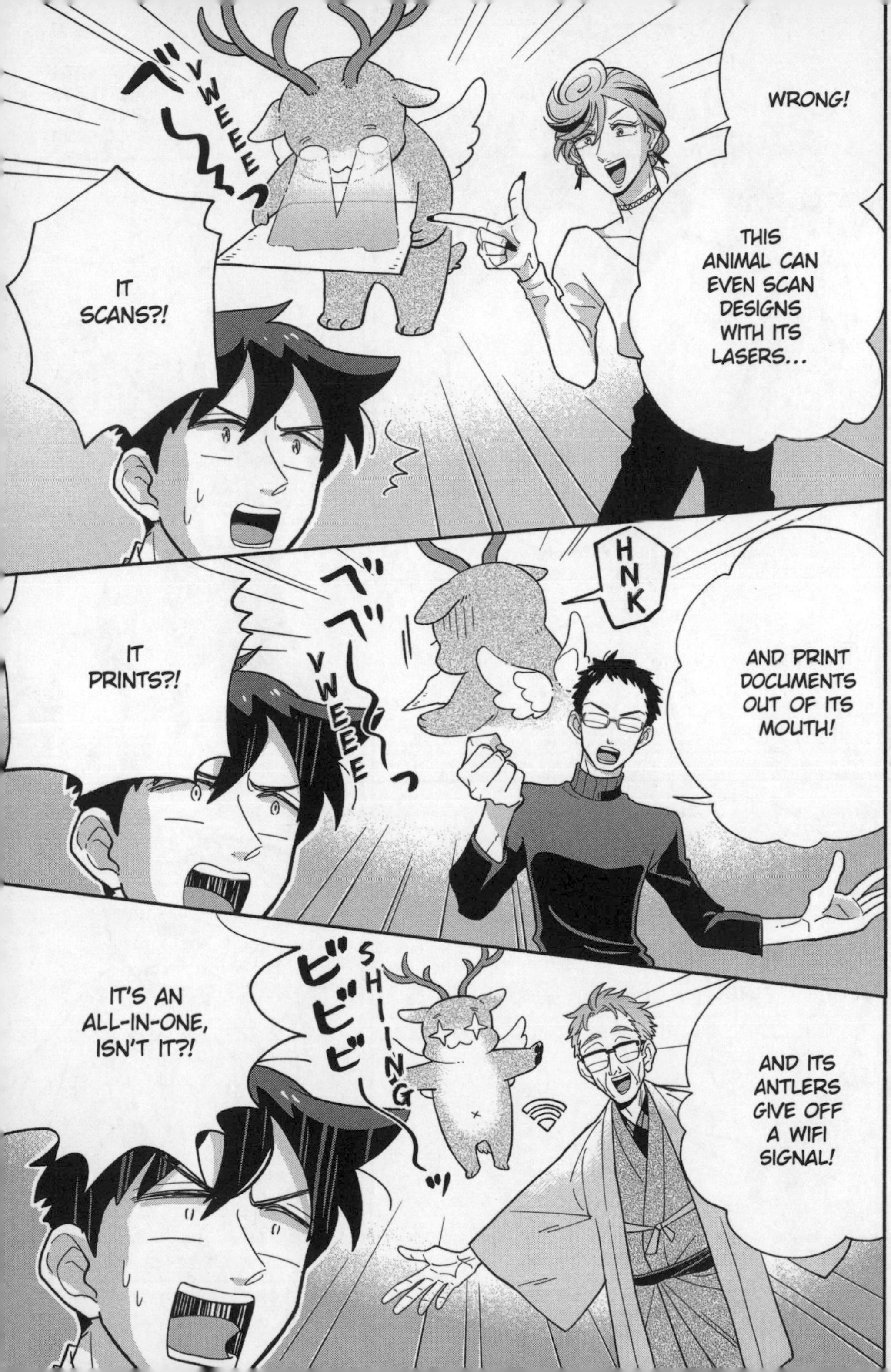
WRONG!
THIS ANIMAL CAN EVEN SCAN DESIGNS WITH ITS LASERS...
べ〜〜っ
VWEEEE
IT SCANS?!
HNK
AND PRINT DOCUMENTS OUT OF ITS MOUTH!
べべ〜っ
VWEEEE
IT PRINTS?!
AND ITS ANTLERS GIVE OFF A WIFI SIGNAL!
ビビビ
SHIING
IT'S AN ALL-IN-ONE, ISN'T IT?!

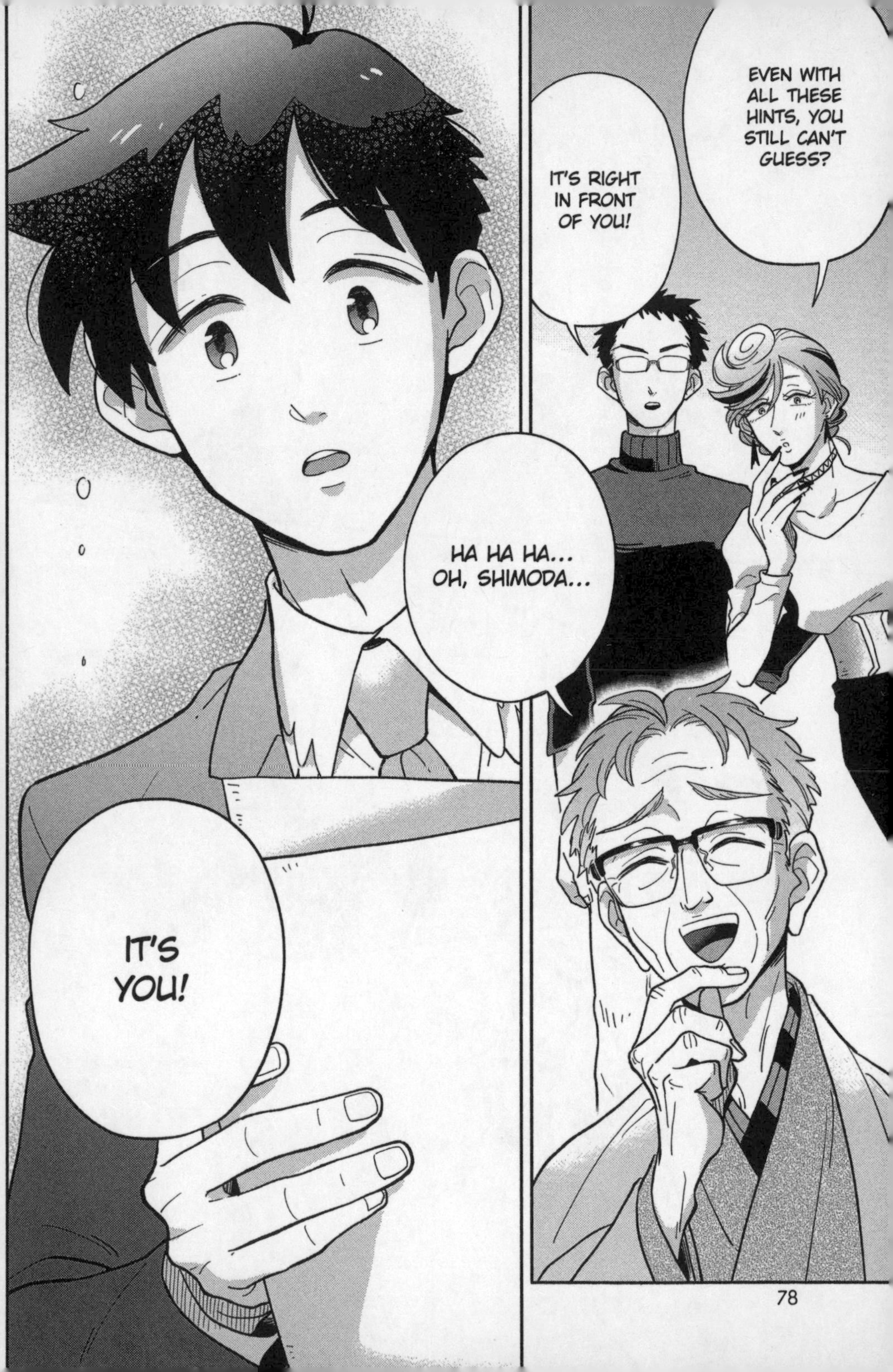
EVEN WITH ALL THESE HINTS, YOU STILL CAN'T GUESS?
IT'S RIGHT IN FRONT OF YOU!
HA HA HA... OH, SHIMODA...
IT'S YOU!

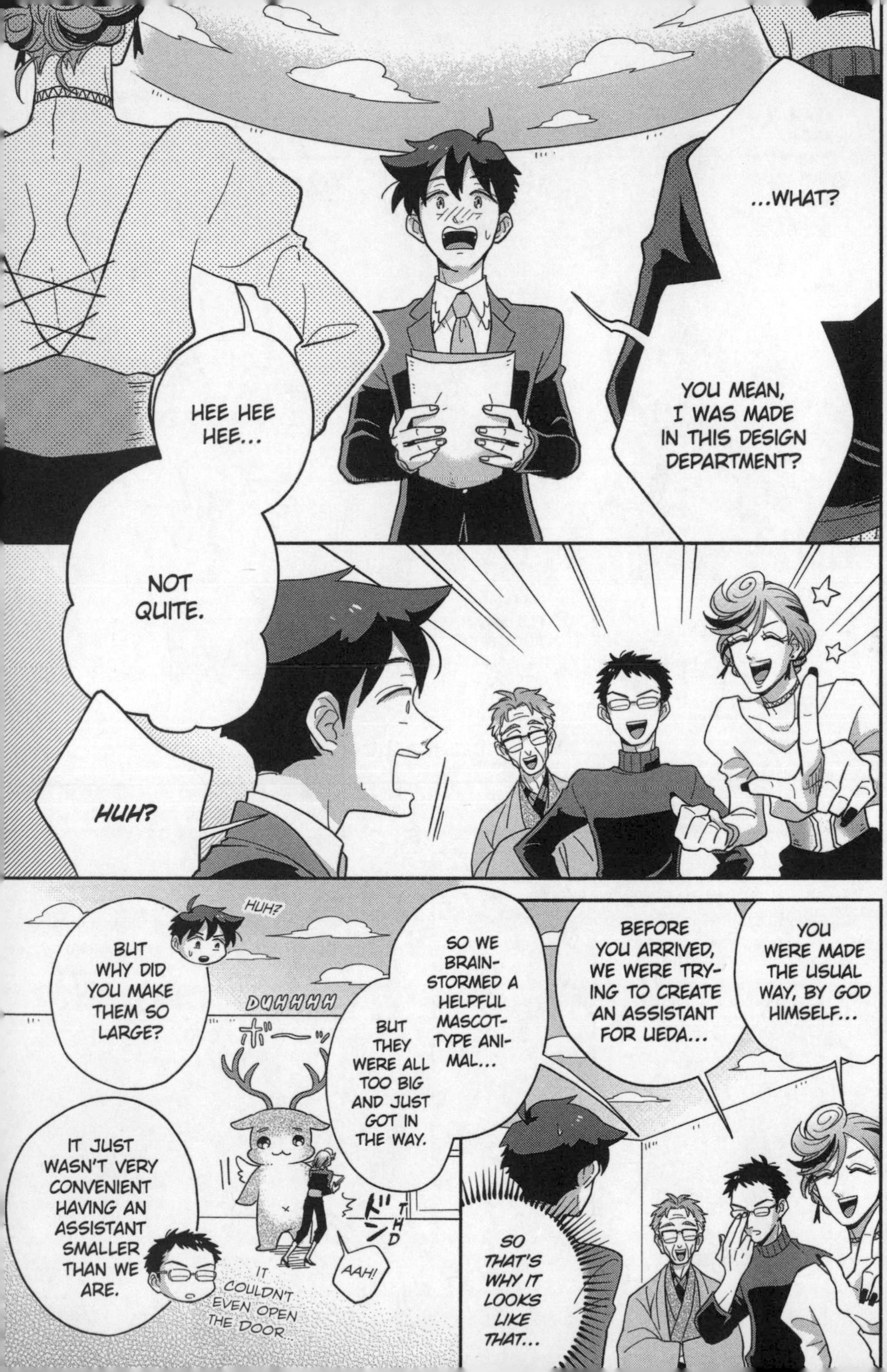
...WHAT?
YOU MEAN, I WAS MADE IN THIS DESIGN DEPARTMENT?
HEE HEE HEE...
NOT QUITE.
HUH?
YOU WERE MADE THE USUAL WAY, BY GOD HIMSELF...
BEFORE YOU ARRIVED, WE WERE TRY-ING TO CREATE AN ASSISTANT FOR UEDA...
SO WE BRAIN-STORMED A HELPFUL MASCOT-TYPE ANI-MAL...
SO THAT'S WHY IT LOOKS LIKE THAT...
BUT THEY WERE ALL TOO BIG AND JUST GOT IN THE WAY.
HUH?
BUT WHY DID YOU MAKE THEM SO LARGE?
DUHHHHH
IT JUST WASN'T VERY CONVENIENT HAVING AN ASSISTANT SMALLER THAN WE ARE.
THD
AAH!
IT COULDN'T EVEN OPEN THE DOOR...

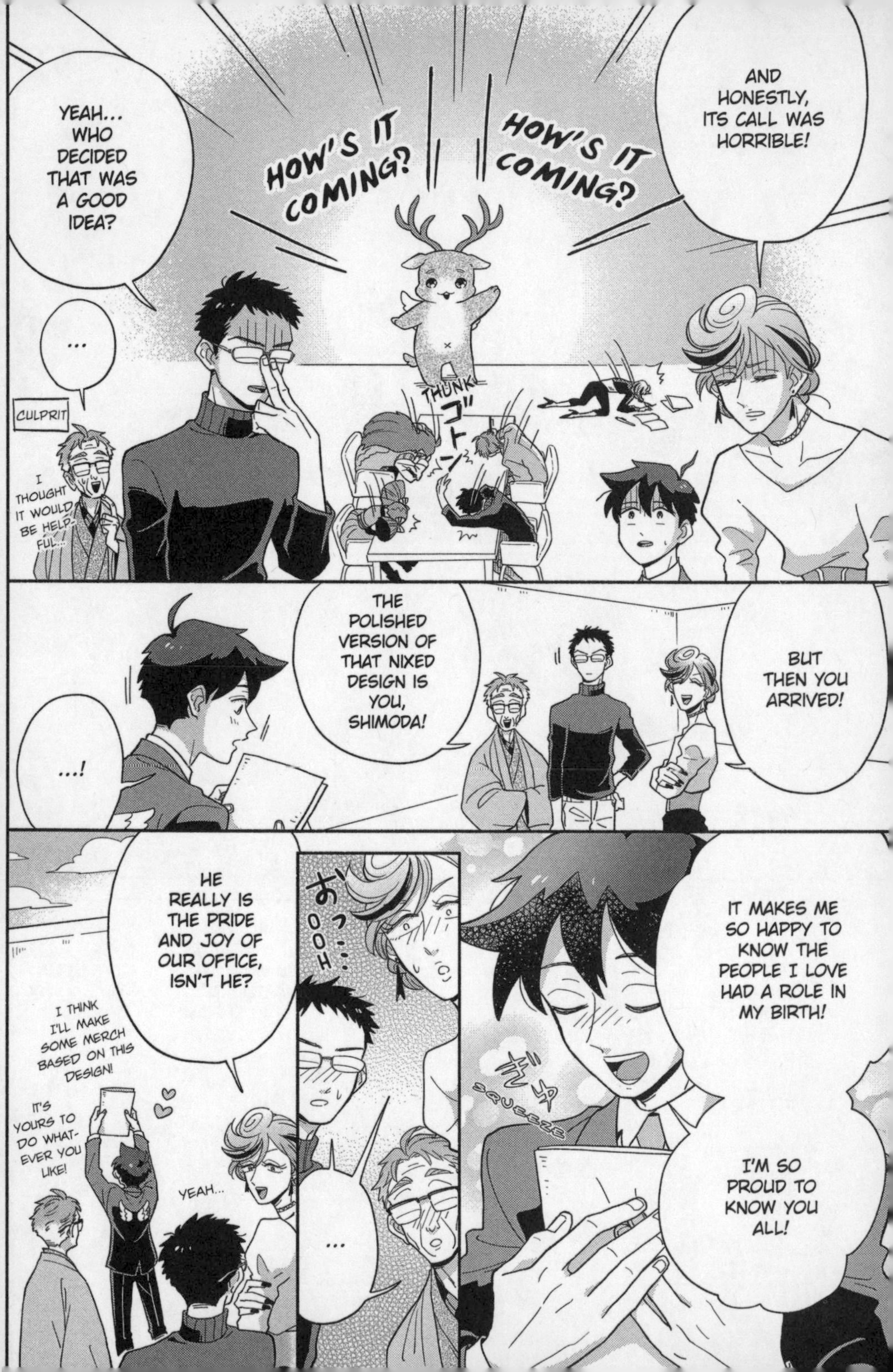
AND HONESTLY, ITS CALL WAS HORRIBLE!
HOW'S IT COMING?
HOW'S IT COMING?
YEAH... WHO DECIDED THAT WAS A GOOD IDEA?
THUNK
...
CULPRIT
I THOUGHT IT WOULD BE HELP-FUL...
BUT THEN YOU ARRIVED!
THE POLISHED VERSION OF THAT NIXED DESIGN IS YOU, SHIMODA!
...!
IT MAKES ME SO HAPPY TO KNOW THE PEOPLE I LOVE HAD A ROLE IN MY BIRTH!
I'M SO PROUD TO KNOW YOU ALL!
SQUEEZE
OOH...
...
HE REALLY IS THE PRIDE AND JOY OF OUR OFFICE, ISN'T HE?
I THINK I'LL MAKE SOME MERCH BASED ON THIS DESIGN!
IT'S YOURS TO DO WHAT-EVER YOU LIKE!
YEAH...

THE ENCYCLOPEDIA OF REAL ANIMALS 18

ANIMAL 48 LION

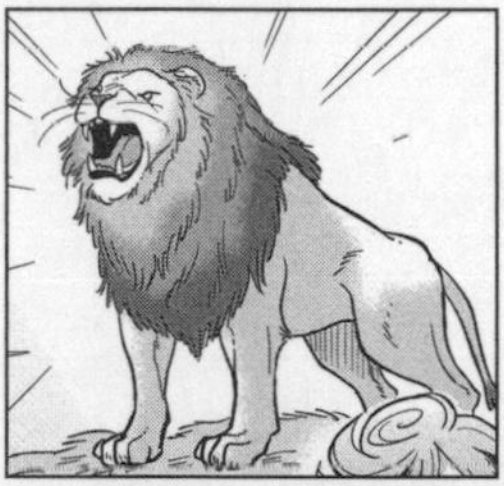

THE REAL THING

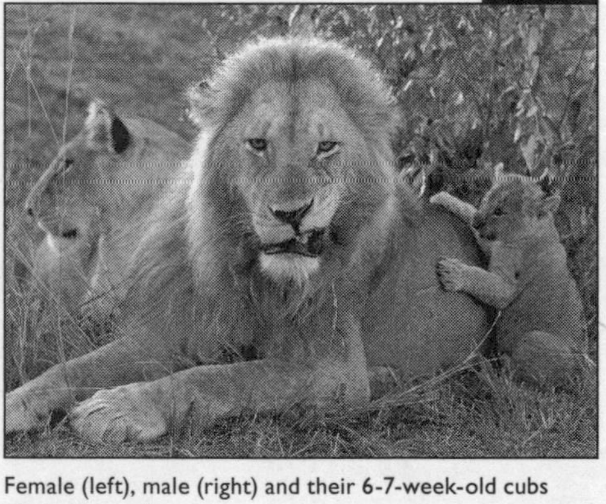

Female (left), male (right) and their 6-7-week-old cubs playing around.

Photo: Minden Pictures/Aflo

[Name] *Panthera leo*
[Classification] Class: Mammalia
Order: Carnivora
Family: Felidae
Genus: *Panthera*
[Habitat] Sub-Saharan Africa, India
[Length] 170-250 cm (5.6-8.2 ft) (males)
140-175 cm (4.6-5.7 ft) (females)

Lions live and hunt in groups known as prides. Resting occurs during the hot daylight hours, while hunting is performed primarily by the females in the cool evening and into the night. An acute sense of smell allows the lionesses to communicate with one another, and their thick paw pads allow them to sneak up on their prey without being heard. They attack with a powerful swipe of their claws or a bite to the throat. They have also been known to enclose their prey's mouth and nose in their jaws to suffocate them.

The volume and color of the males' manes apparently serve as signals of their strength, and the more testosterone a male produces, the larger and darker his mane. The mane also makes the male's body appear larger. Some say the mane may have evolved from a need to protect the neck from an opponent's claws and teeth during fights with other males, but there is some disagreement surrounding this theory.

SPECIAL FEATURE — BIRD NECKS

The bird in this chapter does not exist in real life.

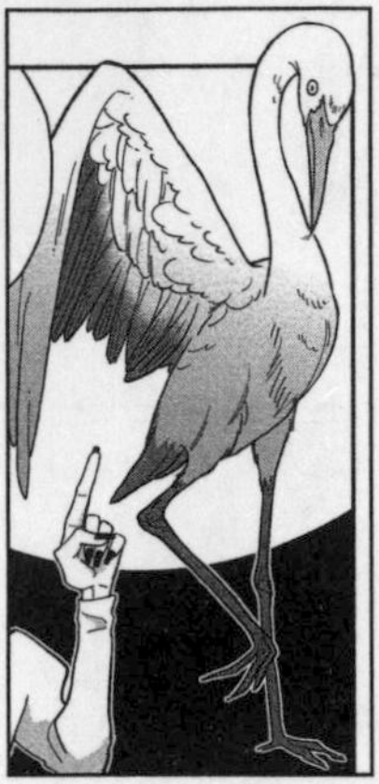

The skeleton of a cormorant, which has 20 neck vertebrae.

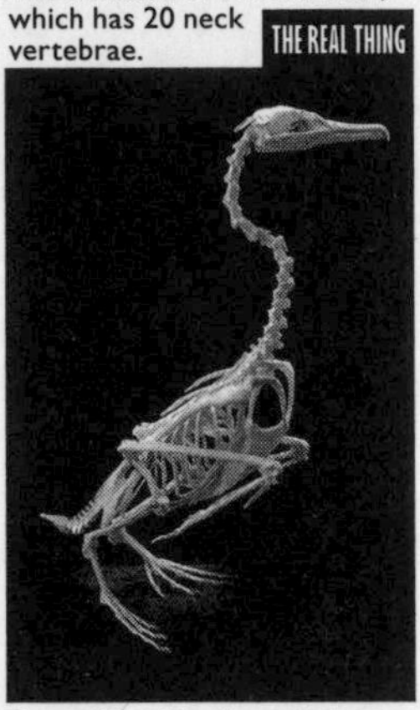
THE REAL THING

Photo: Koji Yonekawa/Aflo

Most mammals' necks are made up of seven cervical vertebrae. Birds, on the other hand, have up to 20 depending on the species, and these are moved with specialized joints, which make their necks very flexible. Because birds have wings, they lack forelegs, but their dextrous necks are able to compensate for the loss.

[Name]	Bird
[Classification]	Class: Aves
[Habitat]	Earth
[Number of neck vertibrae]	9-25

SPECIAL FEATURE — MR. PROGRESS

An expert at managing deadlines, Mr. Progress acts as a companion to the designers when things are progressing smoothly. However, when a deadline is approaching, he has the tendency to harass his co-workers with repeated vocalizations such as: "How's it coming?", "We were hoping for a final draft by tomorrow morning," and "The client would like an update..."

As the deadline gets closer, Mr. Progress's body turns red.

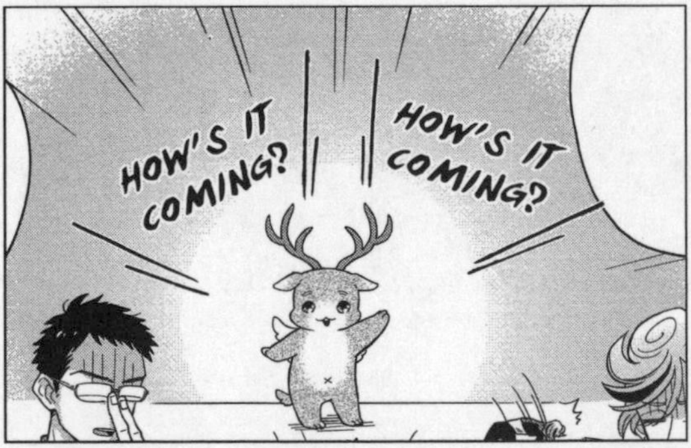
HOW'S IT COMING?
HOW'S IT COMING?

[Name]	Mr. Progress
[Classification]	Unknown
[Habitat]	None
[Length]	Approximately 170 cm (5.6 ft)

HEAVEN'S
DESIGN TEAM

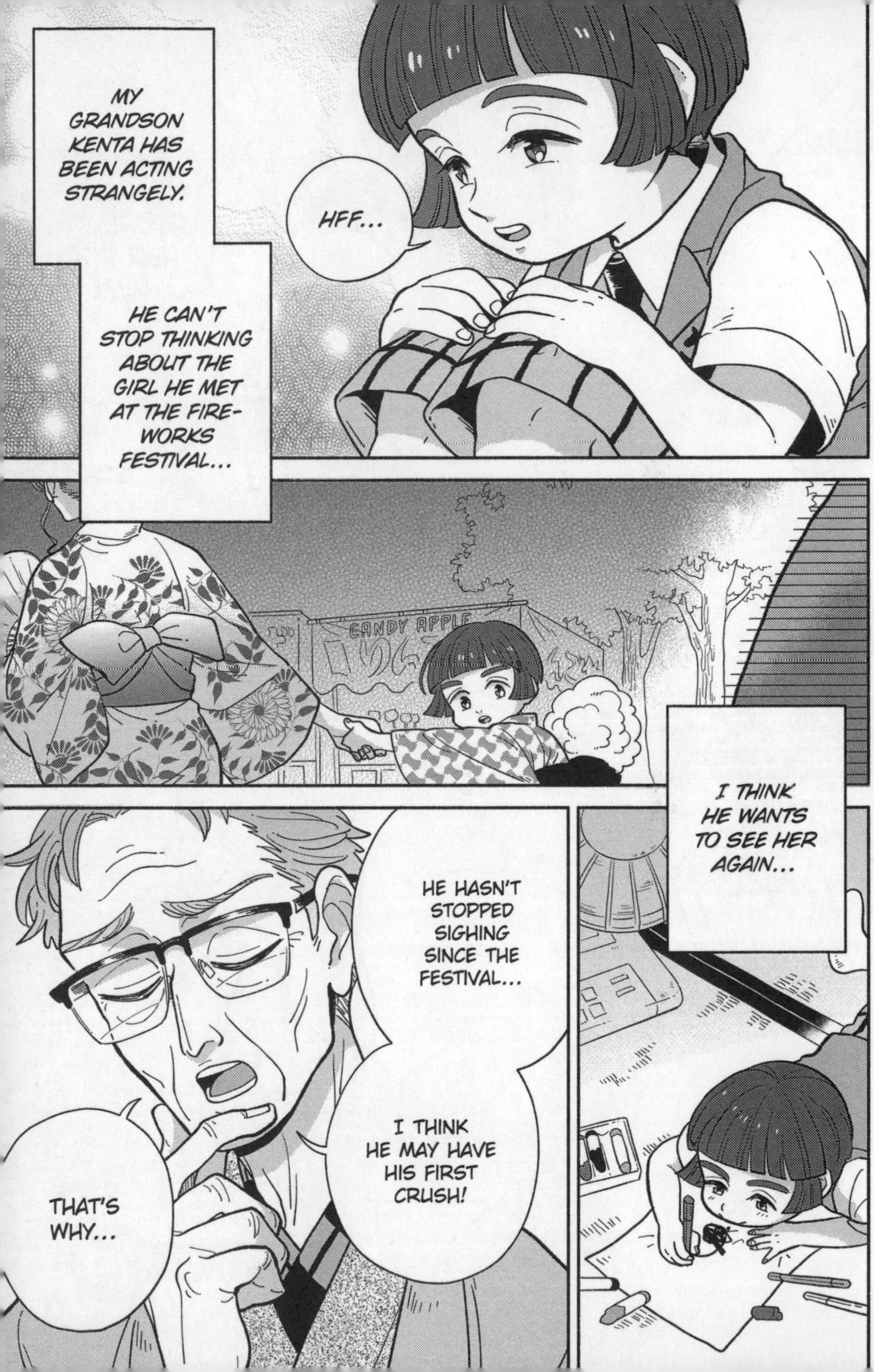
MY GRANDSON KENTA HAS BEEN ACTING STRANGELY.
HFF...
HE CAN'T STOP THINKING ABOUT THE GIRL HE MET AT THE FIRE-WORKS FESTIVAL...
CANDY APPLE
I THINK HE WANTS TO SEE HER AGAIN...
HE HASN'T STOPPED SIGHING SINCE THE FESTIVAL...
I THINK HE MAY HAVE HIS FIRST CRUSH!
THAT'S WHY...

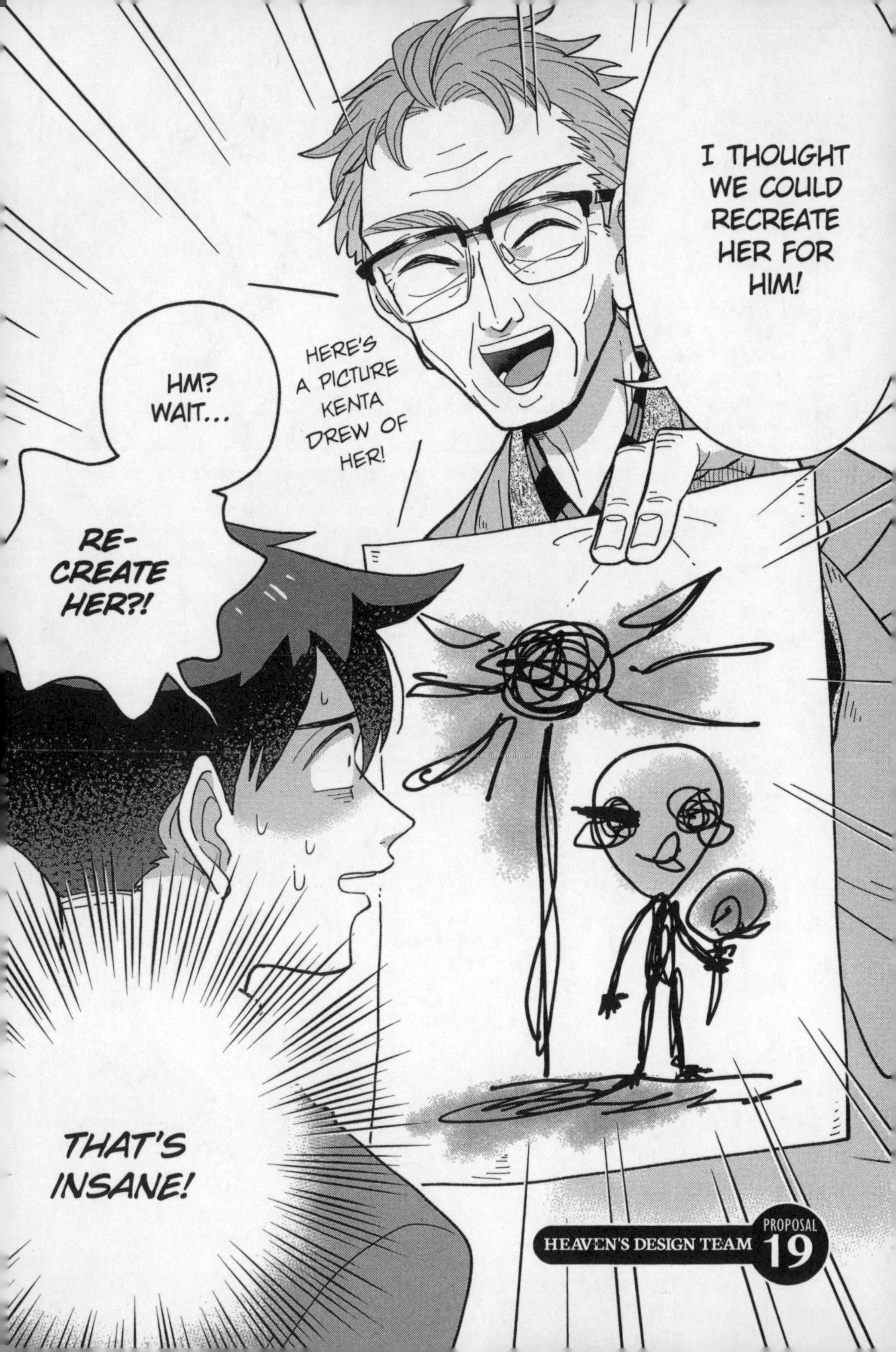
I THOUGHT WE COULD RECREATE HER FOR HIM!
HERE'S A PICTURE KENTA DREW OF HER!
HM? WAIT...
RE-CREATE HER?!
THAT'S INSANE!
HEAVEN'S DESIGN TEAM PROPOSAL 19

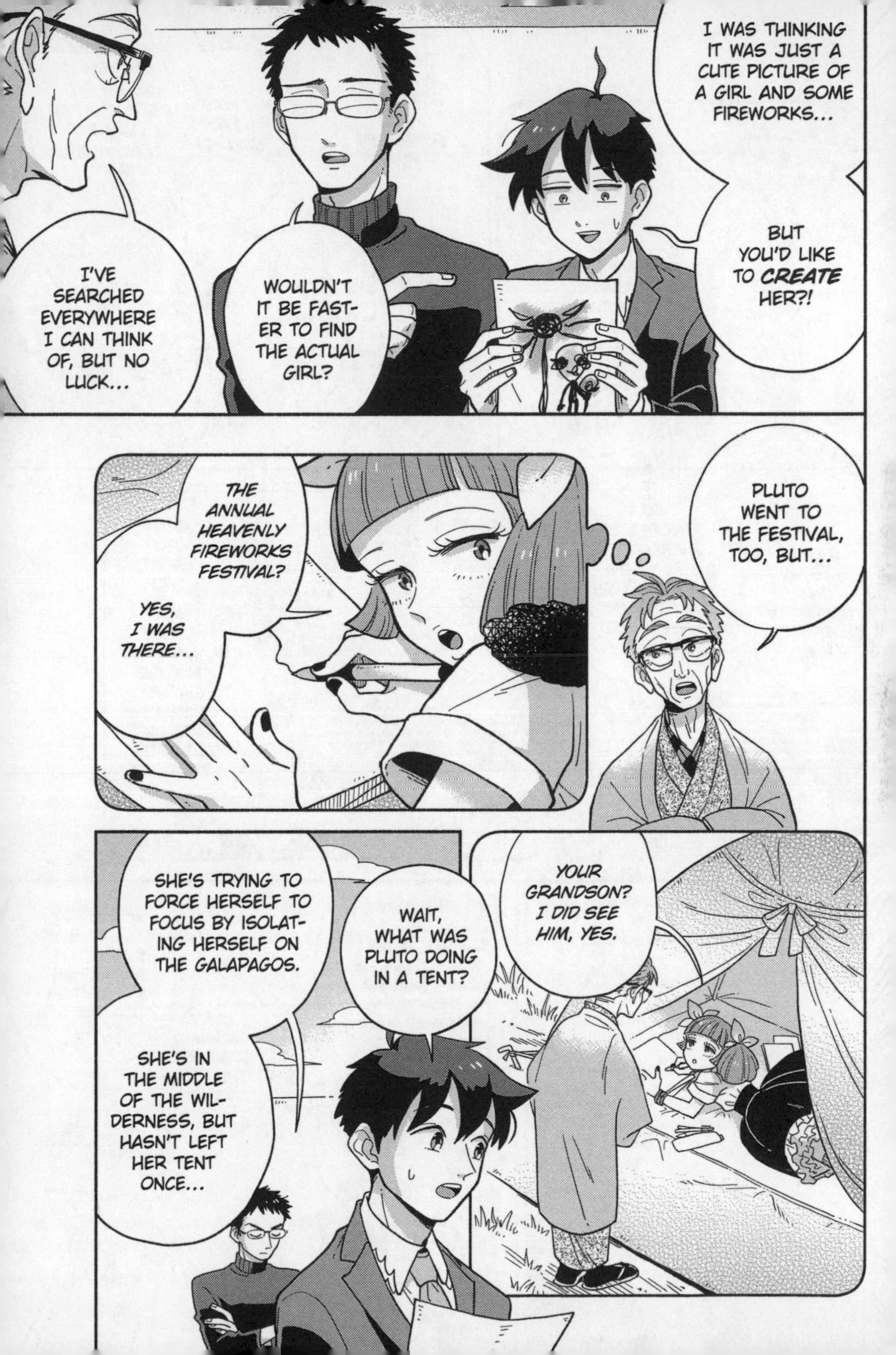
I WAS THINKING IT WAS JUST A CUTE PICTURE OF A GIRL AND SOME FIREWORKS...
BUT YOU'D LIKE TO *CREATE* HER?!
WOULDN'T IT BE FASTER TO FIND THE ACTUAL GIRL?
I'VE SEARCHED EVERYWHERE I CAN THINK OF, BUT NO LUCK...
PLUTO WENT TO THE FESTIVAL, TOO, BUT...
THE ANNUAL HEAVENLY FIREWORKS FESTIVAL?
YES, I WAS THERE...
YOUR GRANDSON? I DID SEE HIM, YES.
WAIT, WHAT WAS PLUTO DOING IN A TENT?
SHE'S TRYING TO FORCE HERSELF TO FOCUS BY ISOLATING HERSELF ON THE GALAPAGOS.
SHE'S IN THE MIDDLE OF THE WILDERNESS, BUT HASN'T LEFT HER TENT ONCE...

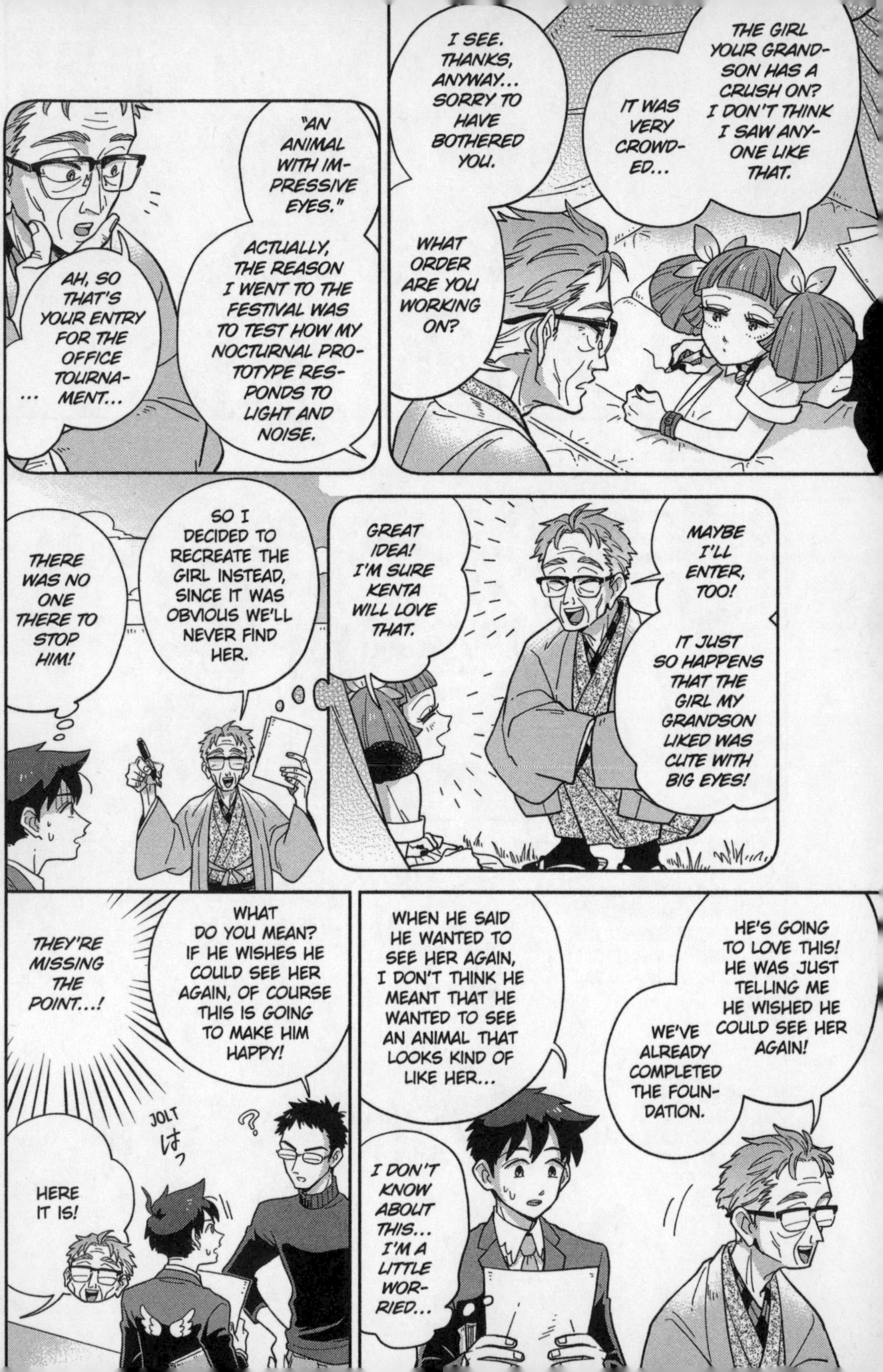
THE GIRL YOUR GRANDSON HAS A CRUSH ON? I DON'T THINK I SAW ANYONE LIKE THAT.
IT WAS VERY CROWDED...
I SEE. THANKS, ANYWAY... SORRY TO HAVE BOTHERED YOU.
WHAT ORDER ARE YOU WORKING ON?
"AN ANIMAL WITH IMPRESSIVE EYES."
ACTUALLY, THE REASON I WENT TO THE FESTIVAL WAS TO TEST HOW MY NOCTURNAL PROTOTYPE RESPONDS TO LIGHT AND NOISE.
AH, SO THAT'S YOUR ENTRY FOR THE OFFICE TOURNAMENT...
...
MAYBE I'LL ENTER, TOO!
IT JUST SO HAPPENS THAT THE GIRL MY GRANDSON LIKED WAS CUTE WITH BIG EYES!
GREAT IDEA! I'M SURE KENTA WILL LOVE THAT.
SO I DECIDED TO RECREATE THE GIRL INSTEAD, SINCE IT WAS OBVIOUS WE'LL NEVER FIND HER.
THERE WAS NO ONE THERE TO STOP HIM!
HE'S GOING TO LOVE THIS! HE WAS JUST TELLING ME HE WISHED HE COULD SEE HER AGAIN!
WE'VE ALREADY COMPLETED THE FOUNDATION.
WHEN HE SAID HE WANTED TO SEE HER AGAIN, I DON'T THINK HE MEANT THAT HE WANTED TO SEE AN ANIMAL THAT LOOKS KIND OF LIKE HER...
I DON'T KNOW ABOUT THIS... I'M A LITTLE WORRIED...
WHAT DO YOU MEAN? IF HE WISHES HE COULD SEE HER AGAIN, OF COURSE THIS IS GOING TO MAKE HIM HAPPY!
THEY'RE MISSING THE POINT...!
JOLT
はっ
?
HERE IT IS!

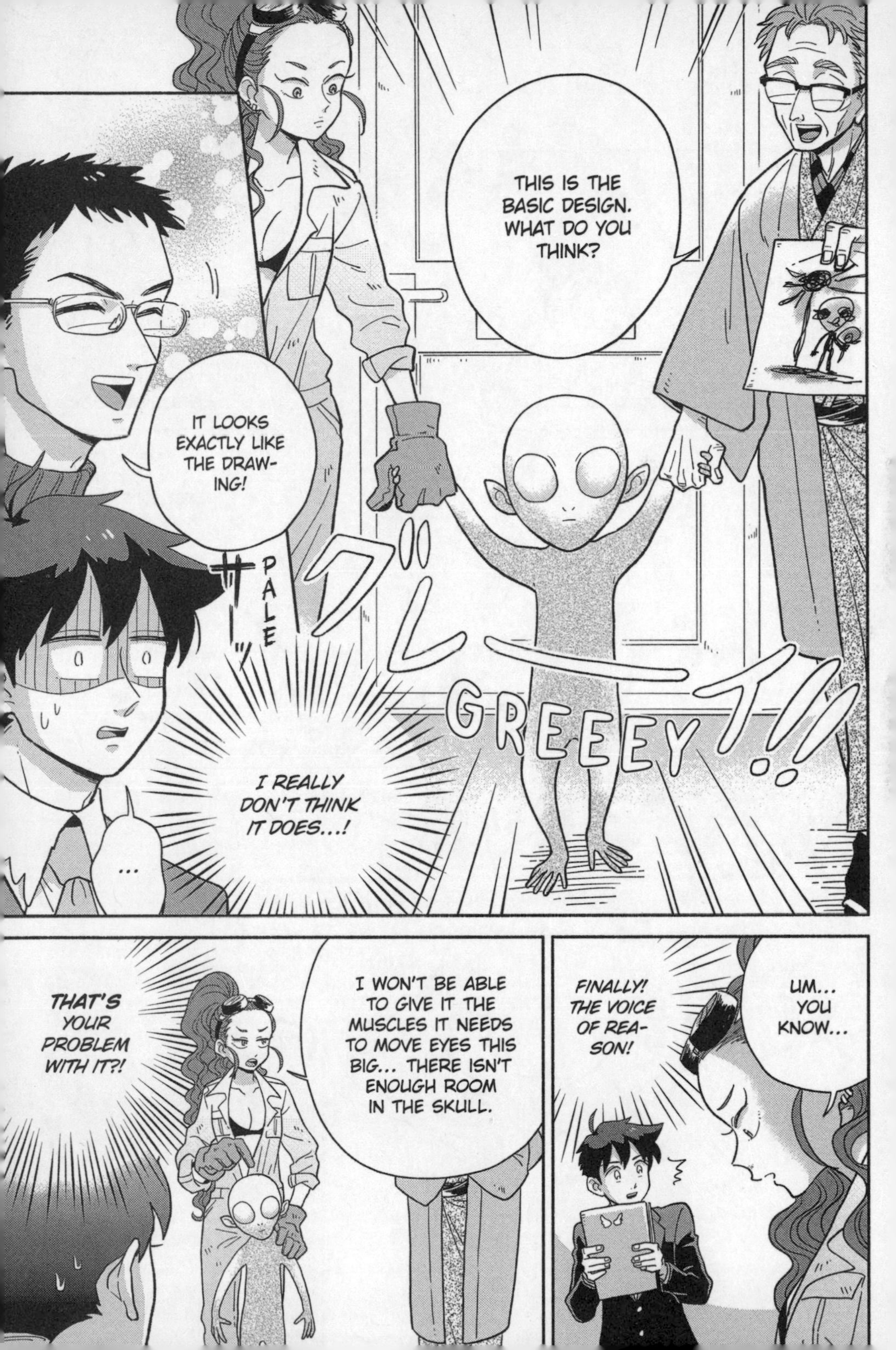
THIS IS THE BASIC DESIGN. WHAT DO YOU THINK?
GREEEY!!
IT LOOKS EXACTLY LIKE THE DRAW-ING!
PALE
I REALLY DON'T THINK IT DOES...!
...
UM... YOU KNOW...
FINALLY! THE VOICE OF REA-SON!
I WON'T BE ABLE TO GIVE IT THE MUSCLES IT NEEDS TO MOVE EYES THIS BIG... THERE ISN'T ENOUGH ROOM IN THE SKULL.
THAT'S YOUR PROBLEM WITH IT?!

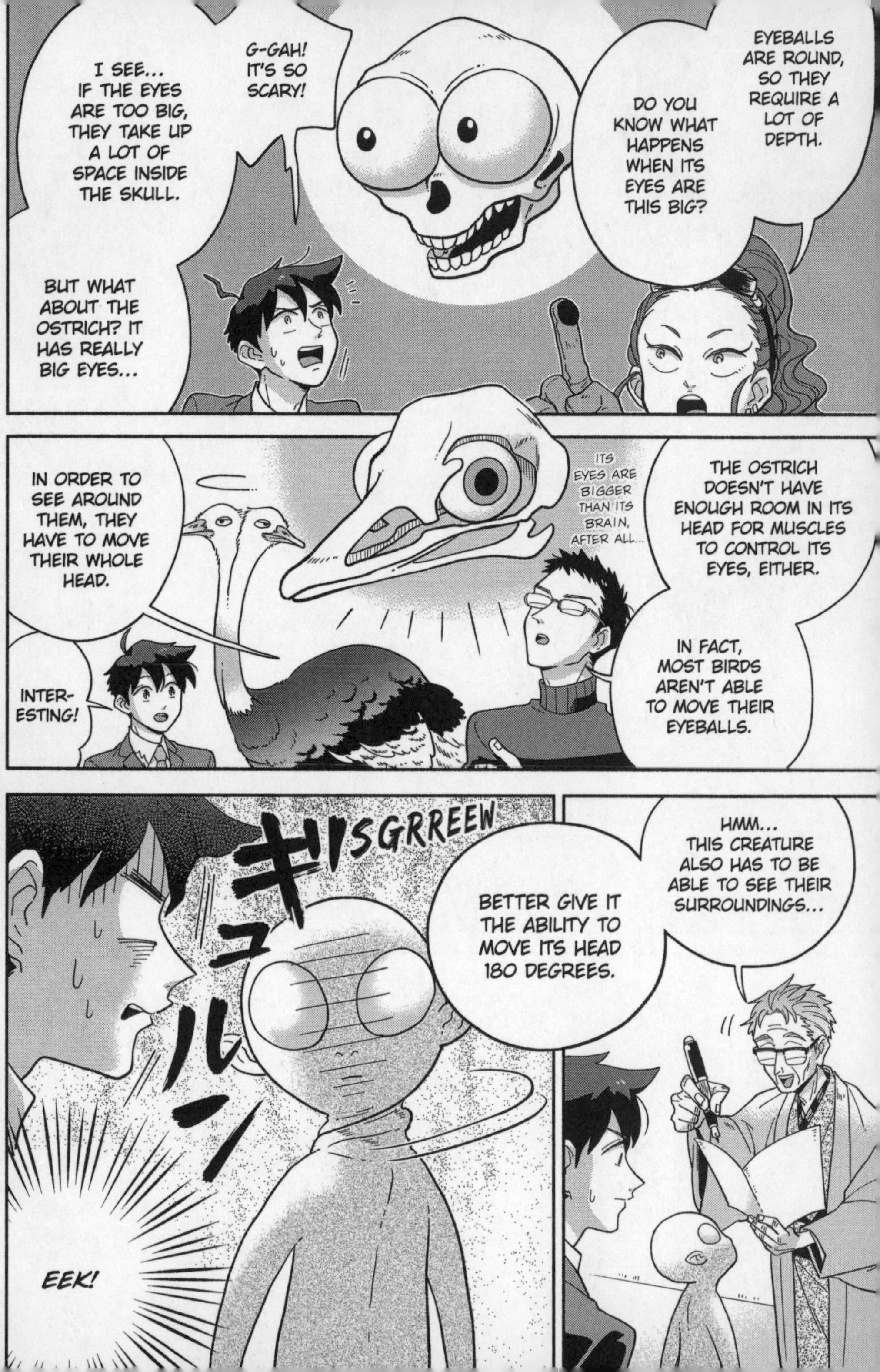
EYEBALLS ARE ROUND, SO THEY REQUIRE A LOT OF DEPTH.
DO YOU KNOW WHAT HAPPENS WHEN ITS EYES ARE THIS BIG?
G-GAH! IT'S SO SCARY!
I SEE... IF THE EYES ARE TOO BIG, THEY TAKE UP A LOT OF SPACE INSIDE THE SKULL.
BUT WHAT ABOUT THE OSTRICH? IT HAS REALLY BIG EYES...
THE OSTRICH DOESN'T HAVE ENOUGH ROOM IN ITS HEAD FOR MUSCLES TO CONTROL ITS EYES, EITHER.
ITS EYES ARE BIGGER THAN ITS BRAIN, AFTER ALL...
IN FACT, MOST BIRDS AREN'T ABLE TO MOVE THEIR EYEBALLS.
IN ORDER TO SEE AROUND THEM, THEY HAVE TO MOVE THEIR WHOLE HEAD.
INTER-ESTING!
HMM... THIS CREATURE ALSO HAS TO BE ABLE TO SEE THEIR SURROUNDINGS...
BETTER GIVE IT THE ABILITY TO MOVE ITS HEAD 180 DEGREES.
ギュルン
SGRREEW
EEK!

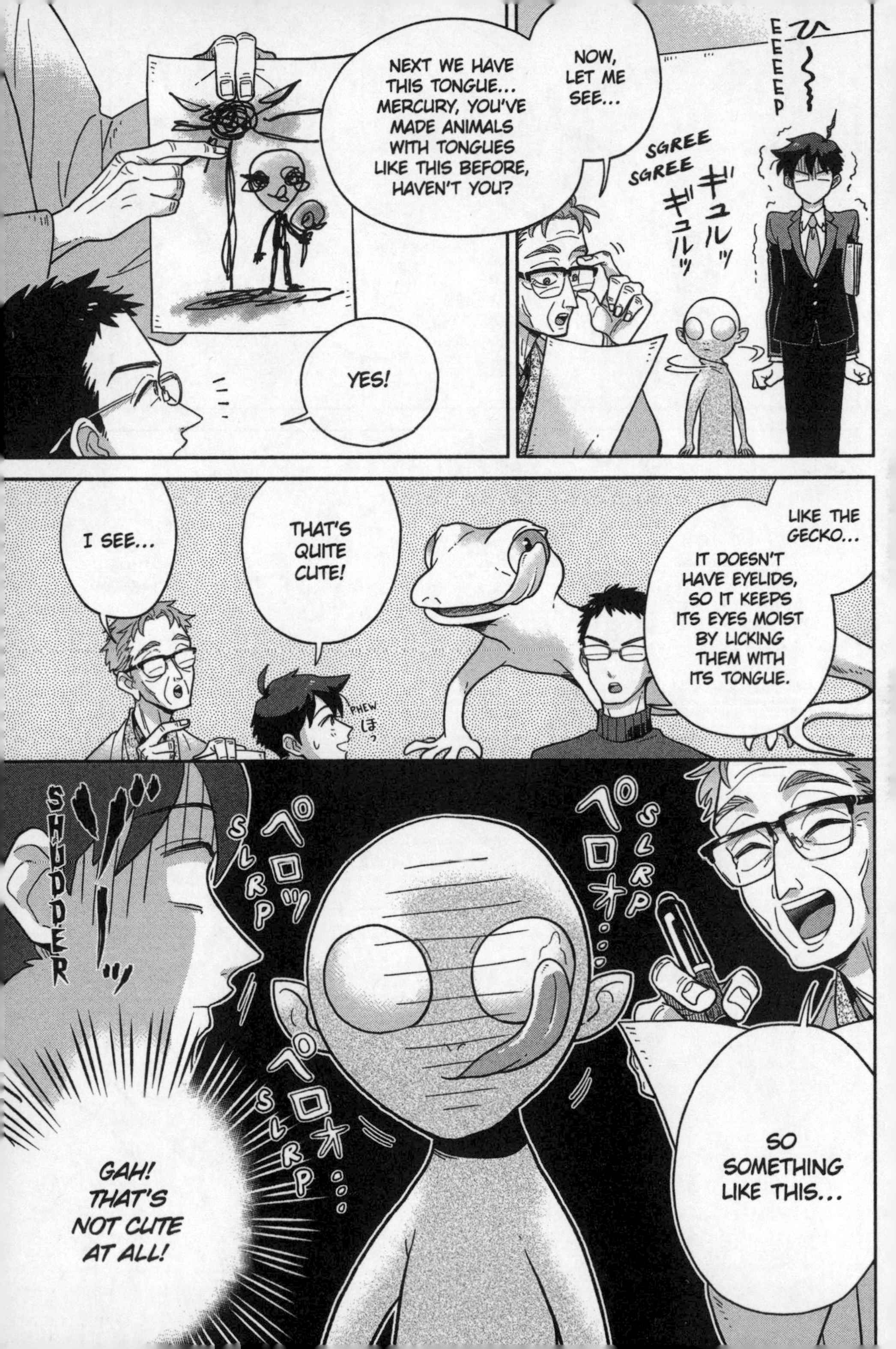

EEEEEP ひ～～
NOW, LET ME SEE...
SGREE SGREE ギュルッ ギュルッ
NEXT WE HAVE THIS TONGUE... MERCURY, YOU'VE MADE ANIMALS WITH TONGUES LIKE THIS BEFORE, HAVEN'T YOU?
YES!
LIKE THE GECKO...
IT DOESN'T HAVE EYELIDS, SO IT KEEPS ITS EYES MOIST BY LICKING THEM WITH ITS TONGUE.
THAT'S QUITE CUTE!
PHEW ほっ
I SEE...
SO SOMETHING LIKE THIS...
SLRP ペロォ…
SLRP ペロォ…
SLRP ペロッ
SHUDDER ゾッ
GAH! THAT'S NOT CUTE AT ALL!

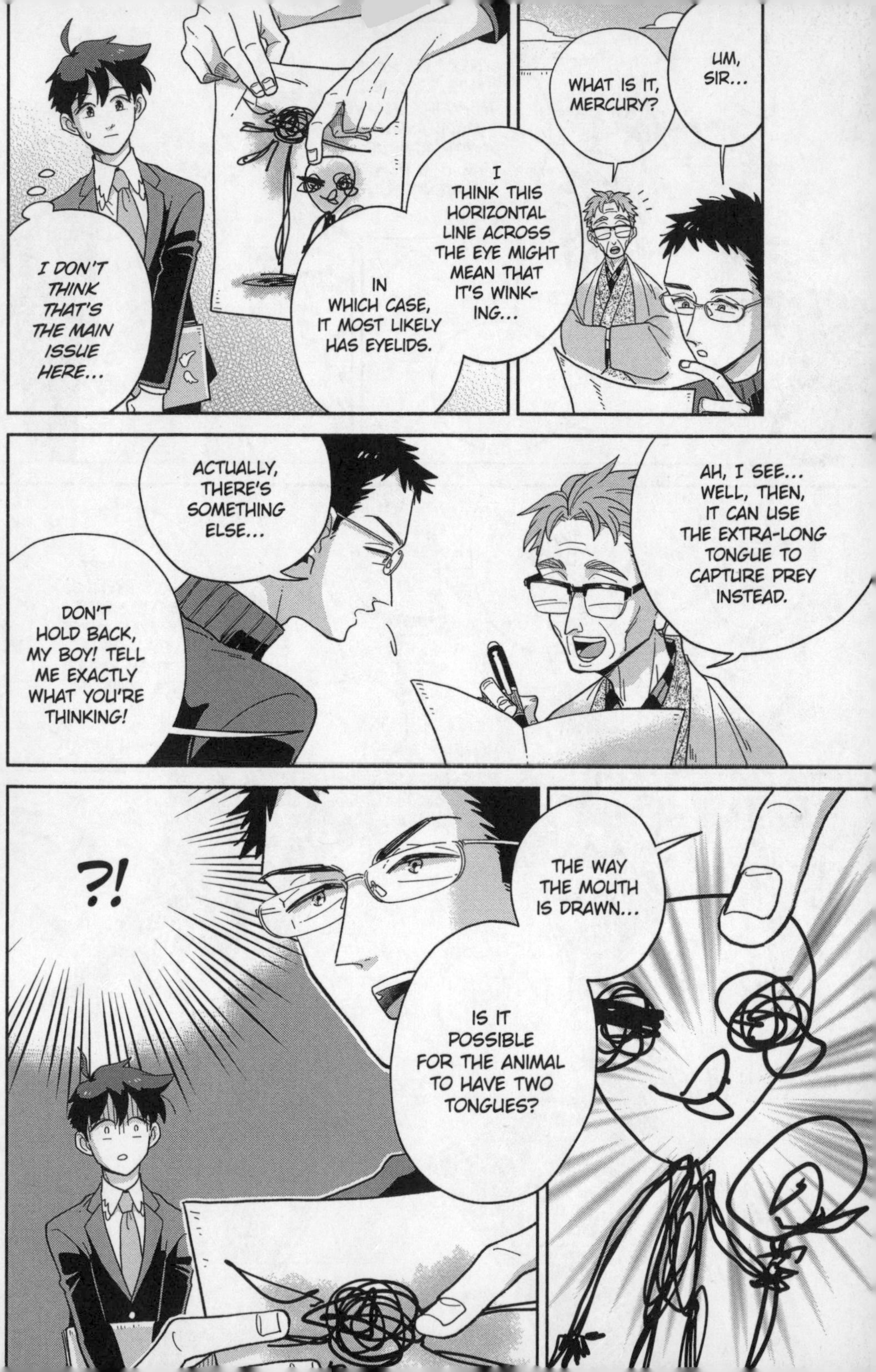
UM, SIR...
WHAT IS IT, MERCURY?
I THINK THIS HORIZONTAL LINE ACROSS THE EYE MIGHT MEAN THAT IT'S WINK-ING...
IN WHICH CASE, IT MOST LIKELY HAS EYELIDS.
I DON'T THINK THAT'S THE MAIN ISSUE HERE...
AH, I SEE... WELL, THEN, IT CAN USE THE EXTRA-LONG TONGUE TO CAPTURE PREY INSTEAD.
ACTUALLY, THERE'S SOMETHING ELSE...
DON'T HOLD BACK, MY BOY! TELL ME EXACTLY WHAT YOU'RE THINKING!
THE WAY THE MOUTH IS DRAWN...
IS IT POSSIBLE FOR THE ANIMAL TO HAVE TWO TONGUES?
?!

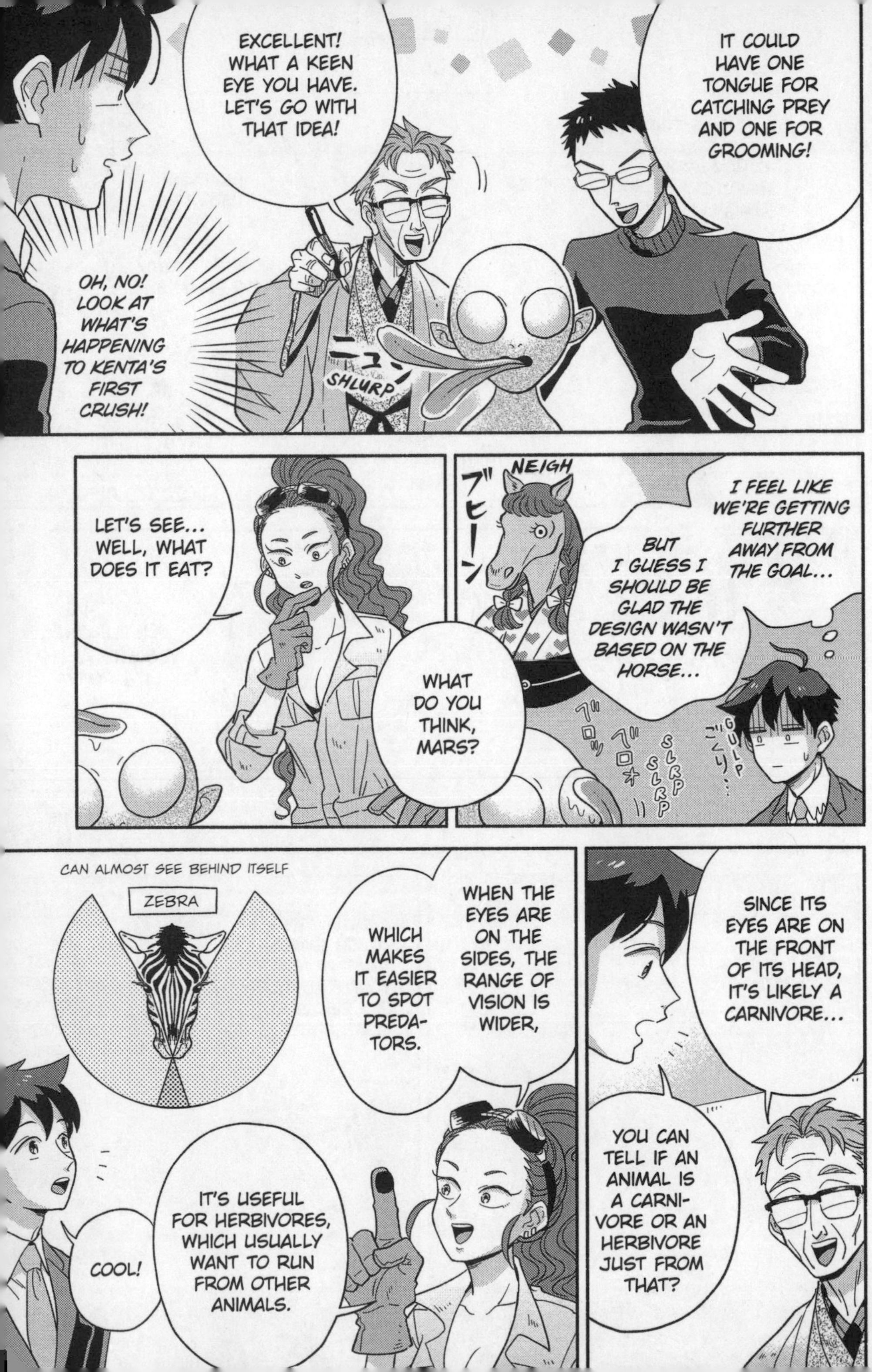
IT COULD HAVE ONE TONGUE FOR CATCHING PREY AND ONE FOR GROOMING!
EXCELLENT! WHAT A KEEN EYE YOU HAVE. LET'S GO WITH THAT IDEA!
ニュン
SHLURP
OH, NO! LOOK AT WHAT'S HAPPENING TO KENTA'S FIRST CRUSH!
NEIGH
ブヒーン
I FEEL LIKE WE'RE GETTING FURTHER AWAY FROM THE GOAL...
BUT I GUESS I SHOULD BE GLAD THE DESIGN WASN'T BASED ON THE HORSE...
ブロッ
ブロオ
SLRP SLRP SLRP
GULP
ごくり...
LET'S SEE... WELL, WHAT DOES IT EAT?
WHAT DO YOU THINK, MARS?
SINCE ITS EYES ARE ON THE FRONT OF ITS HEAD, IT'S LIKELY A CARNIVORE...
YOU CAN TELL IF AN ANIMAL IS A CARNIVORE OR AN HERBIVORE JUST FROM THAT?
WHEN THE EYES ARE ON THE SIDES, THE RANGE OF VISION IS WIDER,
WHICH MAKES IT EASIER TO SPOT PREDATORS.
CAN ALMOST SEE BEHIND ITSELF
ZEBRA
IT'S USEFUL FOR HERBIVORES, WHICH USUALLY WANT TO RUN FROM OTHER ANIMALS.
COOL!

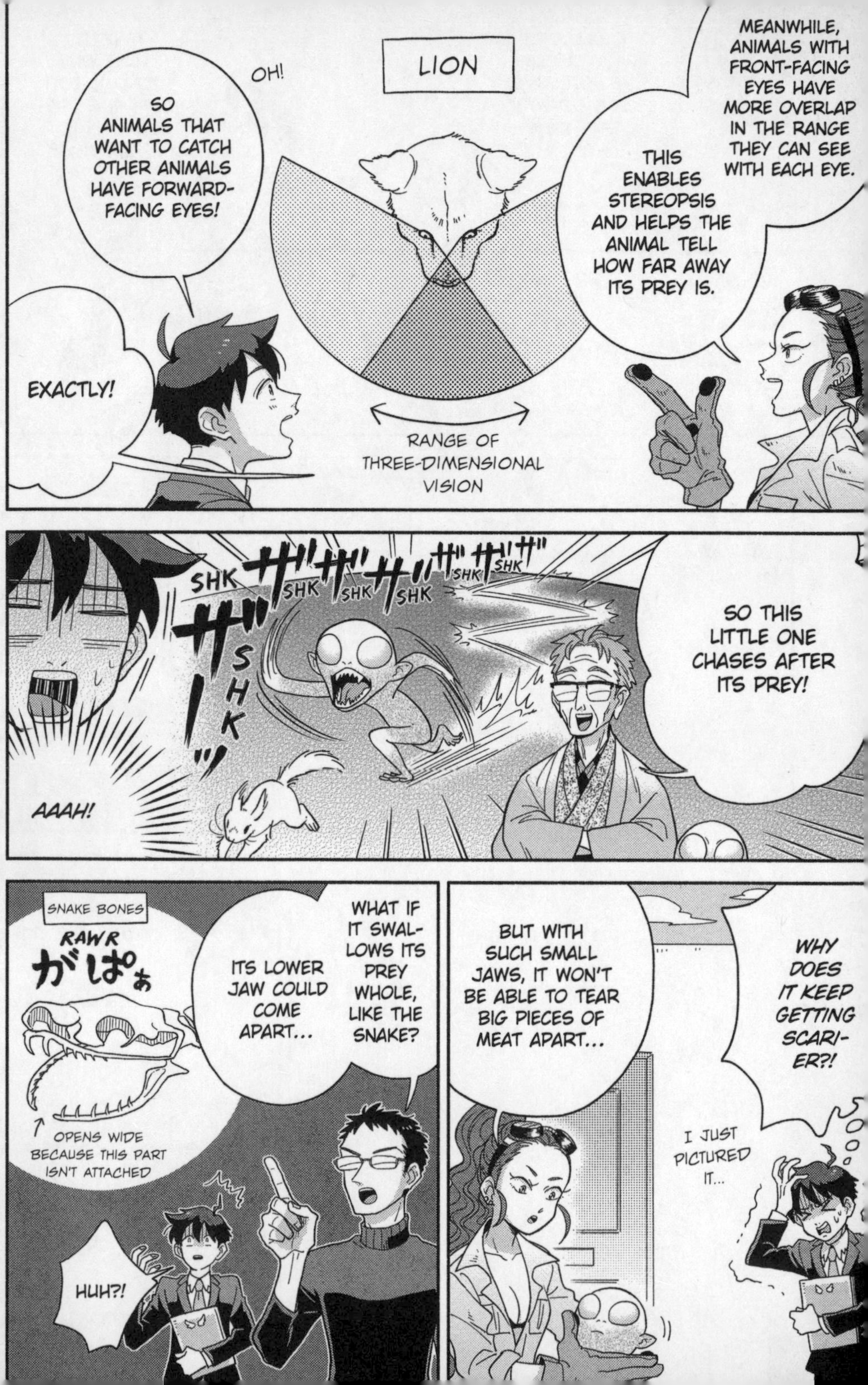
MEANWHILE, ANIMALS WITH FRONT-FACING EYES HAVE MORE OVERLAP IN THE RANGE THEY CAN SEE WITH EACH EYE.
THIS ENABLES STEREOPSIS AND HELPS THE ANIMAL TELL HOW FAR AWAY ITS PREY IS.
LION
OH!
SO ANIMALS THAT WANT TO CATCH OTHER ANIMALS HAVE FORWARD-FACING EYES!
RANGE OF THREE-DIMENSIONAL VISION
EXACTLY!
SO THIS LITTLE ONE CHASES AFTER ITS PREY!
ザザザザザ SHK SHK SHK SHK SHK SHK
ザーッ SHK SHK
AAAH!
BUT WITH SUCH SMALL JAWS, IT WON'T BE ABLE TO TEAR BIG PIECES OF MEAT APART…
WHY DOES IT KEEP GETTING SCARIER?!
I JUST PICTURED IT…
WHAT IF IT SWALLOWS ITS PREY WHOLE, LIKE THE SNAKE?
ITS LOWER JAW COULD COME APART…
SNAKE BONES
RAWR がぱぁ
OPENS WIDE BECAUSE THIS PART ISN'T ATTACHED
HUH?!

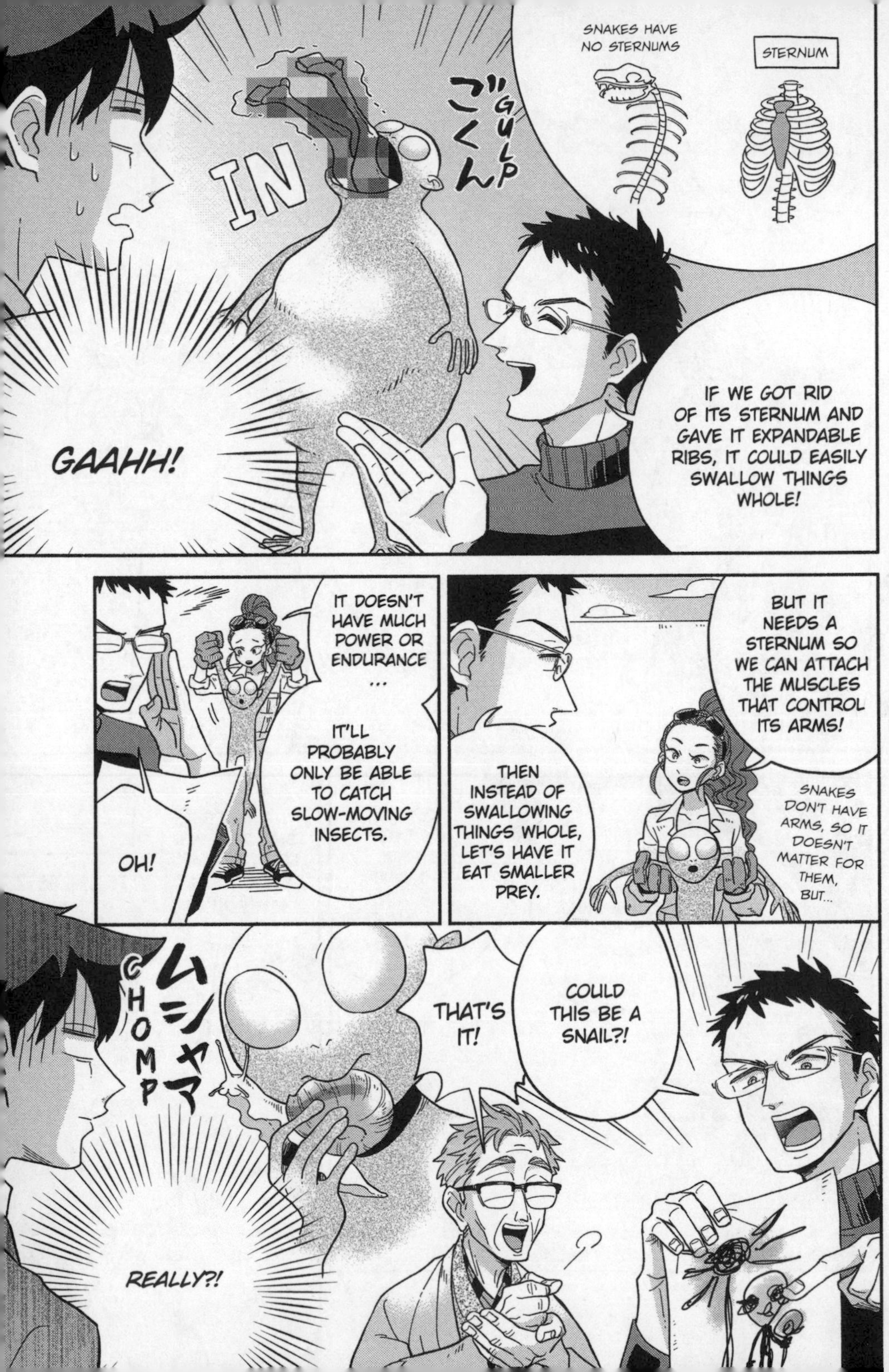
SNAKES HAVE NO STERNUMS
STERNUM
IF WE GOT RID OF ITS STERNUM AND GAVE IT EXPANDABLE RIBS, IT COULD EASILY SWALLOW THINGS WHOLE!
ごくん GULP
IN
GAAHH!
BUT IT NEEDS A STERNUM SO WE CAN ATTACH THE MUSCLES THAT CONTROL ITS ARMS!
SNAKES DON'T HAVE ARMS, SO IT DOESN'T MATTER FOR THEM, BUT...
THEN INSTEAD OF SWALLOWING THINGS WHOLE, LET'S HAVE IT EAT SMALLER PREY.
IT DOESN'T HAVE MUCH POWER OR ENDURANCE ...
IT'LL PROBABLY ONLY BE ABLE TO CATCH SLOW-MOVING INSECTS.
OH!
COULD THIS BE A SNAIL?!
THAT'S IT!
ムシャ CHOMP
REALLY?!

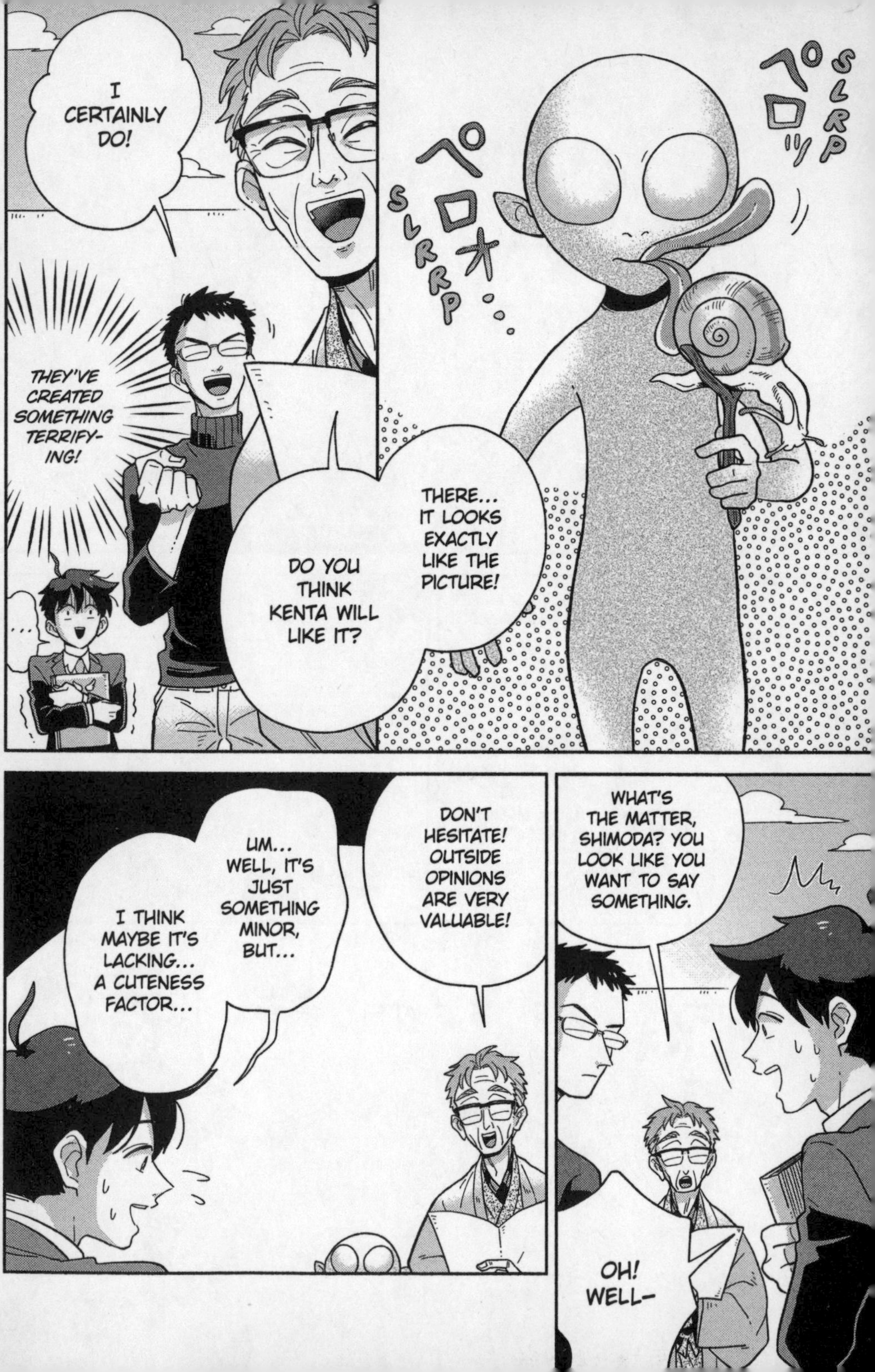

ペロッ
SLRP
ペロォ…
SLRRP
THERE... IT LOOKS EXACTLY LIKE THE PICTURE!
DO YOU THINK KENTA WILL LIKE IT?
I CERTAINLY DO!
THEY'VE CREATED SOMETHING TERRIFY-ING!
...
WHAT'S THE MATTER, SHIMODA? YOU LOOK LIKE YOU WANT TO SAY SOMETHING.
OH! WELL-
DON'T HESITATE! OUTSIDE OPINIONS ARE VERY VALUABLE!
UM... WELL, IT'S JUST SOMETHING MINOR, BUT...
I THINK MAYBE IT'S LACKING... A CUTENESS FACTOR...

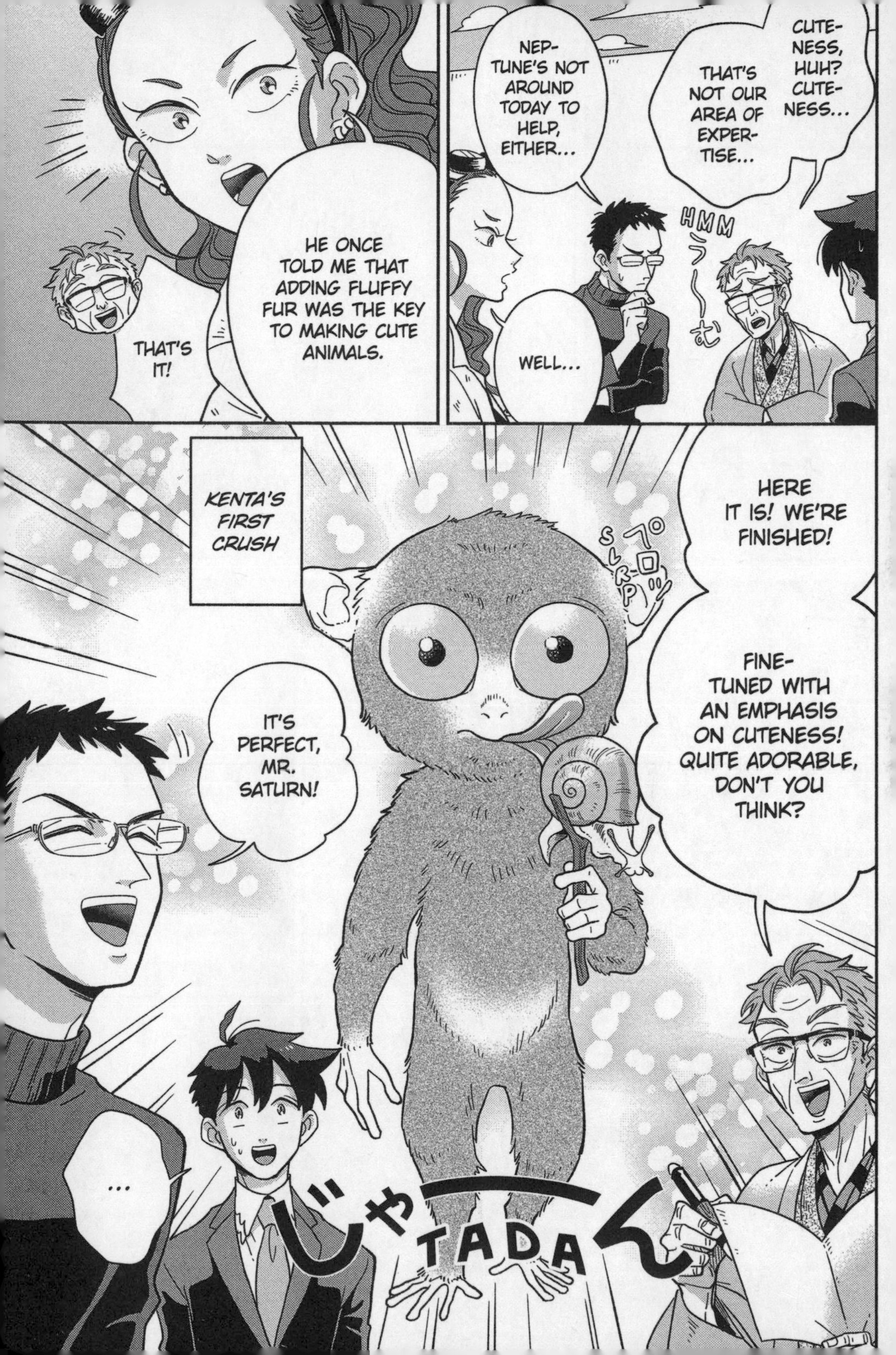
CUTENESS, HUH? CUTENESS...
THAT'S NOT OUR AREA OF EXPERTISE...
NEPTUNE'S NOT AROUND TODAY TO HELP, EITHER...
HMM
WELL...
HE ONCE TOLD ME THAT ADDING FLUFFY FUR WAS THE KEY TO MAKING CUTE ANIMALS.
THAT'S IT!
HERE IT IS! WE'RE FINISHED!
FINE-TUNED WITH AN EMPHASIS ON CUTENESS! QUITE ADORABLE, DON'T YOU THINK?
KENTA'S FIRST CRUSH
SLRP
IT'S PERFECT, MR. SATURN!
...
TADA

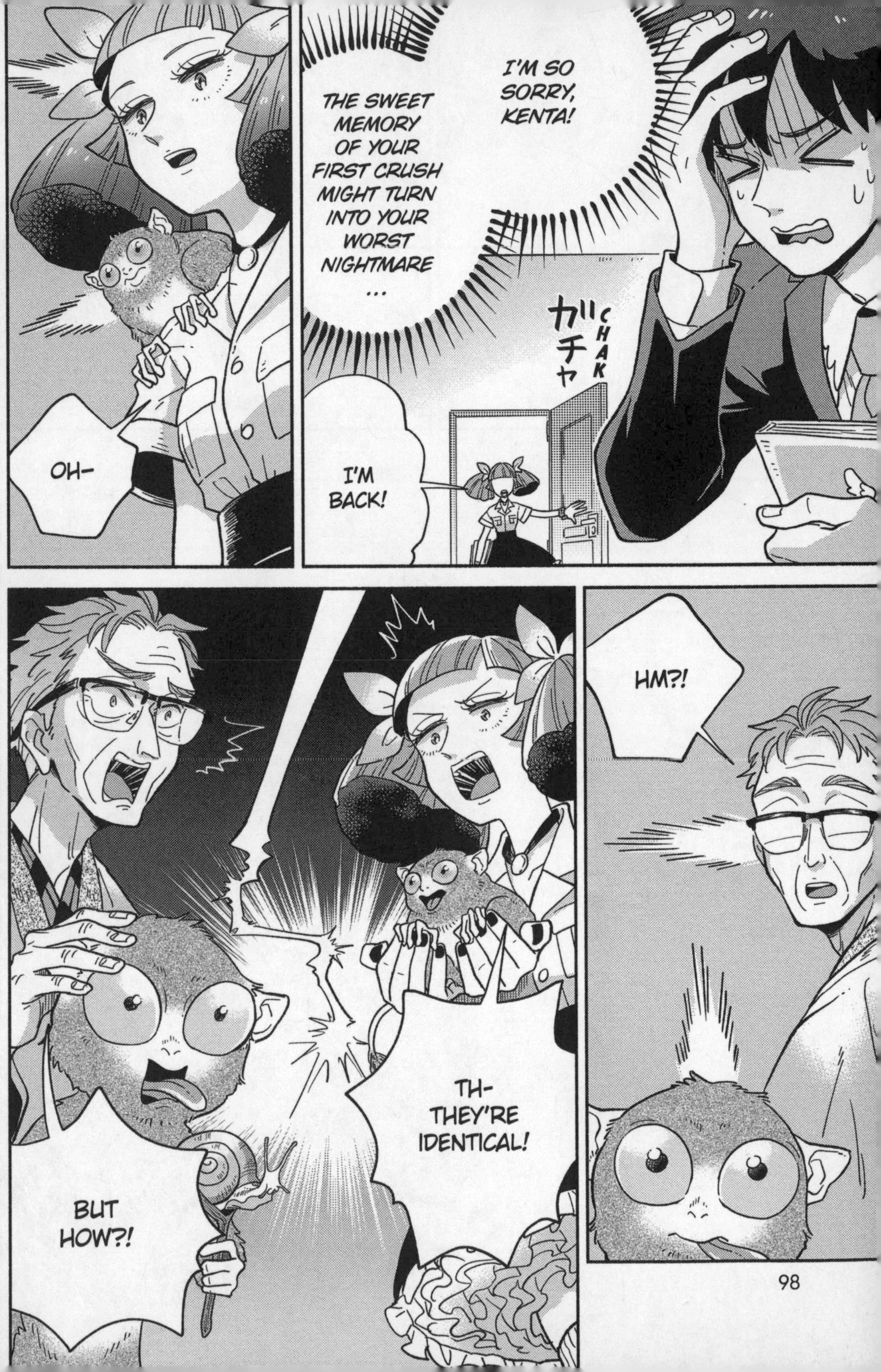
I'M SO SORRY, KENTA!
THE SWEET MEMORY OF YOUR FIRST CRUSH MIGHT TURN INTO YOUR WORST NIGHTMARE ...
ガチャ CHAK
I'M BACK!
OH-
HM?!
TH- THEY'RE IDENTICAL!
BUT HOW?!

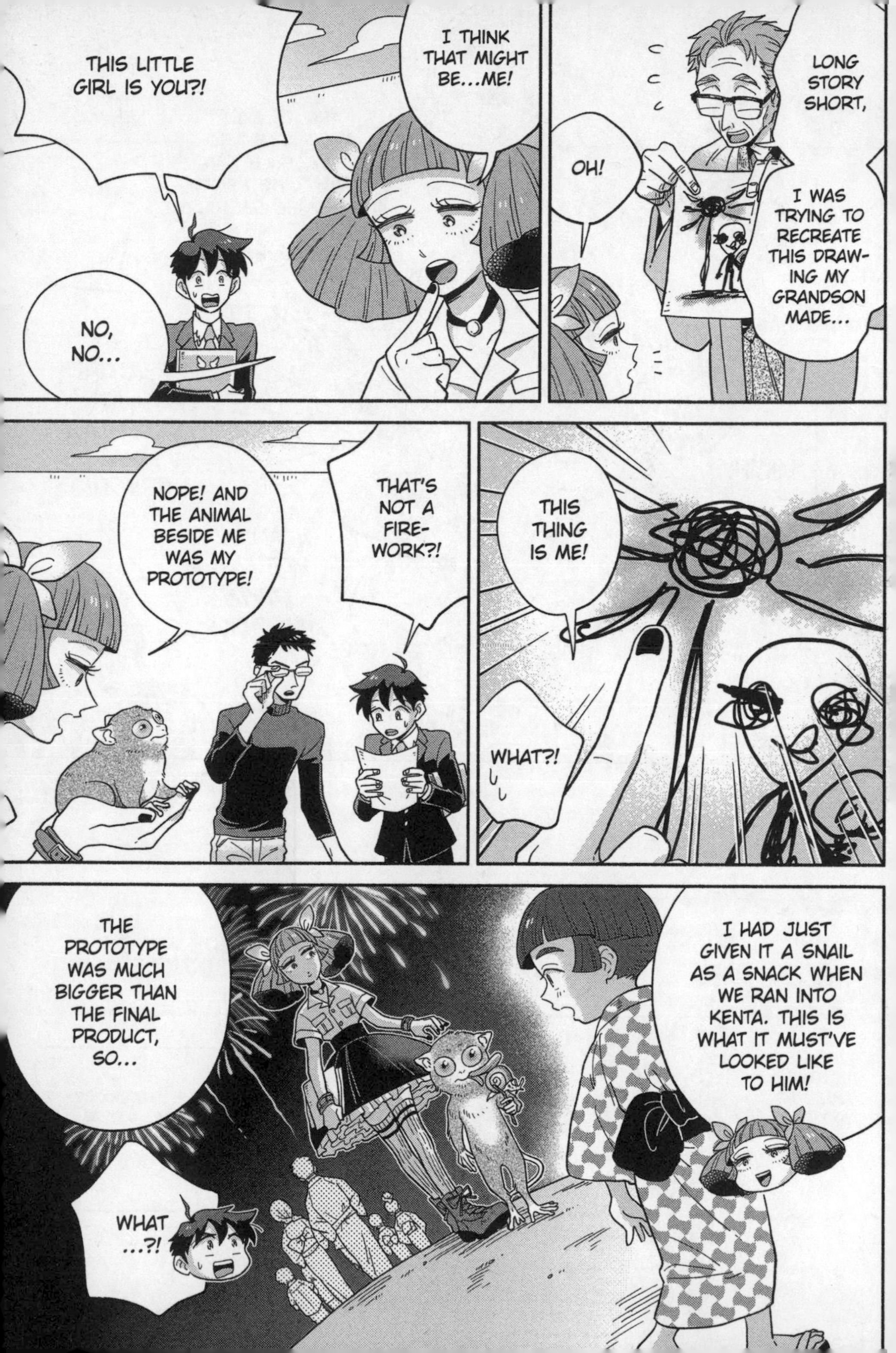
LONG STORY SHORT,
I WAS TRYING TO RECREATE THIS DRAWING MY GRANDSON MADE...
OH!
I THINK THAT MIGHT BE...ME!
THIS LITTLE GIRL IS YOU?!
NO, NO...
THIS THING IS ME!
WHAT?!
THAT'S NOT A FIREWORK?!
NOPE! AND THE ANIMAL BESIDE ME WAS MY PROTOTYPE!
I HAD JUST GIVEN IT A SNAIL AS A SNACK WHEN WE RAN INTO KENTA. THIS IS WHAT IT MUST'VE LOOKED LIKE TO HIM!
THE PROTOTYPE WAS MUCH BIGGER THAN THE FINAL PRODUCT, SO...
WHAT ...?!

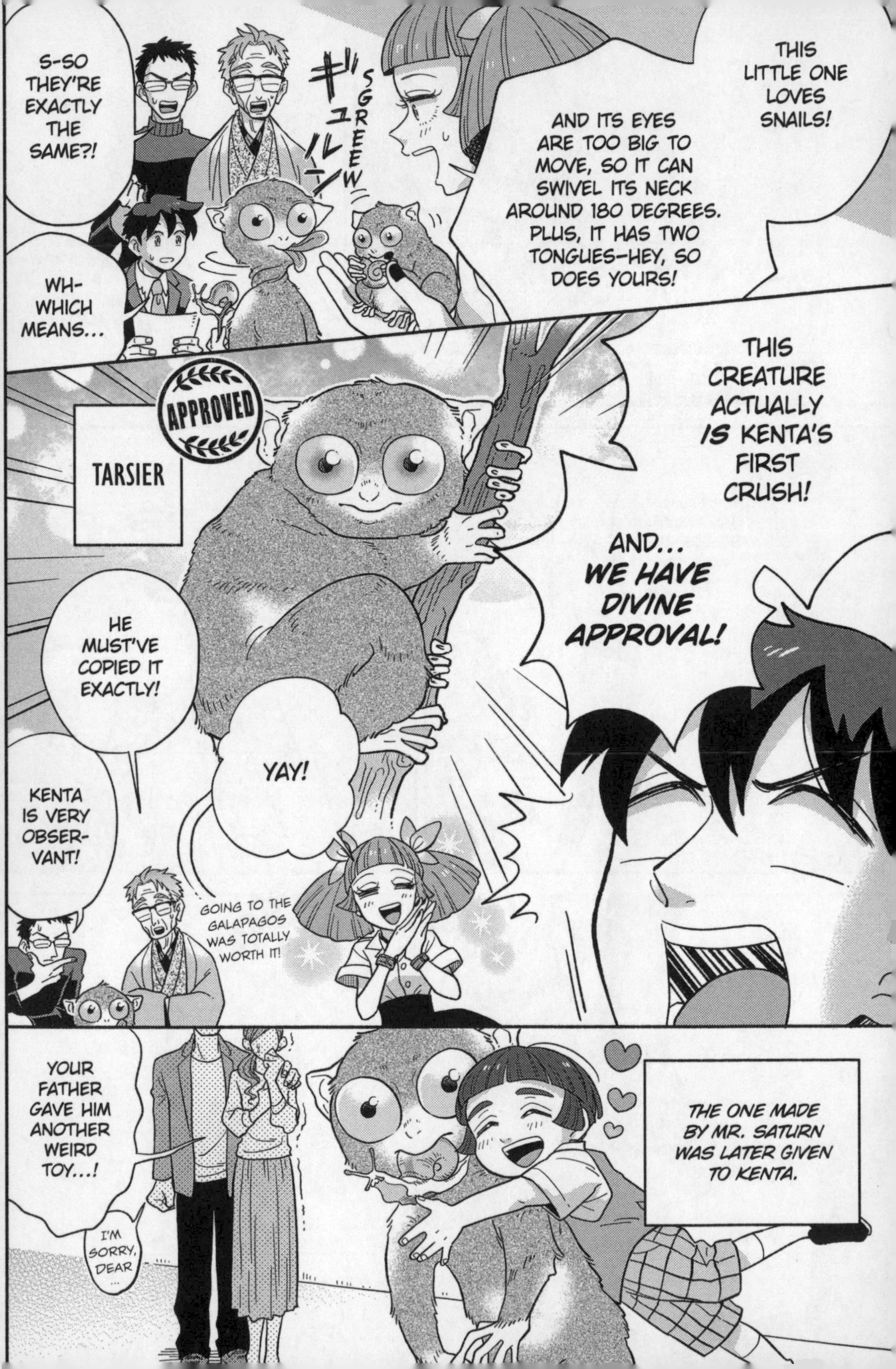
THIS LITTLE ONE LOVES SNAILS!
AND ITS EYES ARE TOO BIG TO MOVE, SO IT CAN SWIVEL ITS NECK AROUND 180 DEGREES. PLUS, IT HAS TWO TONGUES—HEY, SO DOES YOURS!
SGREEEW
S-SO THEY'RE EXACTLY THE SAME?!
WH-WHICH MEANS...
THIS CREATURE ACTUALLY *IS* KENTA'S FIRST CRUSH!
AND... ***WE HAVE DIVINE APPROVAL!***
APPROVED
TARSIER
HE MUST'VE COPIED IT EXACTLY!
YAY!
KENTA IS VERY OBSER-VANT!
GOING TO THE GALAPAGOS WAS TOTALLY WORTH IT!
THE ONE MADE BY MR. SATURN WAS LATER GIVEN TO KENTA.
YOUR FATHER GAVE HIM ANOTHER WEIRD TOY...!
I'M SORRY, DEAR ...

THE ENCYCLOPEDIA OF REAL ANIMALS 19

ANIMAL 49 TARSIER

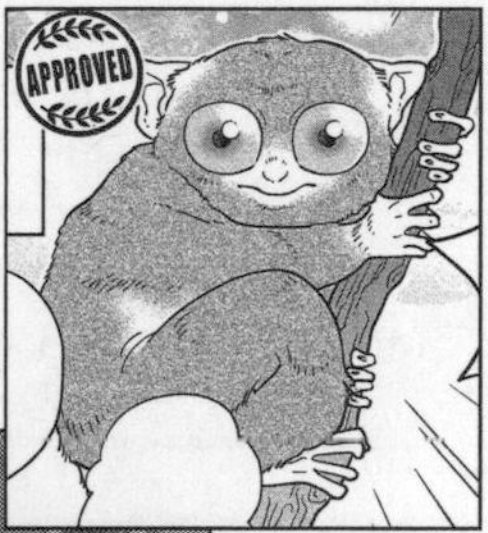
APPROVED

THE REAL THING

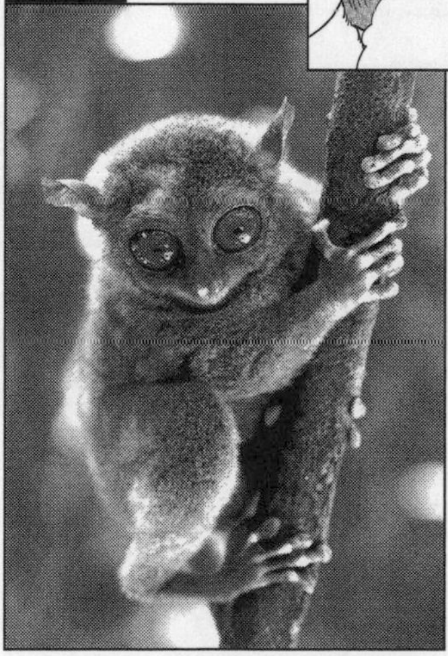

A Philippine tarsier.
Photo: Hiroya Minakuchi/Aflo

With its gigantic eyes, the tarsier can easily perceive objects in three dimensions from trees and at night. Its eyes lack a tapetum lucidum (the layer of tissue in many nocturnal animals, such as cats, which reflects visible light back through the retina, increasing the light available to the photoreceptors and allows for improved night vision), and therefore they do not shine in darkness. It is theorized that to compensate for this, the tarsier's eyes evolved to their large size. Because the tarsier is unable to move its eyeballs, it scans its surroundings by rotating its head 180 degrees. It likes to eat snails, and has two tongues (though their respective roles are not fully understood). It can leap up to two meters (over six feet) away using its powerful and long hind legs.

[Name]	Tarsier
[Classification]	Class: Mammalia Order: Primates Family: Tarsiidae Genus: *Tarsius*
[Habitat]	Southeast Asia
[Length]	8-30 cm (3-12 in)

ANIMAL 50 | GECKO

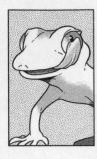

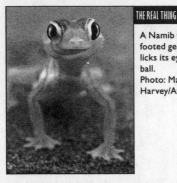

THE REAL THING

A Namib web-footed gecko licks its eyeball.
Photo: Martin Harvey/Aflo

[Name]	Gecko
[Classification]	Class: Reptilia Order: Squamata Family: Gekkonidae
[Habitat]	Tropical, sub-tropical, and warm climates worldwide
[Length]	7-42 cm (2.8-16.5 in)

Schlegel's Japanese gecko is the most common species of gecko found in Japan. The animal eats flies, moths, and other harmful insects.

Generally speaking, the reptilian creatures that lick their eyes to moisten them and remove dust and dirt, adhere to walls and ceilings, and lose their own tails as a defense mechanism are known as geckos. The amphibian animals that don't fit the above description are known as newts.

SPECIAL FEATURE | HERBIVORES' AND CARNIVORES' FIELD OF VISION

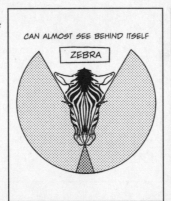

CAN ALMOST SEE BEHIND ITSELF
ZEBRA

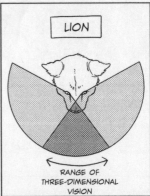

LION
RANGE OF THREE-DIMENSIONAL VISION

The takeaway is that the greater an animal's field of three-dimensional vision, the easier it is for it to determine the distance between itself and other objects. Humans also see two different images at once, as demonstrated by 3D films and virtual reality technology.
By combining the two images, we are able to perceive things in three dimensions and measure distances. Predatory animals that must calculate the distance between themselves and their prey, therefore, have forward-facing eyes, while prey animals require a larger field of vision which allows them to spot predators more easily.

HEAVEN'S DESIGN TEAM

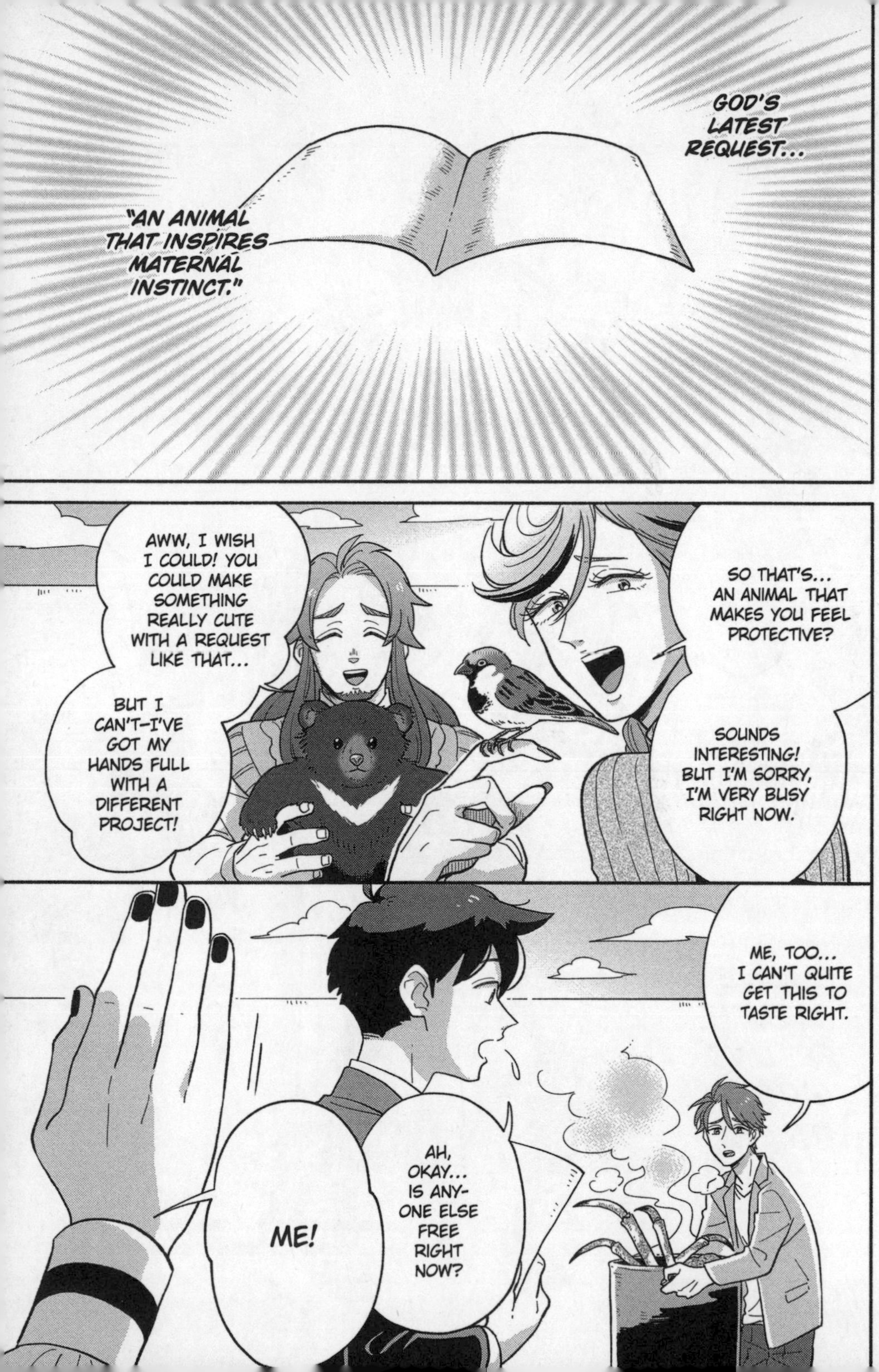
GOD'S LATEST REQUEST...
"AN ANIMAL THAT INSPIRES MATERNAL INSTINCT."
SO THAT'S... AN ANIMAL THAT MAKES YOU FEEL PROTECTIVE?
SOUNDS INTERESTING! BUT I'M SORRY, I'M VERY BUSY RIGHT NOW.
AWW, I WISH I COULD! YOU COULD MAKE SOMETHING REALLY CUTE WITH A REQUEST LIKE THAT...
BUT I CAN'T—I'VE GOT MY HANDS FULL WITH A DIFFERENT PROJECT!
ME, TOO... I CAN'T QUITE GET THIS TO TASTE RIGHT.
AH, OKAY... IS ANY-ONE ELSE FREE RIGHT NOW?
ME!

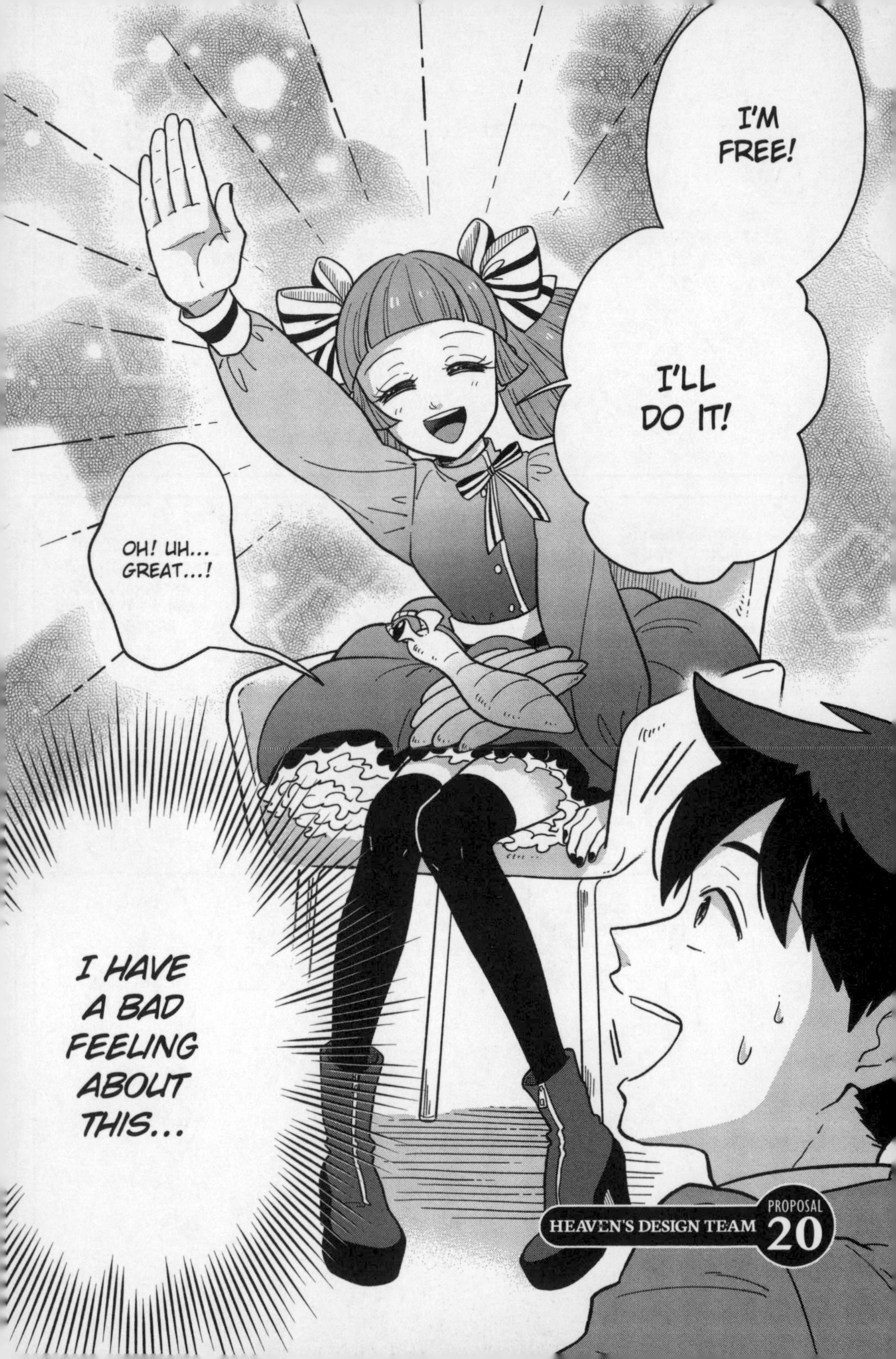
I'M FREE!
I'LL DO IT!
OH! UH... GREAT...!
I HAVE A BAD FEELING ABOUT THIS...
HEAVEN'S DESIGN TEAM PROPOSAL 20

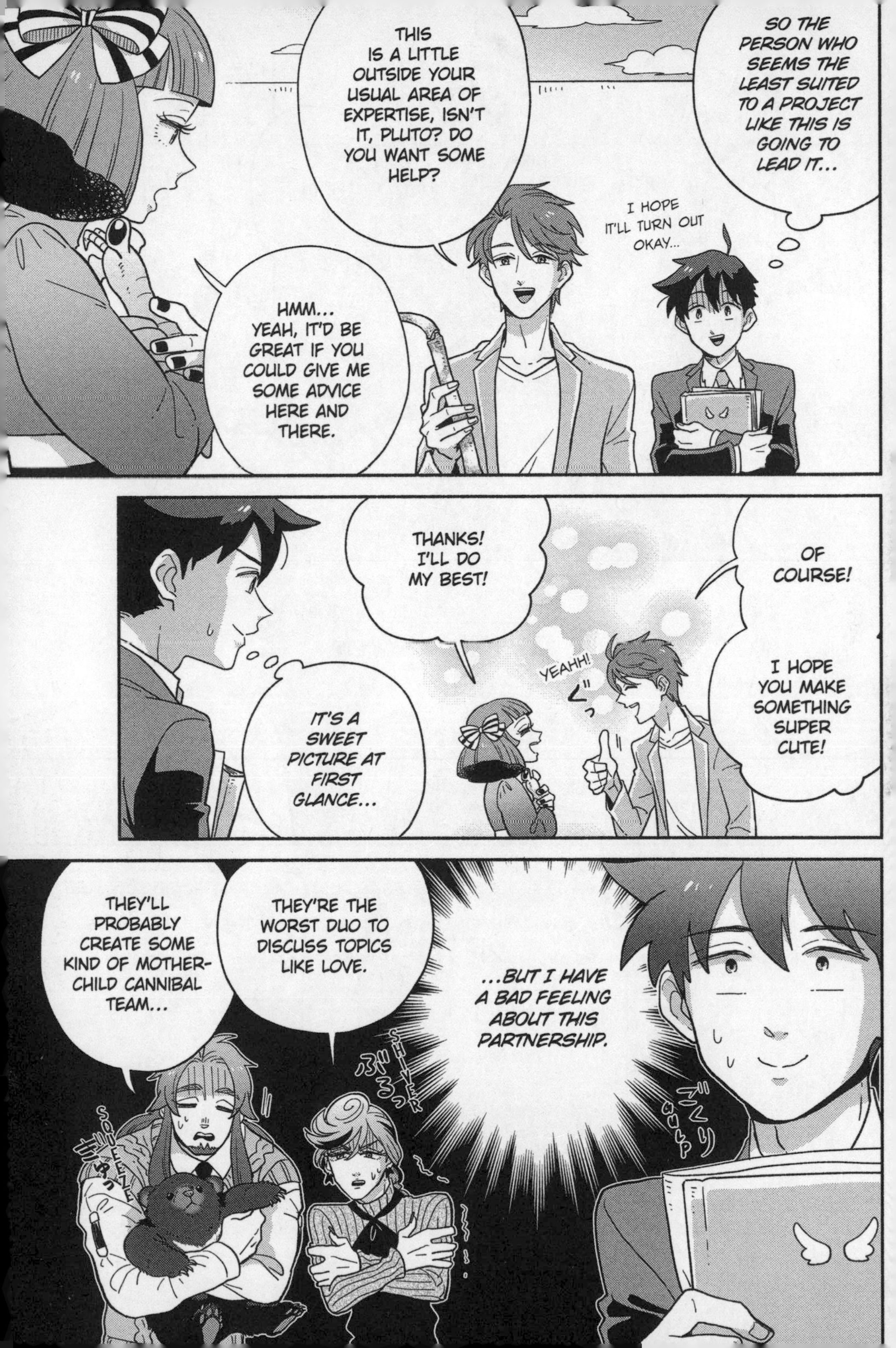
SO THE PERSON WHO SEEMS THE LEAST SUITED TO A PROJECT LIKE THIS IS GOING TO LEAD IT...
I HOPE IT'LL TURN OUT OKAY...
THIS IS A LITTLE OUTSIDE YOUR USUAL AREA OF EXPERTISE, ISN'T IT, PLUTO? DO YOU WANT SOME HELP?
HMM... YEAH, IT'D BE GREAT IF YOU COULD GIVE ME SOME ADVICE HERE AND THERE.
OF COURSE!
I HOPE YOU MAKE SOMETHING SUPER CUTE!
YEAHH!
THANKS! I'LL DO MY BEST!
IT'S A SWEET PICTURE AT FIRST GLANCE...
...BUT I HAVE A BAD FEELING ABOUT THIS PARTNERSHIP.
ごくり
GULP
THEY'RE THE WORST DUO TO DISCUSS TOPICS LIKE LOVE.
ぶるっ
SHIVER
THEY'LL PROBABLY CREATE SOME KIND OF MOTHER-CHILD CANNIBAL TEAM...
ぎゅっ
SQUEEZE

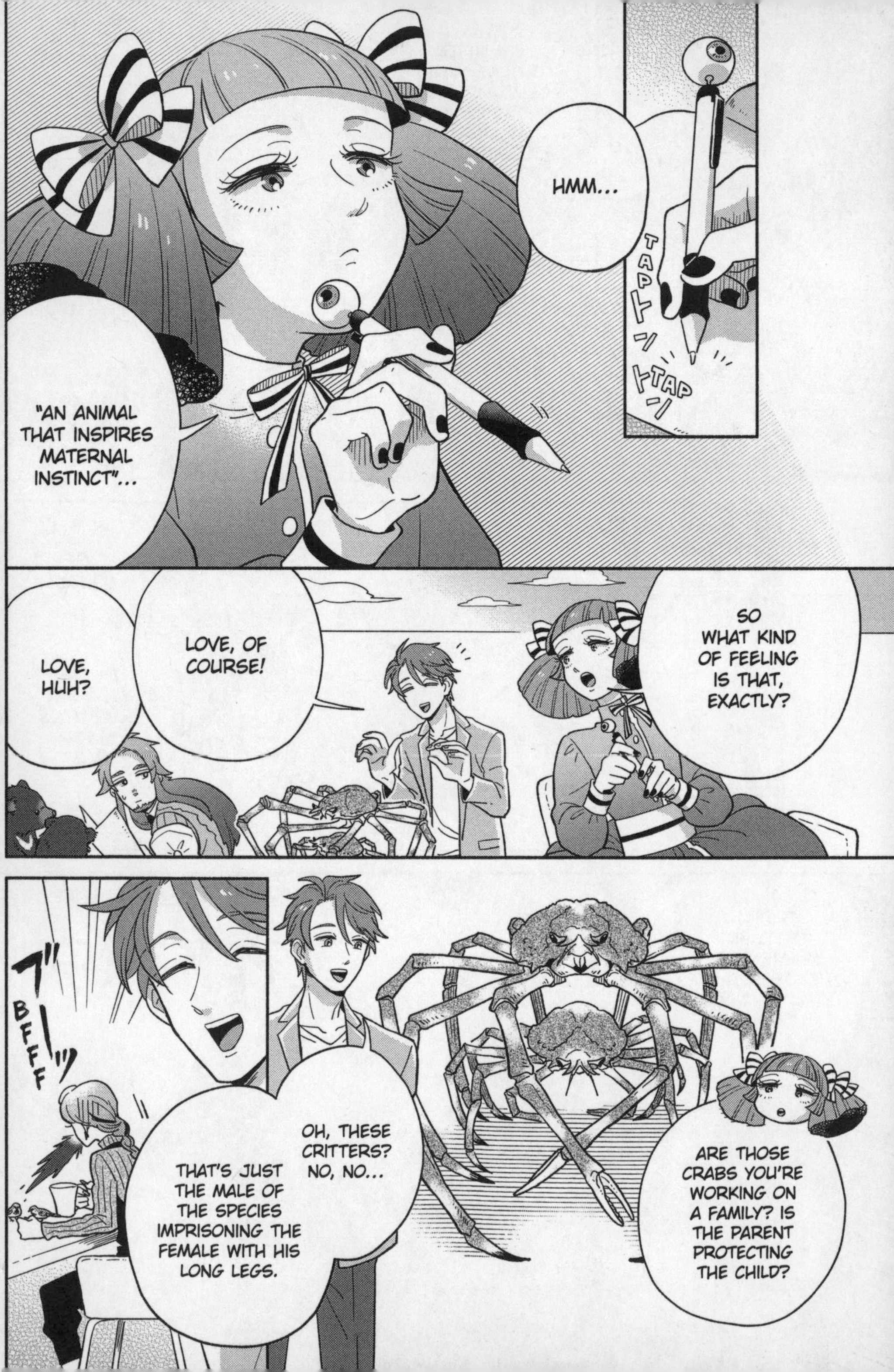
TAP TAP
TAP TAP
HMM...
"AN ANIMAL THAT INSPIRES MATERNAL INSTINCT"...
SO WHAT KIND OF FEELING IS THAT, EXACTLY?
LOVE, OF COURSE!
LOVE, HUH?
ARE THOSE CRABS YOU'RE WORKING ON A FAMILY? IS THE PARENT PROTECTING THE CHILD?
OH, THESE CRITTERS? NO, NO...
THAT'S JUST THE MALE OF THE SPECIES IMPRISONING THE FEMALE WITH HIS LONG LEGS.
BFFF

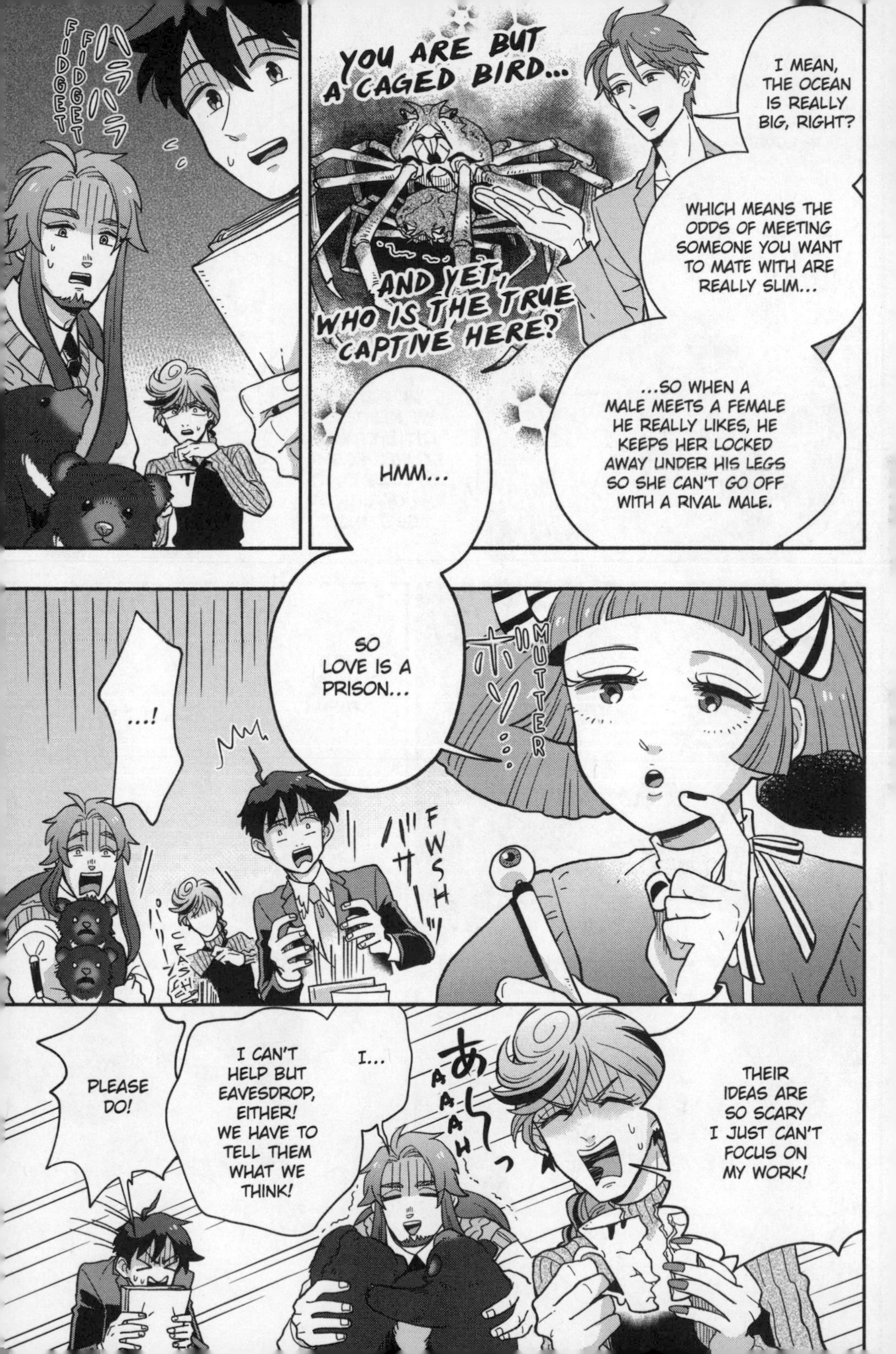
I MEAN, THE OCEAN IS REALLY BIG, RIGHT?
WHICH MEANS THE ODDS OF MEETING SOMEONE YOU WANT TO MATE WITH ARE REALLY SLIM...
...SO WHEN A MALE MEETS A FEMALE HE REALLY LIKES, HE KEEPS HER LOCKED AWAY UNDER HIS LEGS SO SHE CAN'T GO OFF WITH A RIVAL MALE.
YOU ARE BUT A CAGED BIRD...
AND YET, WHO IS THE TRUE CAPTIVE HERE?
HMM...
FIDGET FIDGET
SO LOVE IS A PRISON...
MUTTER
...!
FWSH
CRASH
THEIR IDEAS ARE SO SCARY I JUST CAN'T FOCUS ON MY WORK!
AAAAH
I...
I CAN'T HELP BUT EAVESDROP, EITHER! WE HAVE TO TELL THEM WHAT WE THINK!
PLEASE DO!

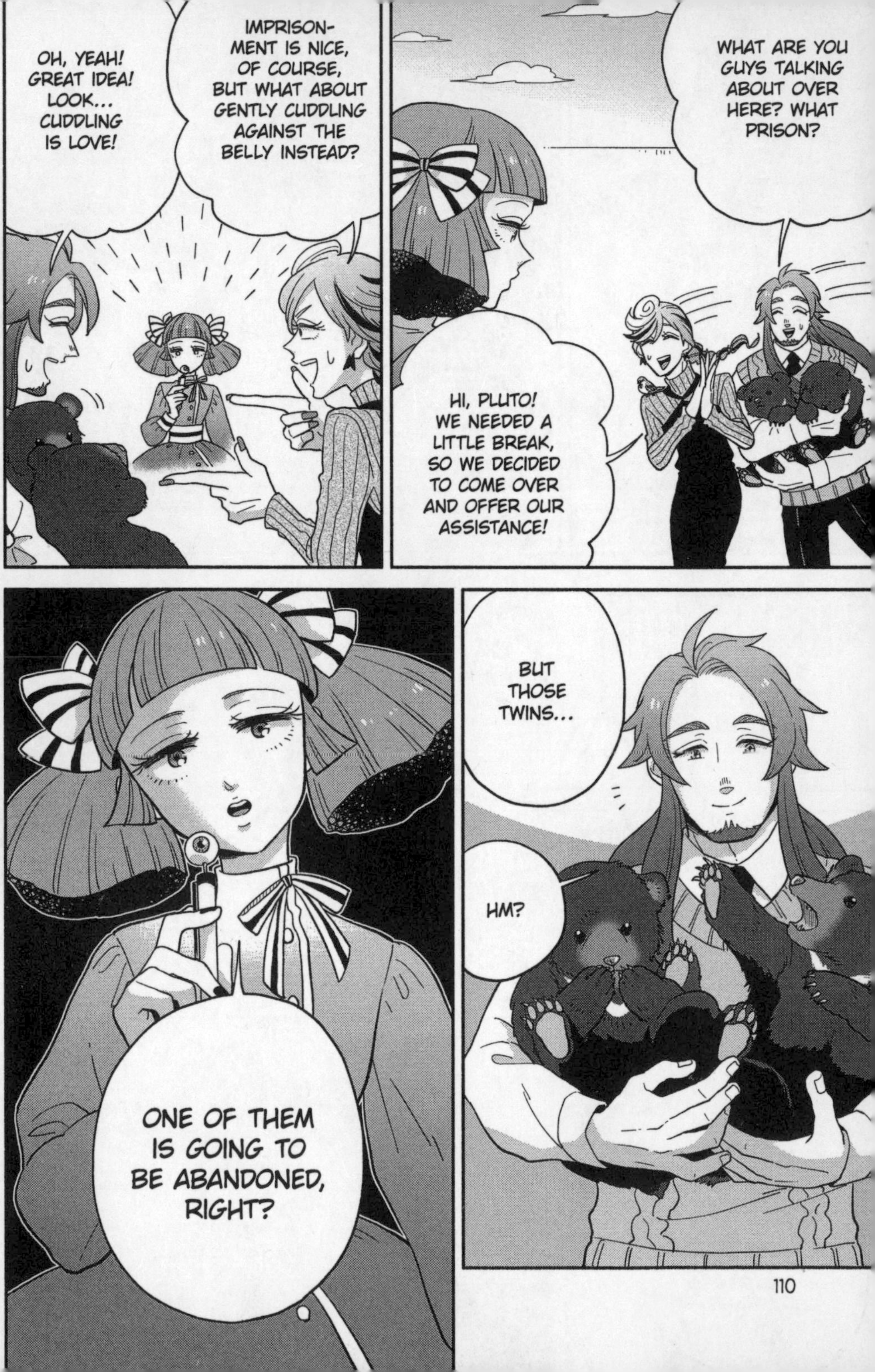
WHAT ARE YOU GUYS TALKING ABOUT OVER HERE? WHAT PRISON?
HI, PLUTO! WE NEEDED A LITTLE BREAK, SO WE DECIDED TO COME OVER AND OFFER OUR ASSISTANCE!
IMPRISON-MENT IS NICE, OF COURSE, BUT WHAT ABOUT GENTLY CUDDLING AGAINST THE BELLY INSTEAD?
OH, YEAH! GREAT IDEA! LOOK... CUDDLING IS LOVE!
BUT THOSE TWINS...
HM?
ONE OF THEM IS GOING TO BE ABANDONED, RIGHT?

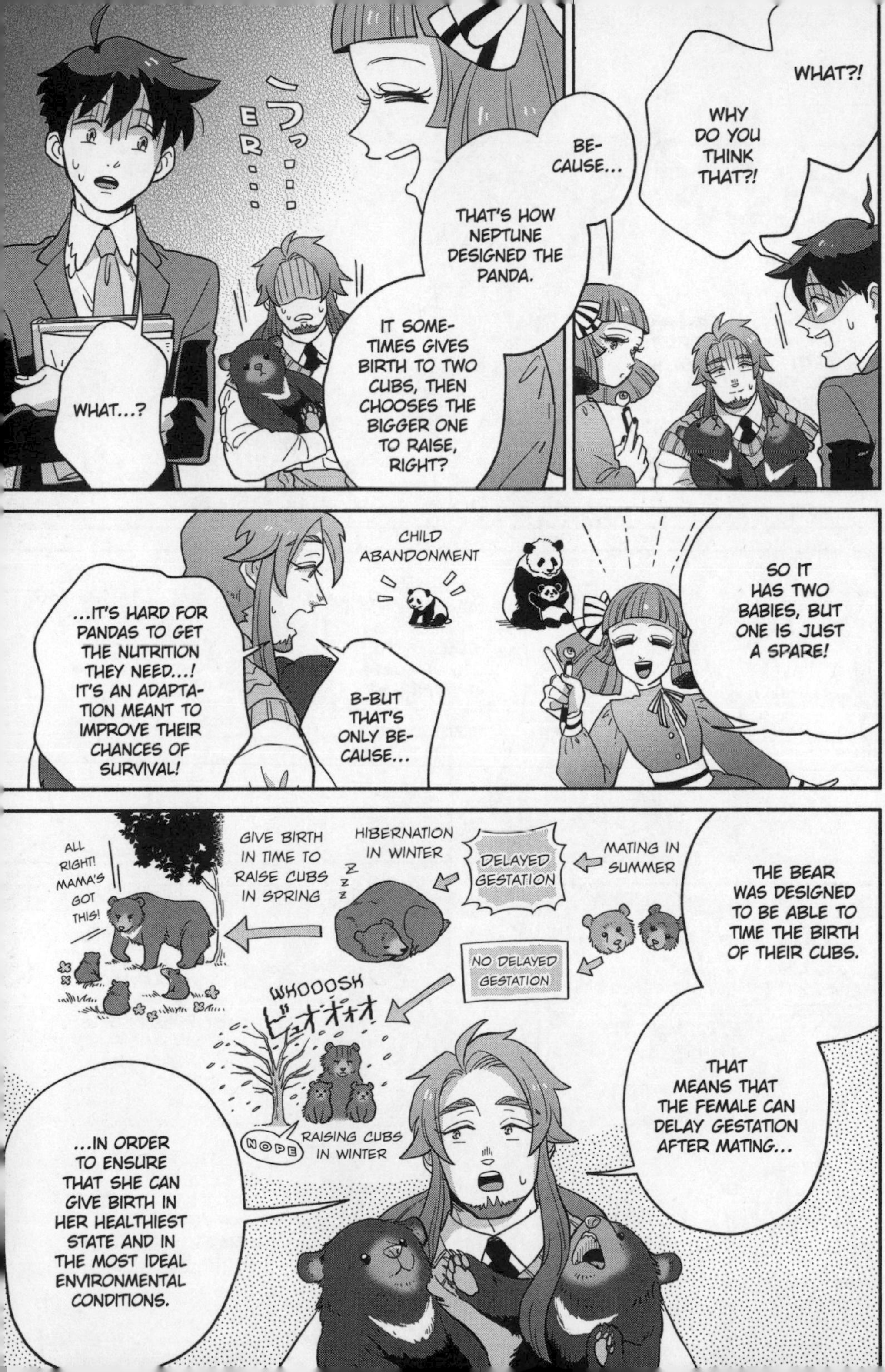
WHAT?!
WHY DO YOU THINK THAT?!
BE-CAUSE...
THAT'S HOW NEPTUNE DESIGNED THE PANDA.
IT SOME-TIMES GIVES BIRTH TO TWO CUBS, THEN CHOOSES THE BIGGER ONE TO RAISE, RIGHT?
ER...
WHAT...?
SO IT HAS TWO BABIES, BUT ONE IS JUST A SPARE!
CHILD ABANDONMENT
B-BUT THAT'S ONLY BE-CAUSE...
...IT'S HARD FOR PANDAS TO GET THE NUTRITION THEY NEED...! IT'S AN ADAPTA-TION MEANT TO IMPROVE THEIR CHANCES OF SURVIVAL!
THE BEAR WAS DESIGNED TO BE ABLE TO TIME THE BIRTH OF THEIR CUBS.
MATING IN SUMMER
DELAYED GESTATION
HIBERNATION IN WINTER
Z Z Z
GIVE BIRTH IN TIME TO RAISE CUBS IN SPRING
ALL RIGHT! MAMA'S GOT THIS!
NO DELAYED GESTATION
WHOOOSH
ジュオオオオ
RAISING CUBS IN WINTER
NOPE
THAT MEANS THAT THE FEMALE CAN DELAY GESTATION AFTER MATING...
...IN ORDER TO ENSURE THAT SHE CAN GIVE BIRTH IN HER HEALTHIEST STATE AND IN THE MOST IDEAL ENVIRONMENTAL CONDITIONS.

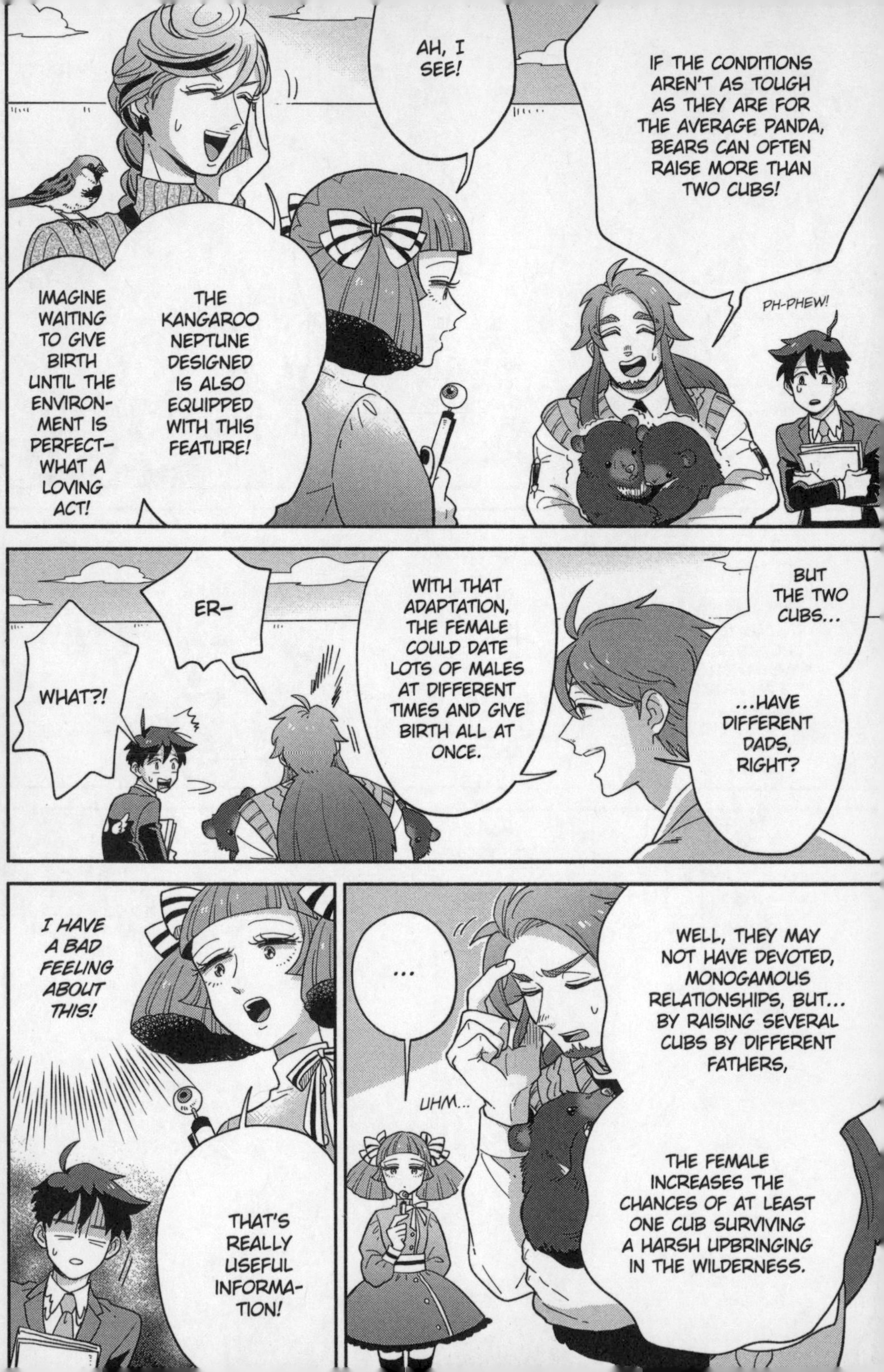
IF THE CONDITIONS AREN'T AS TOUGH AS THEY ARE FOR THE AVERAGE PANDA, BEARS CAN OFTEN RAISE MORE THAN TWO CUBS!
PH-PHEW!
AH, I SEE!
THE KANGAROO NEPTUNE DESIGNED IS ALSO EQUIPPED WITH THIS FEATURE!
IMAGINE WAITING TO GIVE BIRTH UNTIL THE ENVIRONMENT IS PERFECT—WHAT A LOVING ACT!
BUT THE TWO CUBS...
...HAVE DIFFERENT DADS, RIGHT?
WITH THAT ADAPTATION, THE FEMALE COULD DATE LOTS OF MALES AT DIFFERENT TIMES AND GIVE BIRTH ALL AT ONCE.
ER-
WHAT?!
WELL, THEY MAY NOT HAVE DEVOTED, MONOGAMOUS RELATIONSHIPS, BUT... BY RAISING SEVERAL CUBS BY DIFFERENT FATHERS,
THE FEMALE INCREASES THE CHANCES OF AT LEAST ONE CUB SURVIVING A HARSH UPBRINGING IN THE WILDERNESS.
...
UHM...
I HAVE A BAD FEELING ABOUT THIS!
THAT'S REALLY USEFUL INFORMATION!

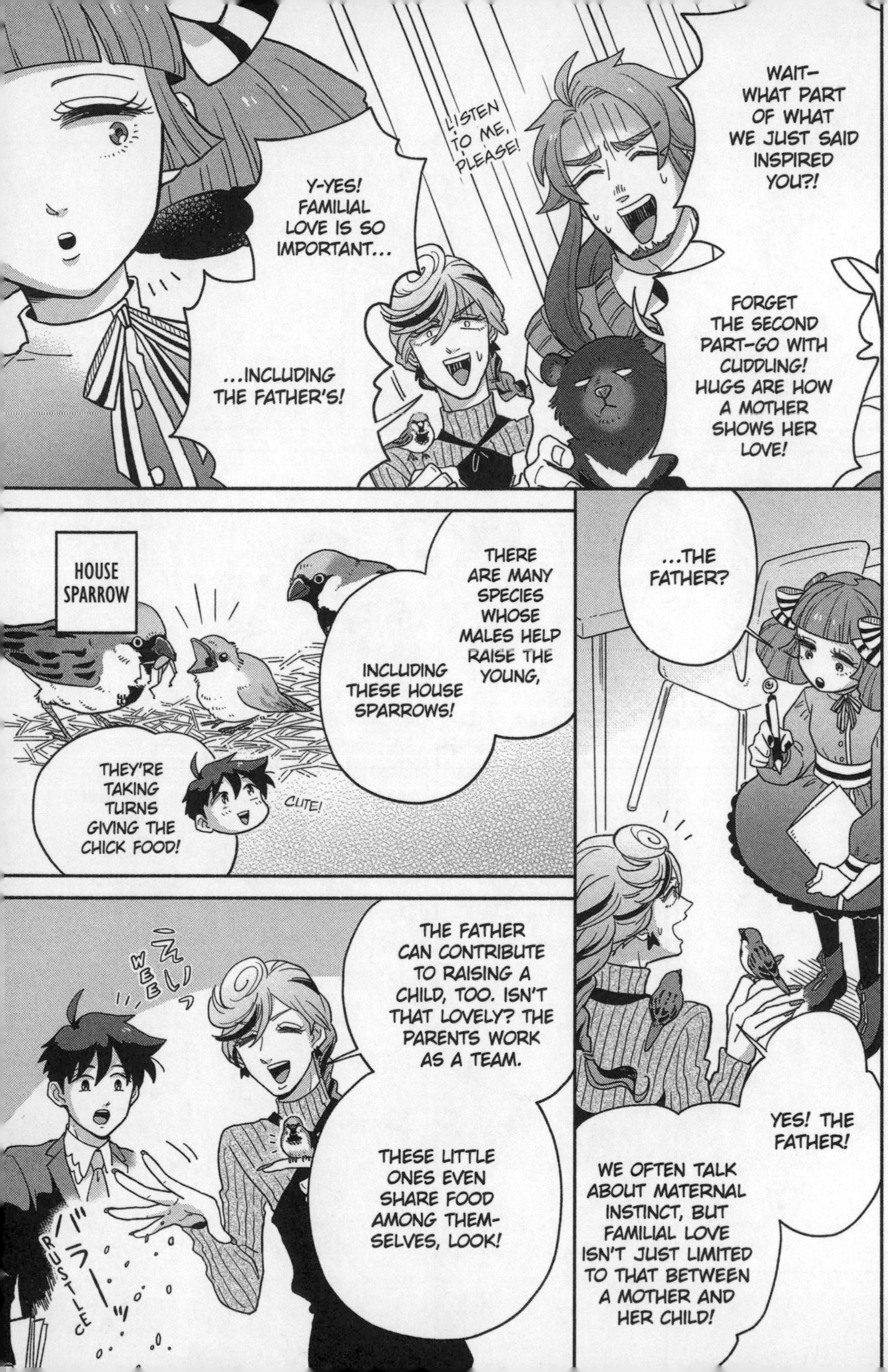
WAIT— WHAT PART OF WHAT WE JUST SAID INSPIRED YOU?!
FORGET THE SECOND PART—GO WITH CUDDLING! HUGS ARE HOW A MOTHER SHOWS HER LOVE!
LISTEN TO ME, PLEASE!
Y-YES! FAMILIAL LOVE IS SO IMPORTANT...
...INCLUDING THE FATHER'S!
...THE FATHER?
YES! THE FATHER!
WE OFTEN TALK ABOUT MATERNAL INSTINCT, BUT FAMILIAL LOVE ISN'T JUST LIMITED TO THAT BETWEEN A MOTHER AND HER CHILD!
THERE ARE MANY SPECIES WHOSE MALES HELP RAISE THE YOUNG,
INCLUDING THESE HOUSE SPARROWS!
HOUSE SPARROW
THEY'RE TAKING TURNS GIVING THE CHICK FOOD!
CUTE!
THE FATHER CAN CONTRIBUTE TO RAISING A CHILD, TOO. ISN'T THAT LOVELY? THE PARENTS WORK AS A TEAM.
THESE LITTLE ONES EVEN SHARE FOOD AMONG THEMSELVES, LOOK!
WEE
RUSTLE

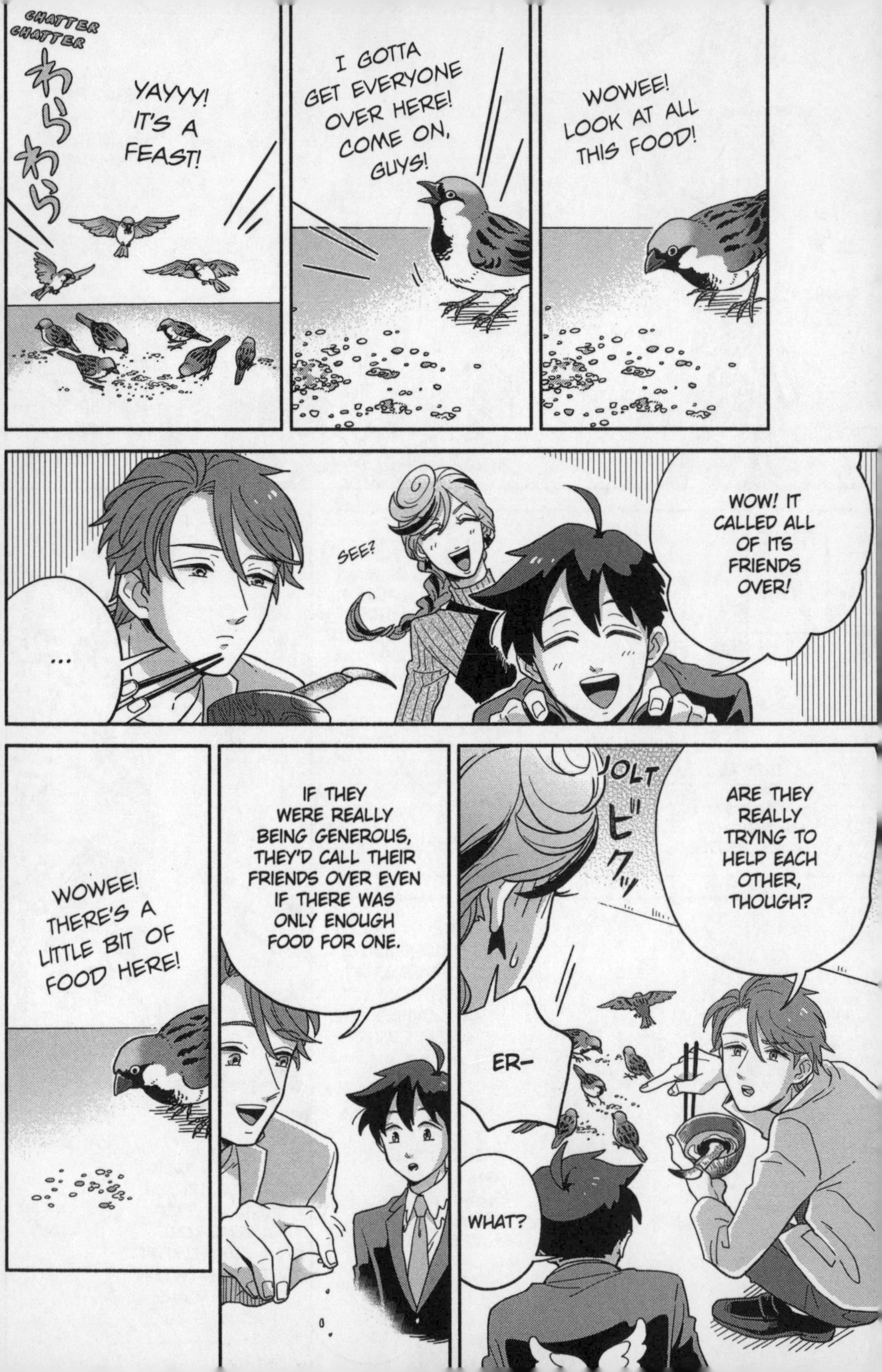
WOWEE! LOOK AT ALL THIS FOOD!
I GOTTA GET EVERYONE OVER HERE! COME ON, GUYS!
CHATTER CHATTER
わらわら
YAYYY! IT'S A FEAST!
WOW! IT CALLED ALL OF ITS FRIENDS OVER!
SEE?
...
ARE THEY REALLY TRYING TO HELP EACH OTHER, THOUGH?
JOLT
ビクッ
ER-
WHAT?
IF THEY WERE REALLY BEING GENEROUS, THEY'D CALL THEIR FRIENDS OVER EVEN IF THERE WAS ONLY ENOUGH FOOD FOR ONE.
WOWEE! THERE'S A LITTLE BIT OF FOOD HERE!

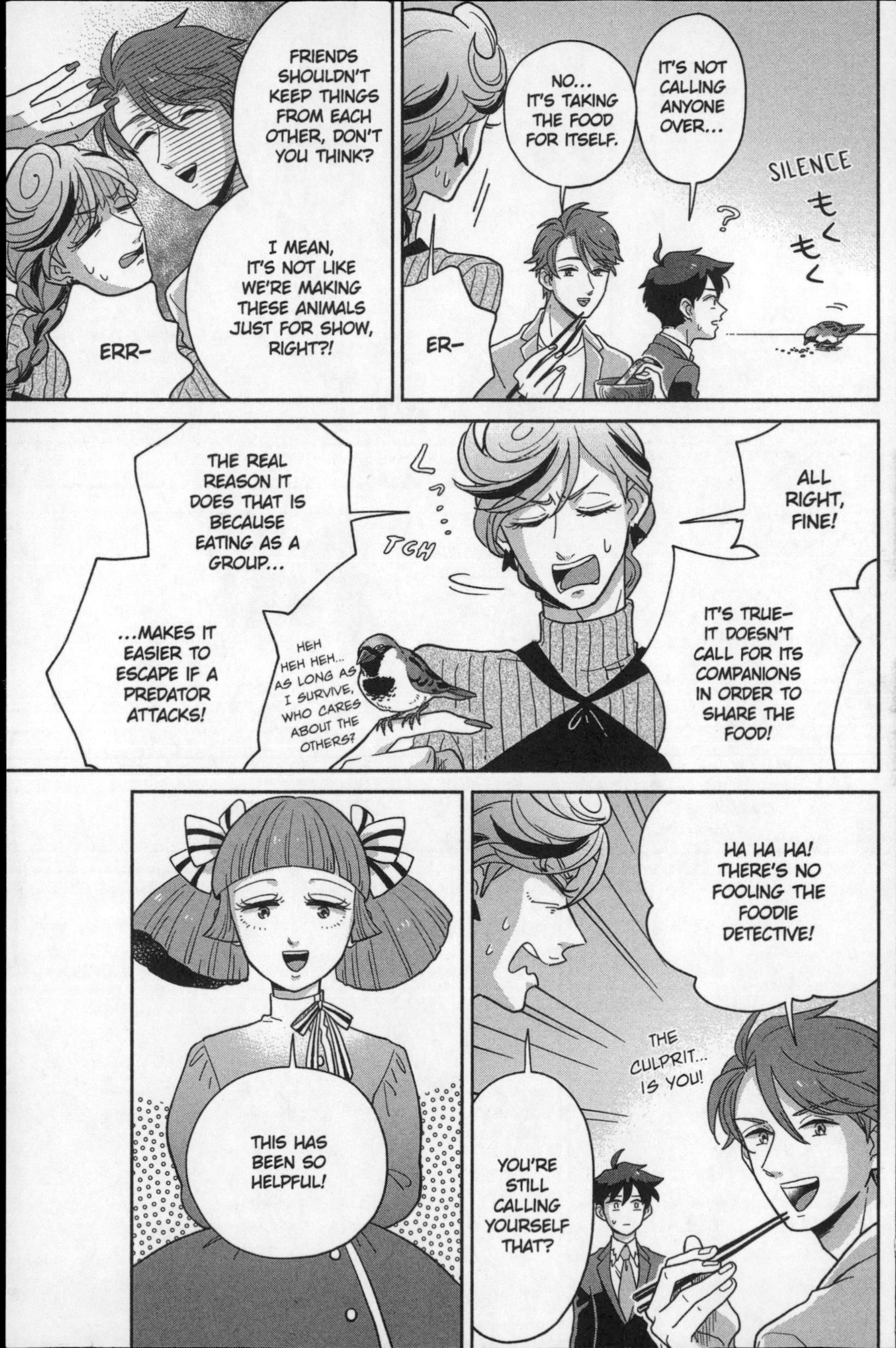
IT'S NOT CALLING ANYONE OVER...
NO... IT'S TAKING THE FOOD FOR ITSELF.
SILENCE
もく もく
?
ER–
FRIENDS SHOULDN'T KEEP THINGS FROM EACH OTHER, DON'T YOU THINK?
I MEAN, IT'S NOT LIKE WE'RE MAKING THESE ANIMALS JUST FOR SHOW, RIGHT?!
ERR–
ALL RIGHT, FINE!
IT'S TRUE– IT DOESN'T CALL FOR ITS COMPANIONS IN ORDER TO SHARE THE FOOD!
TCH
THE REAL REASON IT DOES THAT IS BECAUSE EATING AS A GROUP...
HEH HEH HEH... AS LONG AS I SURVIVE, WHO CARES ABOUT THE OTHERS?
...MAKES IT EASIER TO ESCAPE IF A PREDATOR ATTACKS!
HA HA HA! THERE'S NO FOOLING THE FOODIE DETECTIVE!
THE CULPRIT... IS YOU!
YOU'RE STILL CALLING YOURSELF THAT?
THIS HAS BEEN SO HELPFUL!

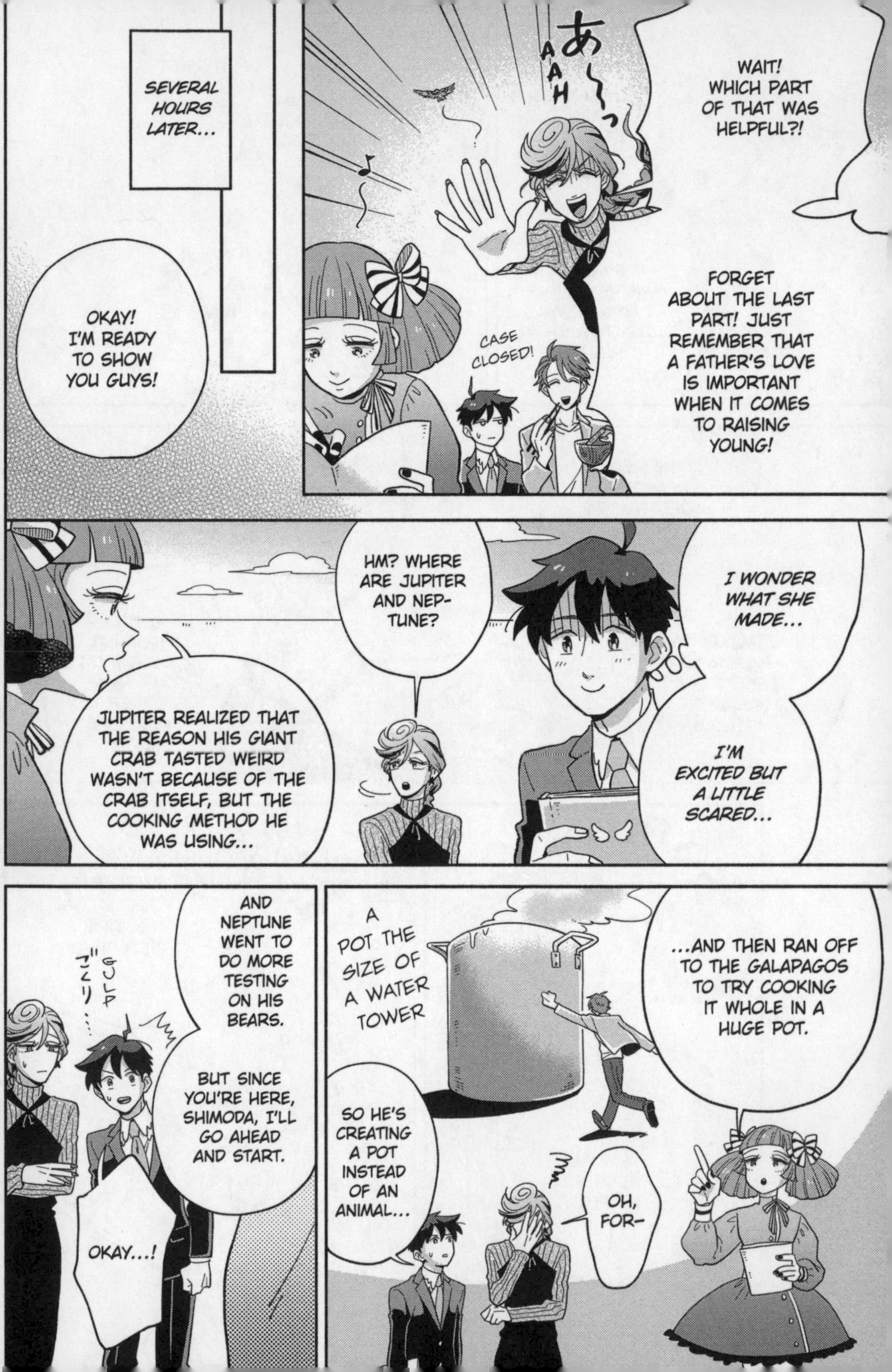
あ~っ
AAH
WAIT! WHICH PART OF THAT WAS HELPFUL?!
FORGET ABOUT THE LAST PART! JUST REMEMBER THAT A FATHER'S LOVE IS IMPORTANT WHEN IT COMES TO RAISING YOUNG!
CASE CLOSED!
SEVERAL HOURS LATER...
OKAY! I'M READY TO SHOW YOU GUYS!
I WONDER WHAT SHE MADE...
I'M EXCITED BUT A LITTLE SCARED...
HM? WHERE ARE JUPITER AND NEP-TUNE?
JUPITER REALIZED THAT THE REASON HIS GIANT CRAB TASTED WEIRD WASN'T BECAUSE OF THE CRAB ITSELF, BUT THE COOKING METHOD HE WAS USING...
...AND THEN RAN OFF TO THE GALAPAGOS TO TRY COOKING IT WHOLE IN A HUGE POT.
A POT THE SIZE OF A WATER TOWER
OH, FOR-
SO HE'S CREATING A POT INSTEAD OF AN ANIMAL...
AND NEPTUNE WENT TO DO MORE TESTING ON HIS BEARS.
BUT SINCE YOU'RE HERE, SHIMODA, I'LL GO AHEAD AND START.
ゴクリ…
GULP
OKAY...!

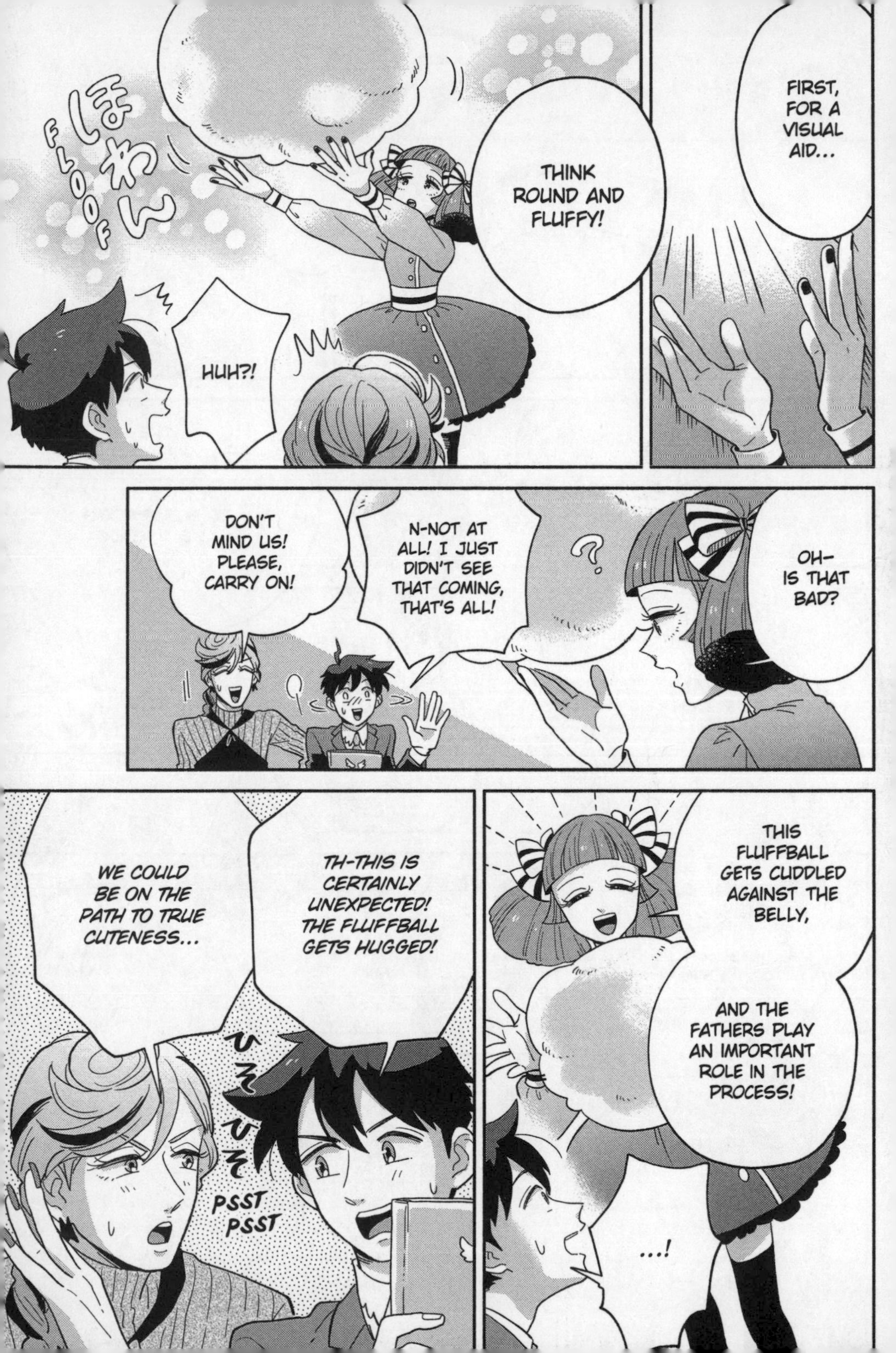
FIRST, FOR A VISUAL AID…
THINK ROUND AND FLUFFY!
ほわん
FLOOF
HUH?!
OH- IS THAT BAD?
N-NOT AT ALL! I JUST DIDN'T SEE THAT COMING, THAT'S ALL!
DON'T MIND US! PLEASE, CARRY ON!
THIS FLUFFBALL GETS CUDDLED AGAINST THE BELLY,
AND THE FATHERS PLAY AN IMPORTANT ROLE IN THE PROCESS!
…!
TH-THIS IS CERTAINLY UNEXPECTED! THE FLUFFBALL GETS HUGGED!
WE COULD BE ON THE PATH TO TRUE CUTENESS…
ひそひそ
PSST PSST

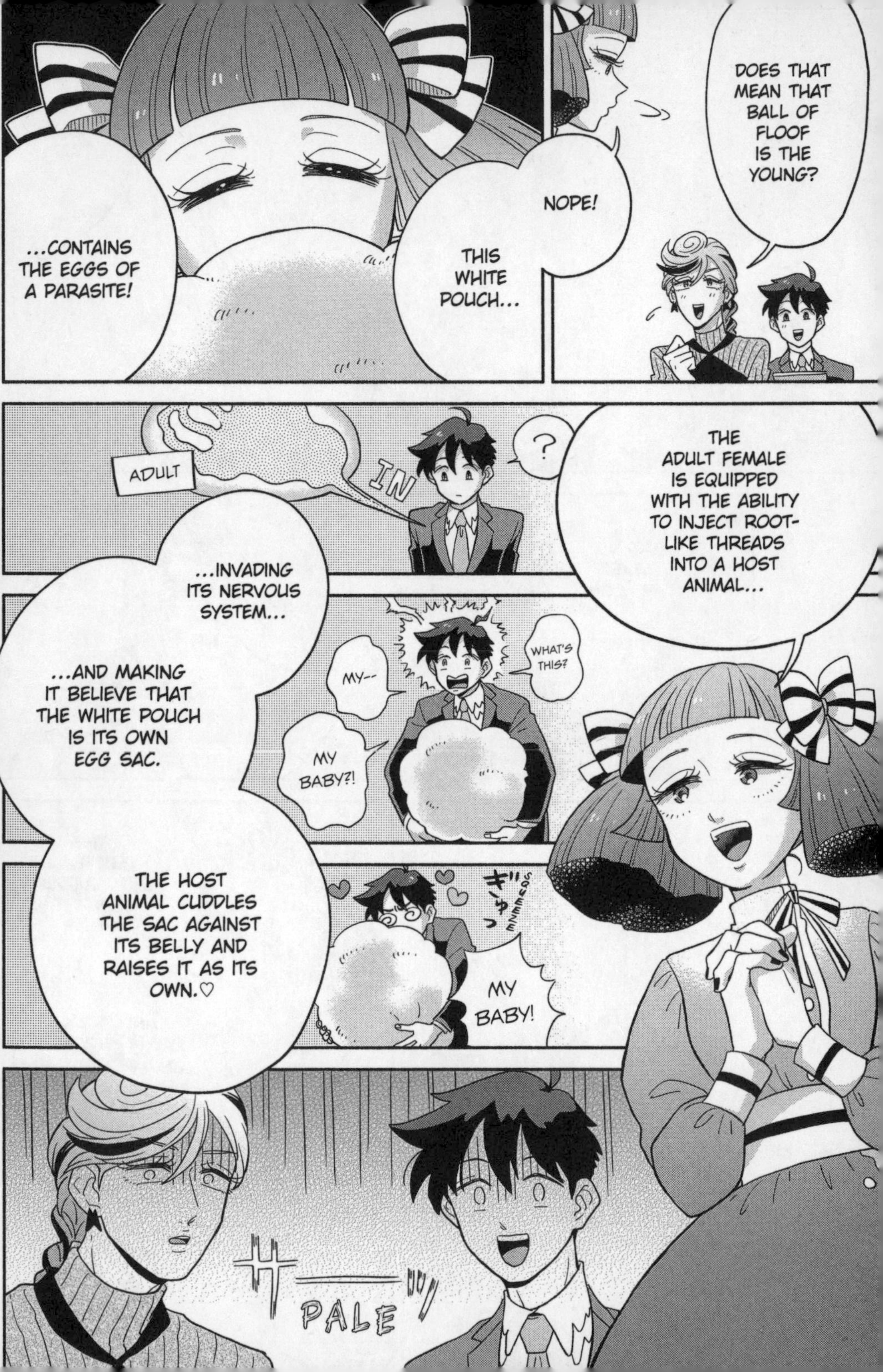
DOES THAT MEAN THAT BALL OF FLOOF IS THE YOUNG?
NOPE!
THIS WHITE POUCH...
...CONTAINS THE EGGS OF A PARASITE!
THE ADULT FEMALE IS EQUIPPED WITH THE ABILITY TO INJECT ROOT-LIKE THREADS INTO A HOST ANIMAL...
?
IN
ADULT
...INVADING ITS NERVOUS SYSTEM...
WHAT'S THIS?
MY--
MY BABY?!
...AND MAKING IT BELIEVE THAT THE WHITE POUCH IS ITS OWN EGG SAC.
ギュッ SQUEEZE
MY BABY!
THE HOST ANIMAL CUDDLES THE SAC AGAINST ITS BELLY AND RAISES IT AS ITS OWN.♡
PALE

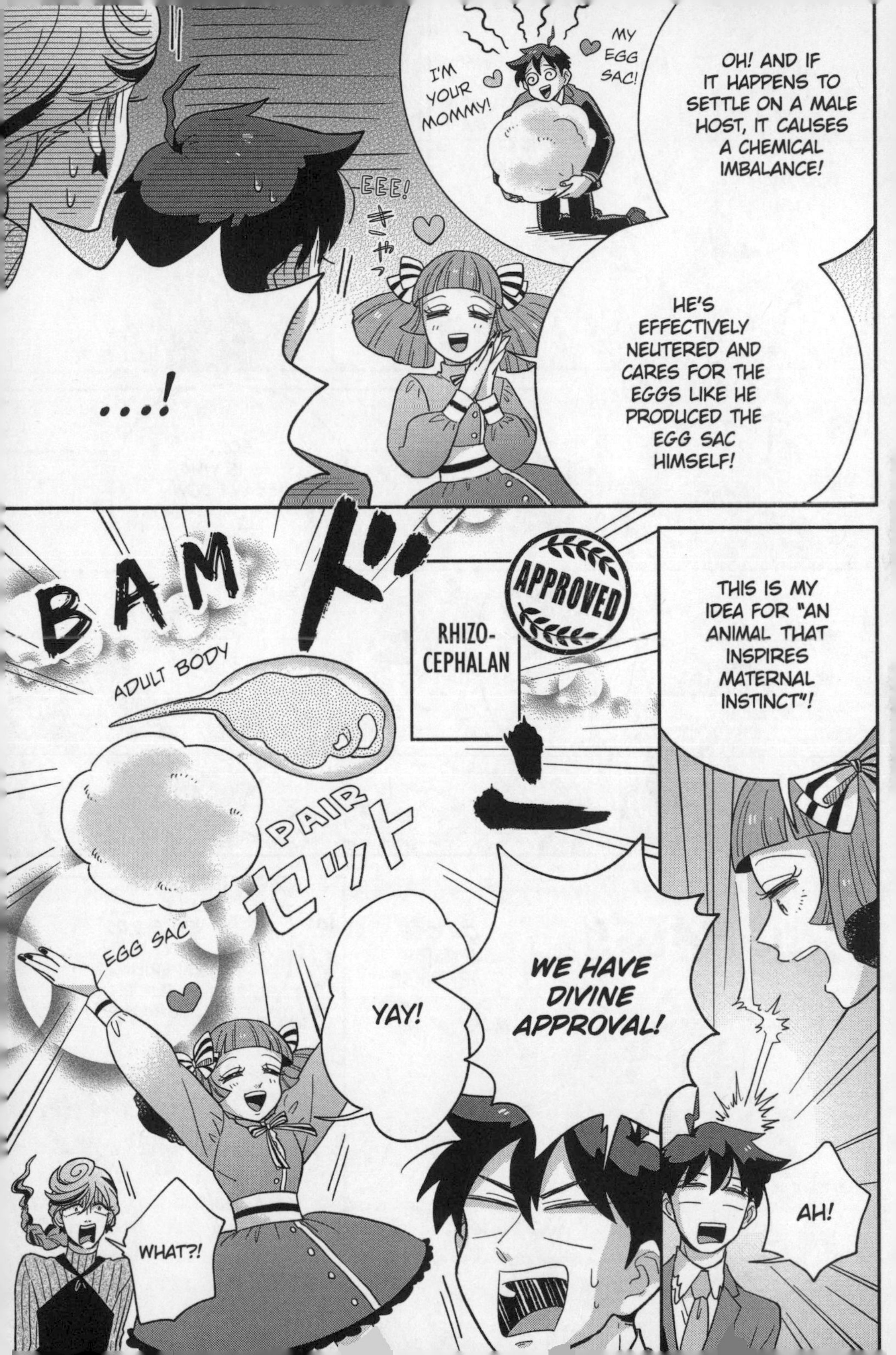
OH! AND IF IT HAPPENS TO SETTLE ON A MALE HOST, IT CAUSES A CHEMICAL IMBALANCE!
MY EGG SAC!
I'M YOUR MOMMY!
HE'S EFFECTIVELY NEUTERED AND CARES FOR THE EGGS LIKE HE PRODUCED THE EGG SAC HIMSELF!
-EEE!
...!
THIS IS MY IDEA FOR "AN ANIMAL THAT INSPIRES MATERNAL INSTINCT"!
APPROVED
RHIZO-CEPHALAN
ド
BAM
ADULT BODY
PAIR
セット
EGG SAC
WE HAVE DIVINE APPROVAL!
YAY!
AH!
WHAT?!

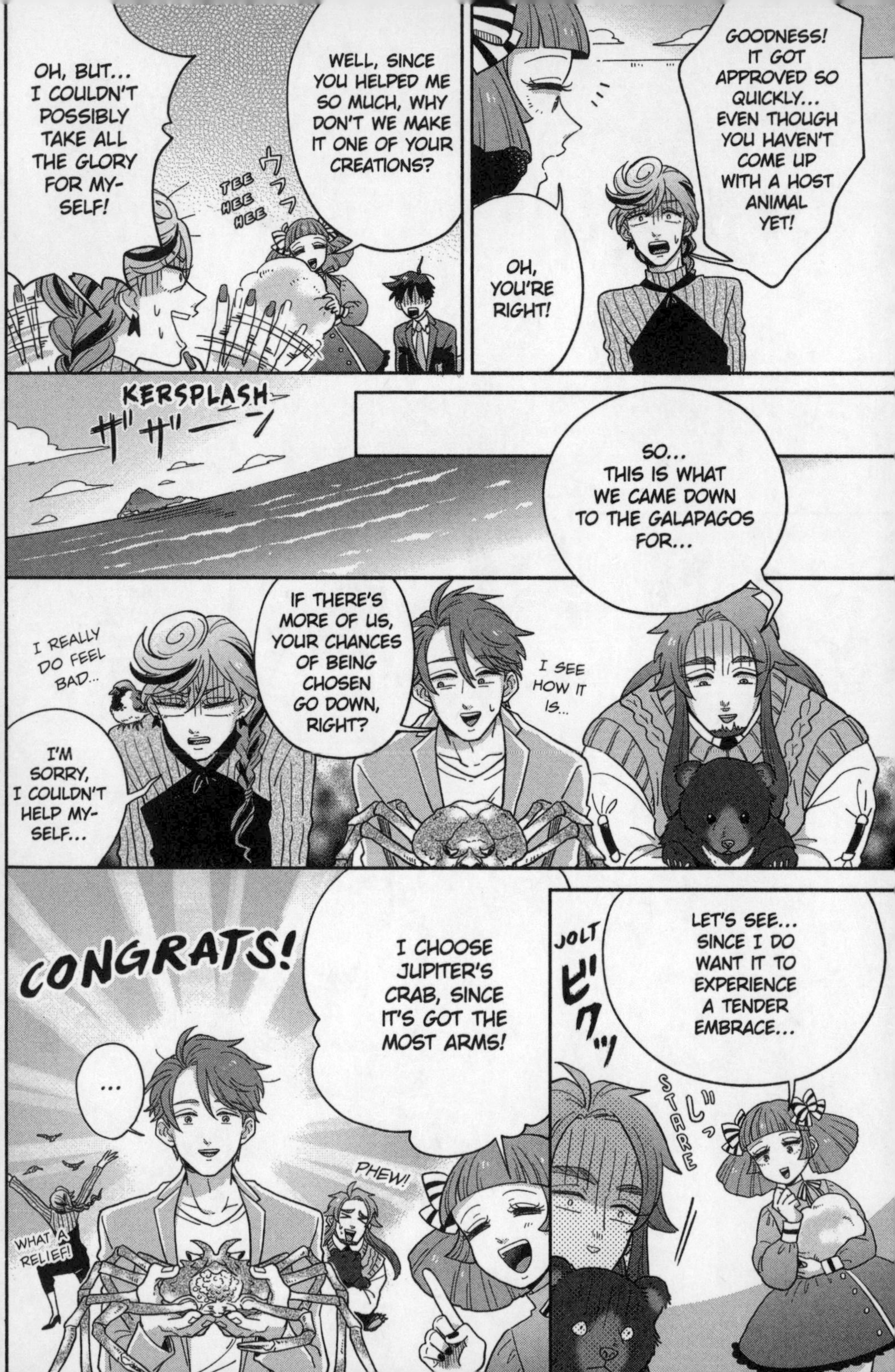
GOODNESS! IT GOT APPROVED SO QUICKLY... EVEN THOUGH YOU HAVEN'T COME UP WITH A HOST ANIMAL YET!
OH, YOU'RE RIGHT!
WELL, SINCE YOU HELPED ME SO MUCH, WHY DON'T WE MAKE IT ONE OF YOUR CREATIONS?
OH, BUT... I COULDN'T POSSIBLY TAKE ALL THE GLORY FOR MY-SELF!
ウフフ
TEE HEE HEE
SO... THIS IS WHAT WE CAME DOWN TO THE GALAPAGOS FOR...
KERSPLASH
ザザーン
I SEE HOW IT IS...
IF THERE'S MORE OF US, YOUR CHANCES OF BEING CHOSEN GO DOWN, RIGHT?
I REALLY DO FEEL BAD...
I'M SORRY, I COULDN'T HELP MY-SELF...
LET'S SEE... SINCE I DO WANT IT TO EXPERIENCE A TENDER EMBRACE...
JOLT
ビクッ
じっ
STARE
I CHOOSE JUPITER'S CRAB, SINCE IT'S GOT THE MOST ARMS!
CONGRATS!
...
PHEW!
WHAT A RELIEF!

THE ENCYCLOPEDIA OF REAL ANIMALS 20

ANIMAL 51 RHIZOCEPHALAN

Larva
Female
Male
stab
Enters through hole in pouch and joins female
Crab
Injects roots into the host and absorbs nutrients
Pouch containing eggs develops outside of the host's body
Crab doesn't die

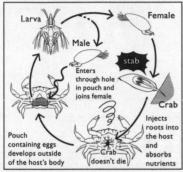

Illustration: Hebi-zou

THE REAL THING

A rhizocephalan on a Japanese shore crab.
Photo: Ayumu Fukui (Walk Photo Atelier)/Aflo

Though it hardly resembles one, the rhizocephalan is a kind of crustacean that includes approximately 250 species. As shown in the diagram, it can take on many forms depending on its stage of growth. It is classified as a type of barnacle, though it settles on other animals rather than on rocks. Most often, it parasitizes decapods like shrimp and crabs, manipulating their nervous systems and forcing them to care for its egg sac as their own. If the host animal is male, a hormone imbalance occurs, effectively castrating it and causing it to protect the rhizocephalan and its egg sac as a female would. Interestingly, the neutered host animal then often ends up living longer, as it no longer has to spend its energy reproducing. Only the adult female rhizocephalan is able to settle directly on the host, and after the eggs are fertilized, the males are discarded with the old shell when the host animal molts.

[Name] Rhizocephalan
[Classification] Class: Maxillopoda
Superorder: Rhizocephala
[Habitat] The ocean

| # BEAR

THE REAL THING

A grizzly bear mother and her two cubs.

Photo: Minden Pictures/Aflo

The female bear undergoes a reproductive strategy known as delayed implantation. In mammals, the embryonic blastocyst usually implants immediately in the uterus after sexual reproduction. The bear, however, has the ability to keep the embryo suspended within the uterus in order to delay gestation. Because of this, the animal can avoid giving birth during its hibernation period. It's also thought that delayed implantation allows the female to mate with several different males to increase the genetic diversity of her young.

[Name]	Bear
[Classification]	Class: Mammalia
	Order: Carnivora
	Family: Ursidae
[Habitat]	The Americas, Eurasia, Japan, the North Pole
[Length]	1.2-2.8 m (4-9.2 ft)

| # JAPANESE SPIDER CRAB

The largest extant arthropod, the male Japanese spider crab's tendency to imprison the female during breeding is a characteristic shared among many crab species. Mating can only occur right after the female crab has molted, when her shell is still soft, and the odds of finding a recently molted female are quite slim. For that reason, the male often traps an available female until she is ready to mate.

Because its flesh seems to melt away as soon as it is taken from the water, the Japanese spider crab is difficult to cook; however, it is delicious steamed in a big pot.

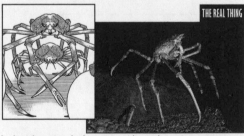

THE REAL THING

Its long legs give the Japanese spider crab a unique appearance. Normally, it lives at depths of 200-600 m (656-1968 ft), but in spring can move up to depths of 20 m (65 ft).

Photo: Photoshot/Aflo

[Name]	*Macrocheira kaempferi*
[Classification]	Class: Malacostraca
	Order: Decapoda
	Family: Majidae
	Genus: *Macrocheira*
[Habitat]	Waters around Japan
[Length]	30 cm (12 in) (body), 4 m (13 ft) (leg span)

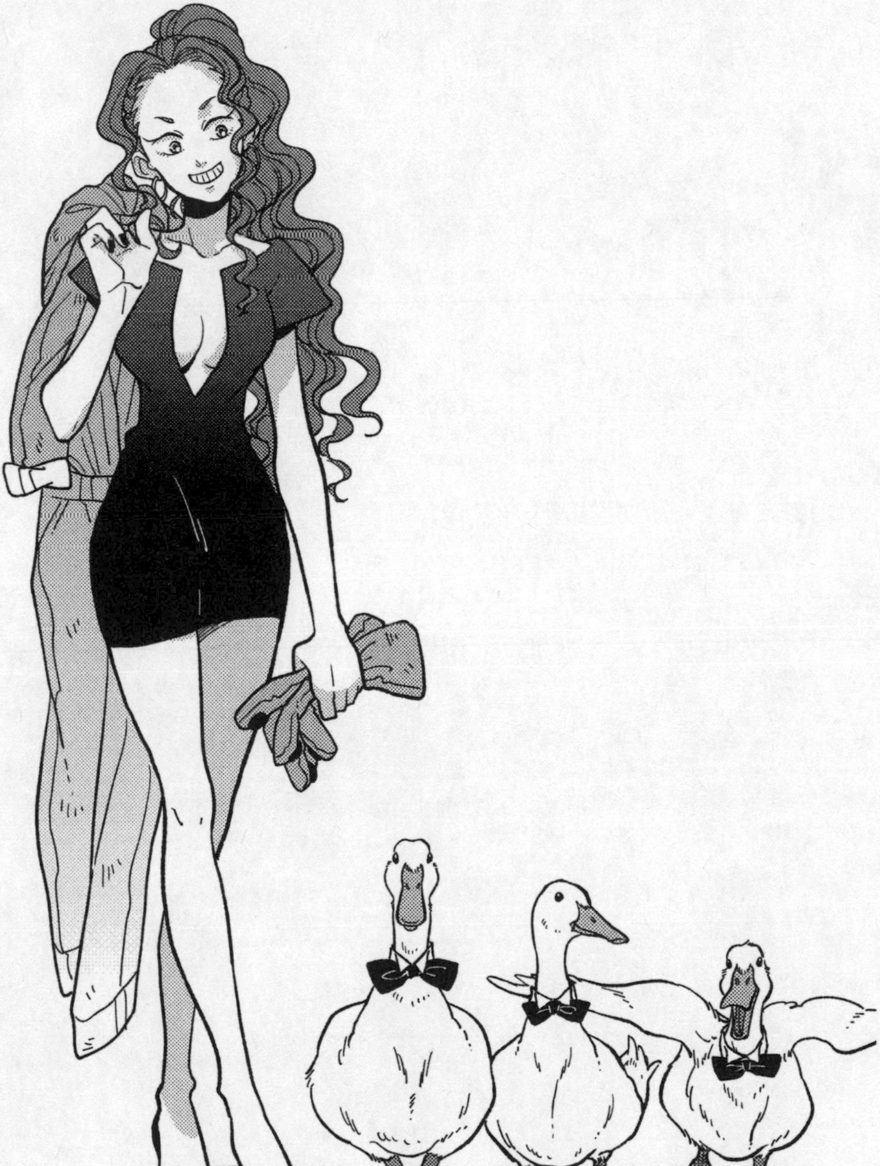

HEAVEN'S
DESIGN TEAM

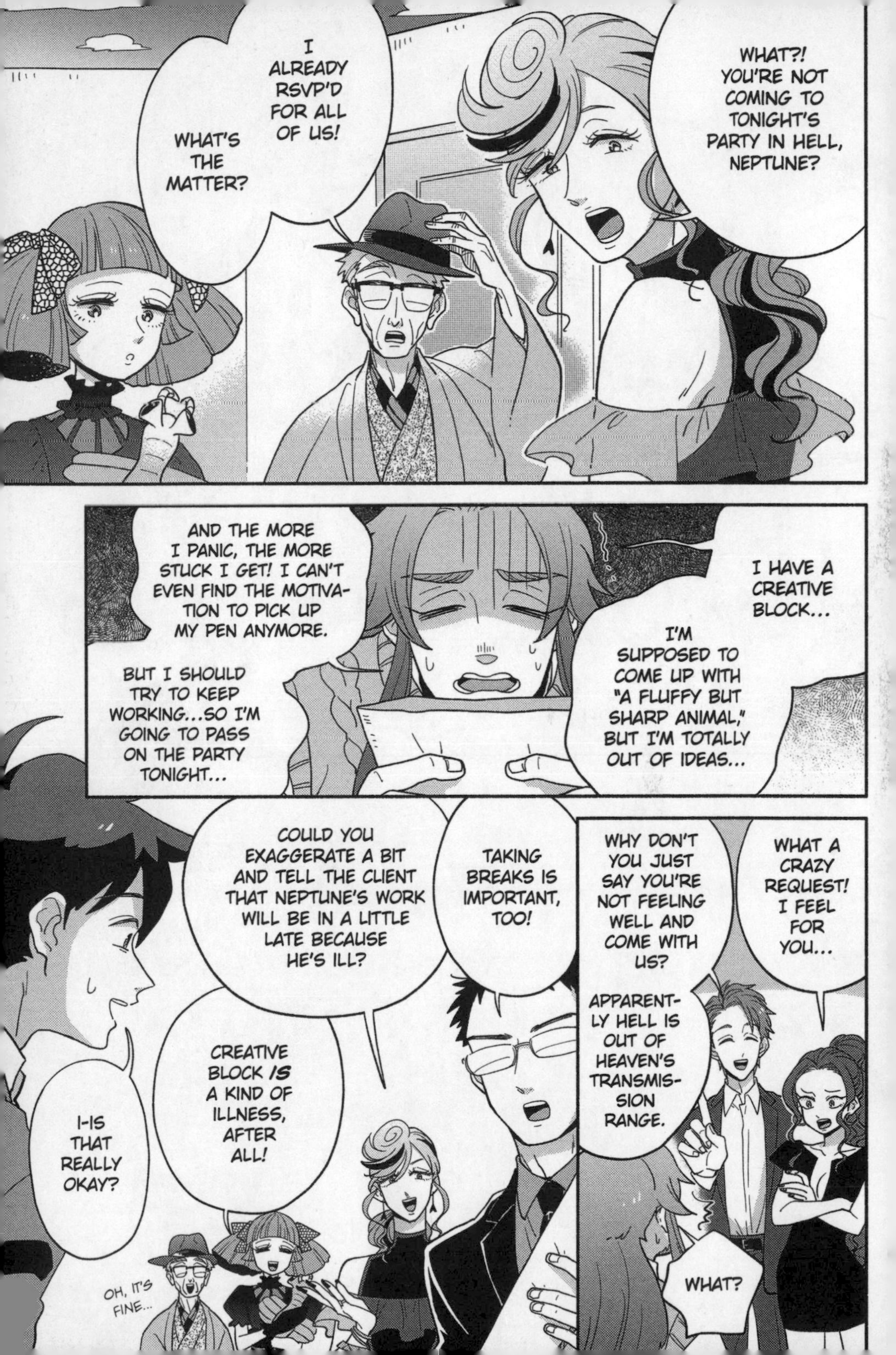
WHAT?! YOU'RE NOT COMING TO TONIGHT'S PARTY IN HELL, NEPTUNE?
I ALREADY RSVP'D FOR ALL OF US!
WHAT'S THE MATTER?
I HAVE A CREATIVE BLOCK...
I'M SUPPOSED TO COME UP WITH "A FLUFFY BUT SHARP ANIMAL," BUT I'M TOTALLY OUT OF IDEAS...
AND THE MORE I PANIC, THE MORE STUCK I GET! I CAN'T EVEN FIND THE MOTIVATION TO PICK UP MY PEN ANYMORE.
BUT I SHOULD TRY TO KEEP WORKING...SO I'M GOING TO PASS ON THE PARTY TONIGHT...
WHAT A CRAZY REQUEST! I FEEL FOR YOU...
WHY DON'T YOU JUST SAY YOU'RE NOT FEELING WELL AND COME WITH US?
APPARENTLY HELL IS OUT OF HEAVEN'S TRANSMISSION RANGE.
WHAT?
TAKING BREAKS IS IMPORTANT, TOO!
COULD YOU EXAGGERATE A BIT AND TELL THE CLIENT THAT NEPTUNE'S WORK WILL BE IN A LITTLE LATE BECAUSE HE'S ILL?
CREATIVE BLOCK *IS* A KIND OF ILLNESS, AFTER ALL!
I-IS THAT REALLY OKAY?
OH, IT'S FINE...

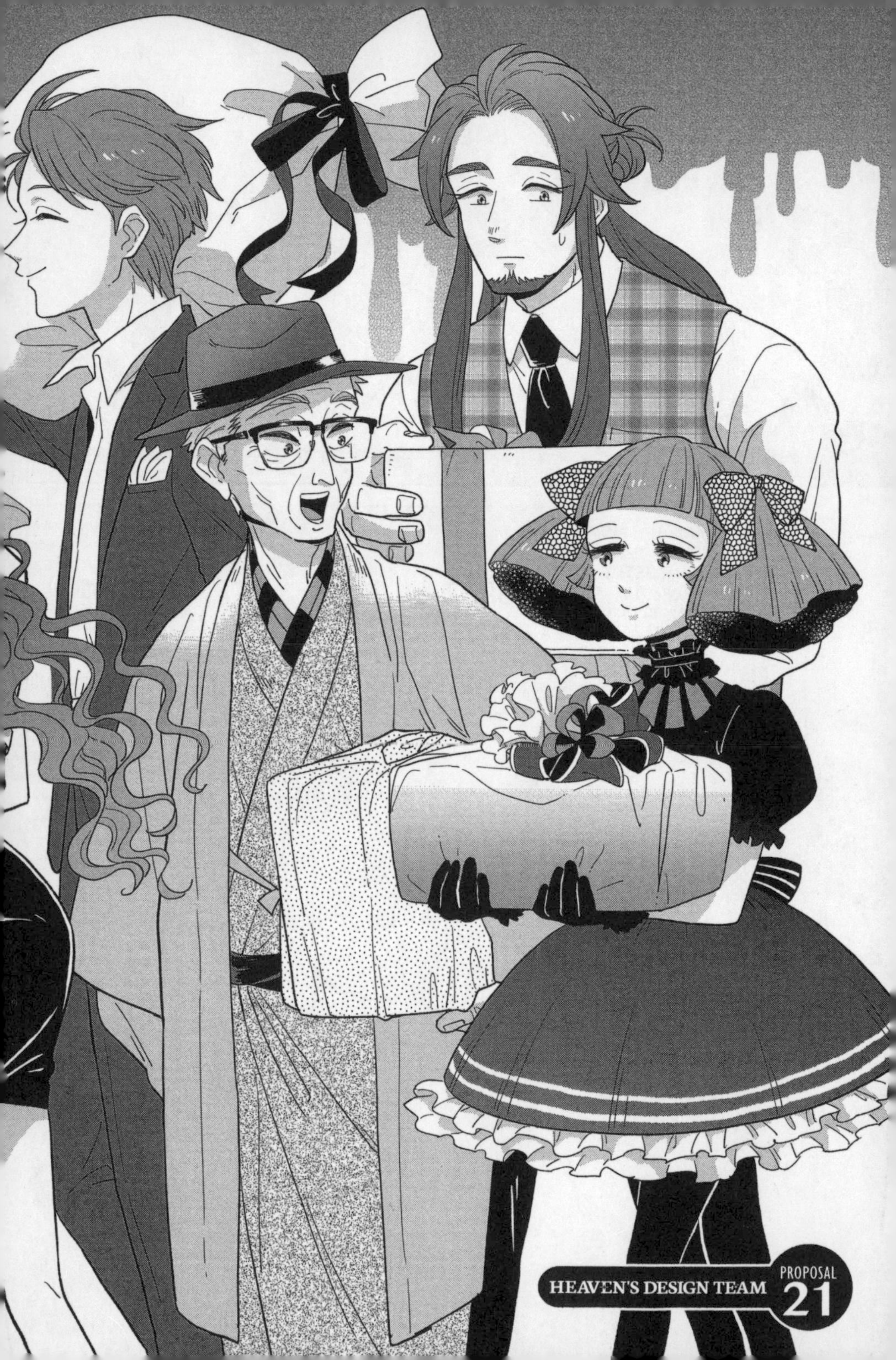
HEAVEN'S DESIGN TEAM
PROPOSAL
21

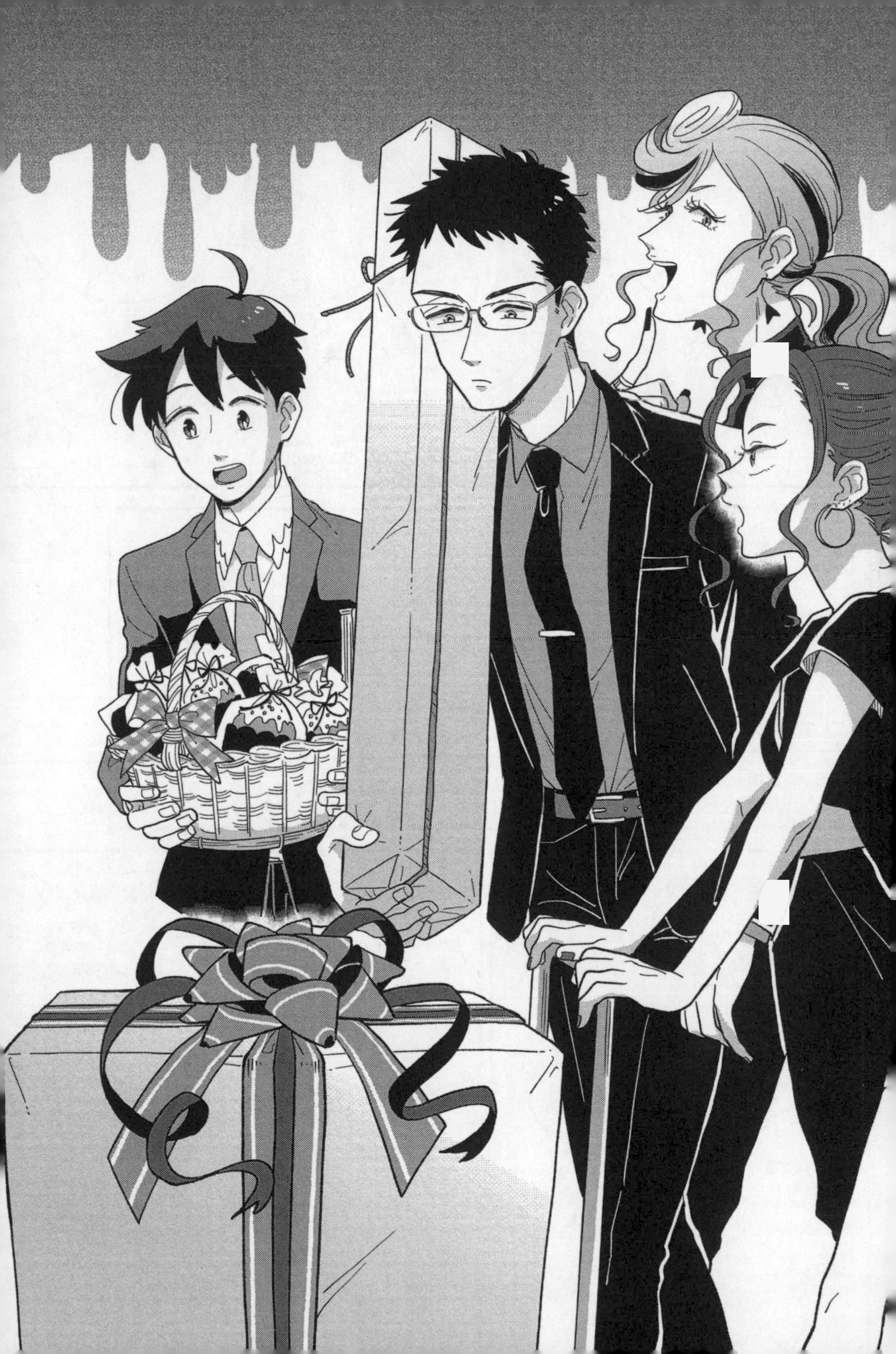

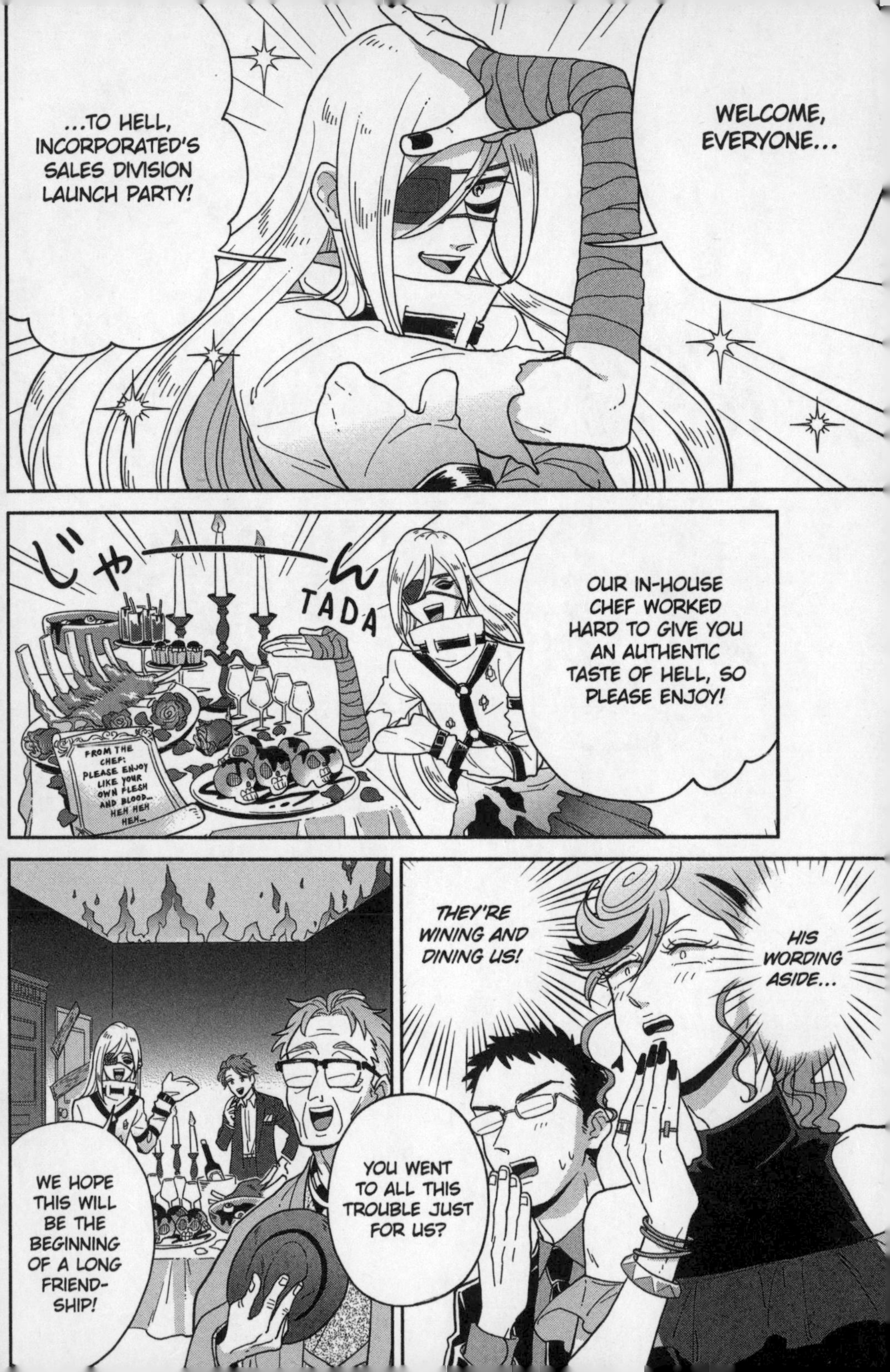
WELCOME, EVERYONE...
...TO HELL, INCORPORATED'S SALES DIVISION LAUNCH PARTY!
OUR IN-HOUSE CHEF WORKED HARD TO GIVE YOU AN AUTHENTIC TASTE OF HELL, SO PLEASE ENJOY!
TADA
じゃーーーん
FROM THE CHEF: PLEASE ENJOY LIKE YOUR OWN FLESH AND BLOOD... HEH HEH HEH...
HIS WORDING ASIDE...
THEY'RE WINING AND DINING US!
YOU WENT TO ALL THIS TROUBLE JUST FOR US?
WE HOPE THIS WILL BE THE BEGINNING OF A LONG FRIEND-SHIP!

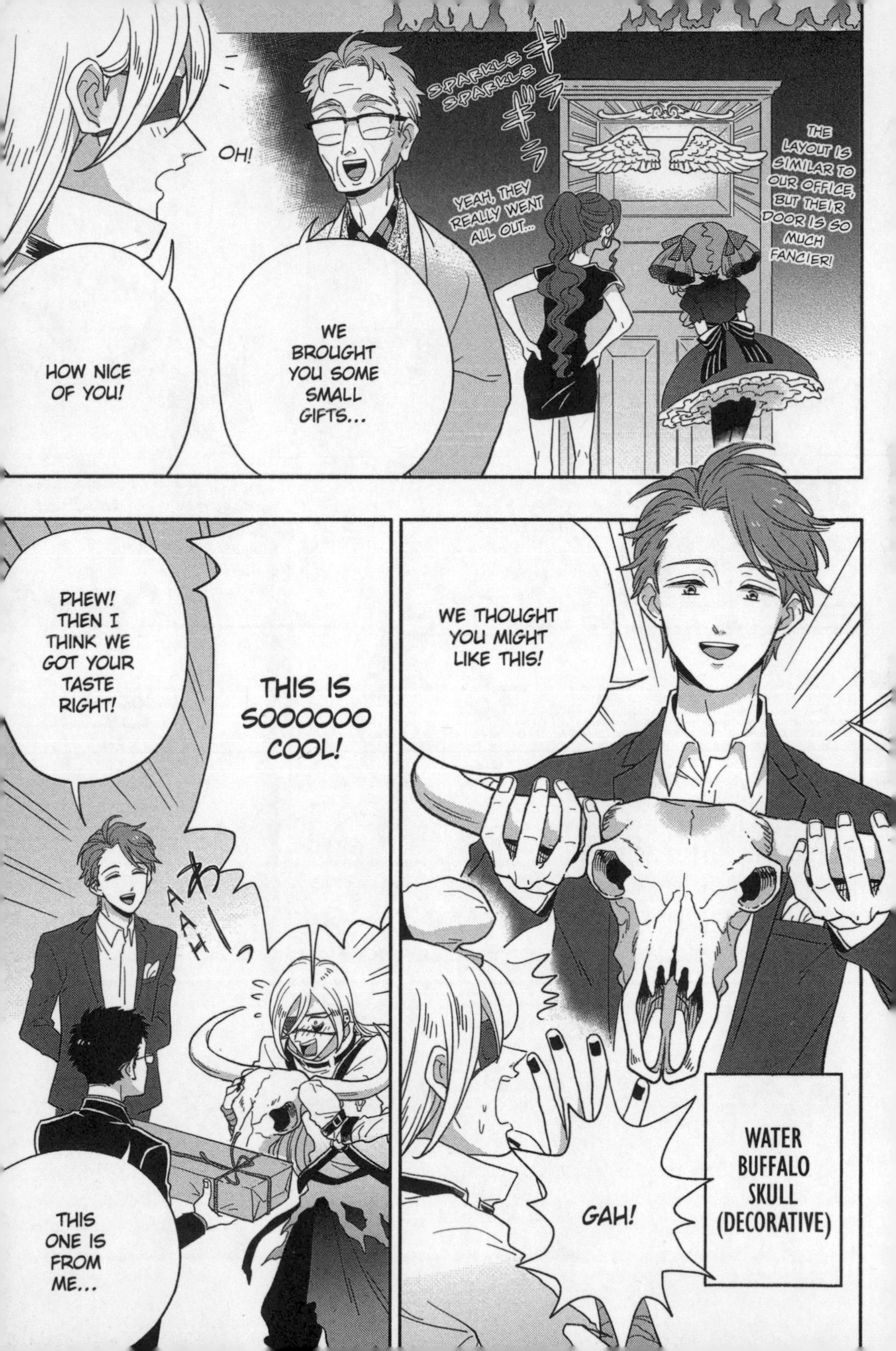
SPARKLE SPARKLE
THE LAYOUT IS SIMILAR TO OUR OFFICE, BUT THEIR DOOR IS SO MUCH FANCIER!
YEAH, THEY REALLY WENT ALL OUT...
OH!
WE BROUGHT YOU SOME SMALL GIFTS...
HOW NICE OF YOU!
WE THOUGHT YOU MIGHT LIKE THIS!
WATER BUFFALO SKULL (DECORATIVE)
GAH!
THIS IS SOOOOOO COOL!
PHEW! THEN I THINK WE GOT YOUR TASTE RIGHT!
AAAH
THIS ONE IS FROM ME...

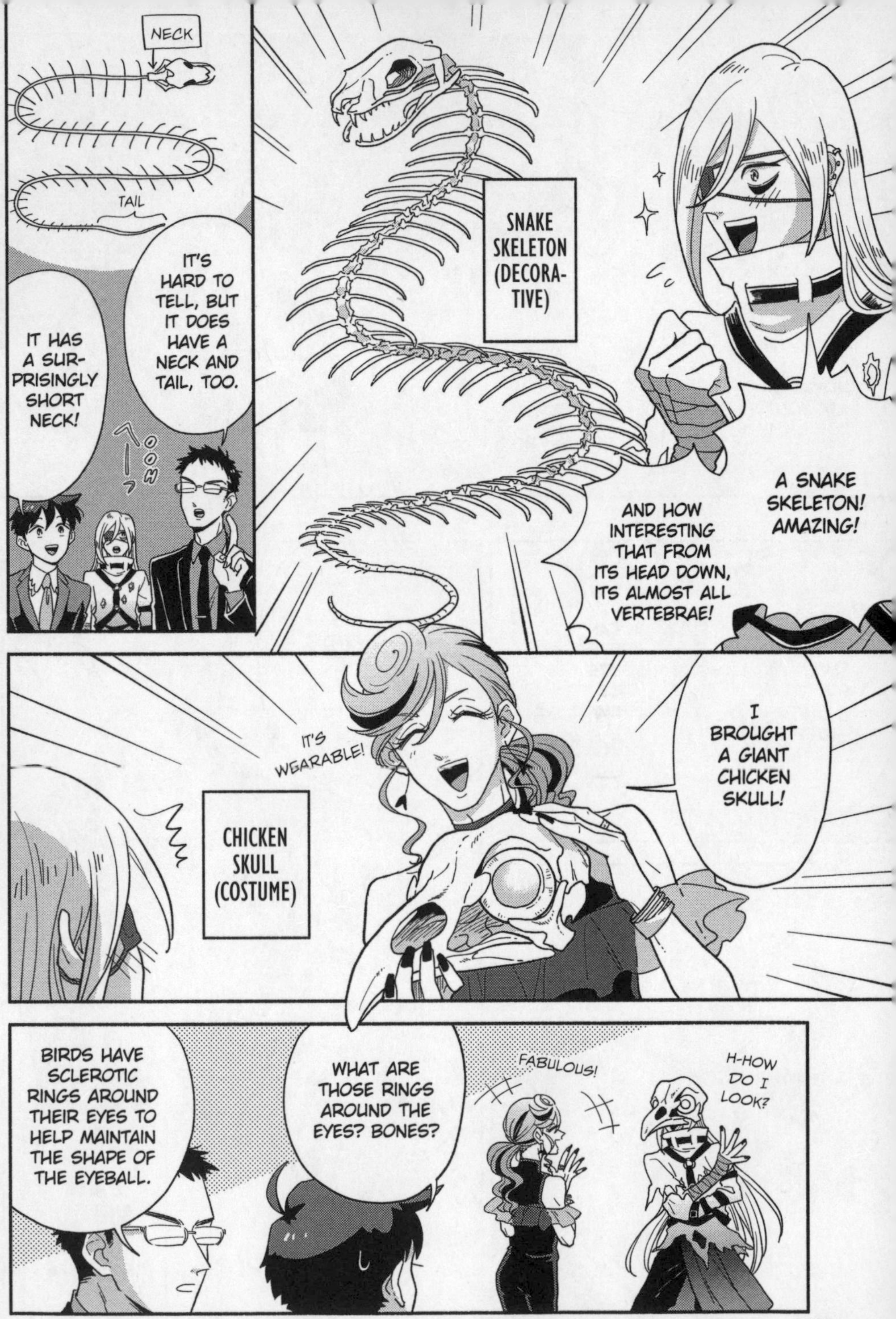
A SNAKE SKELETON! AMAZING!
AND HOW INTERESTING THAT FROM ITS HEAD DOWN, ITS ALMOST ALL VERTEBRAE!
SNAKE SKELETON (DECORATIVE)
NECK
TAIL
IT'S HARD TO TELL, BUT IT DOES HAVE A NECK AND TAIL, TOO.
OOOH
IT HAS A SURPRISINGLY SHORT NECK!
I BROUGHT A GIANT CHICKEN SKULL!
IT'S WEARABLE!
CHICKEN SKULL (COSTUME)
H-HOW DO I LOOK?
FABULOUS!
WHAT ARE THOSE RINGS AROUND THE EYES? BONES?
BIRDS HAVE SCLEROTIC RINGS AROUND THEIR EYES TO HELP MAINTAIN THE SHAPE OF THE EYEBALL.

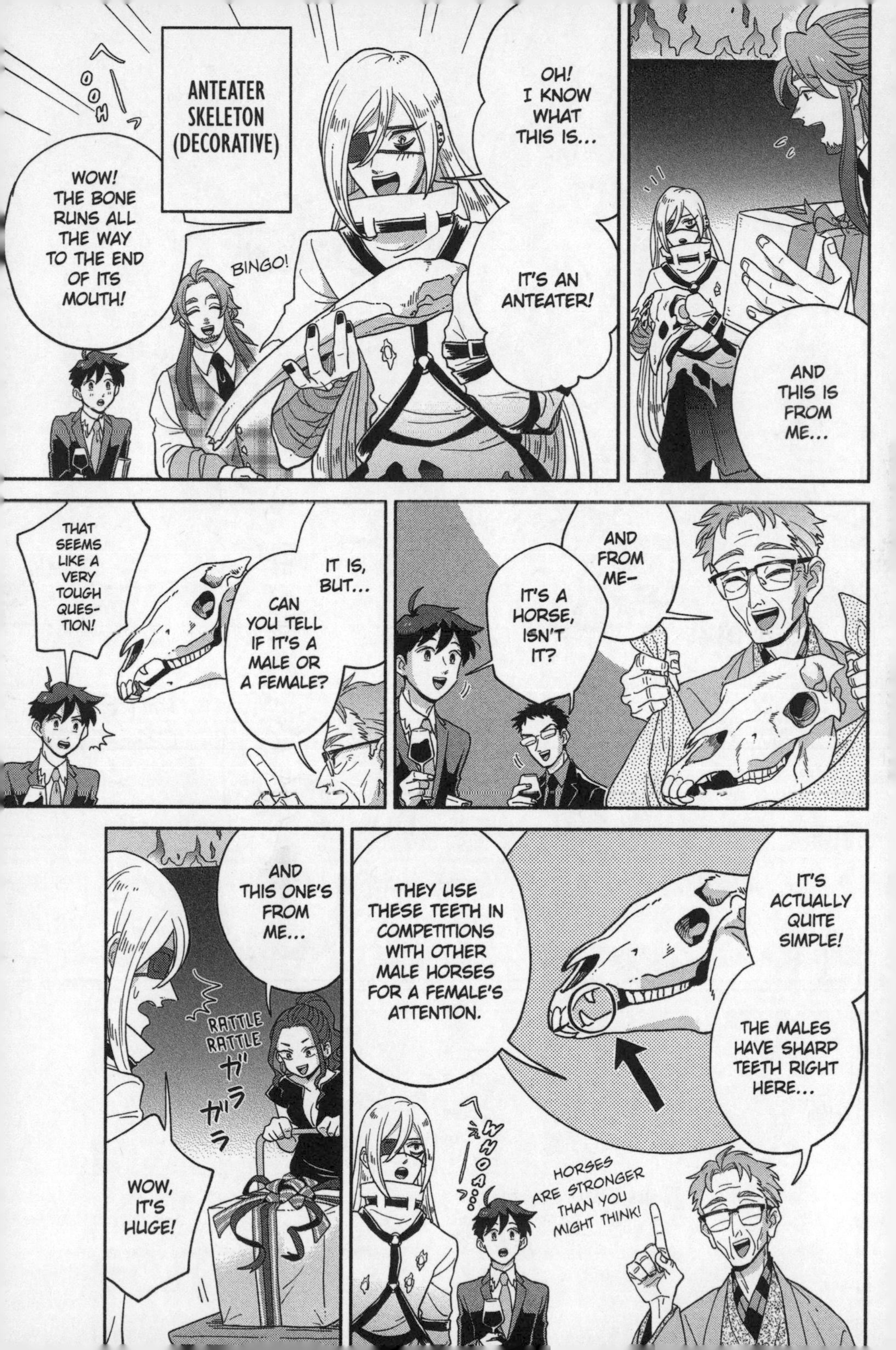
AND THIS IS FROM ME...
OH! I KNOW WHAT THIS IS...
IT'S AN ANTEATER!
ANTEATER SKELETON (DECORATIVE)
OOOH
WOW! THE BONE RUNS ALL THE WAY TO THE END OF ITS MOUTH!
BINGO!
AND FROM ME-
IT'S A HORSE, ISN'T IT?
IT IS, BUT...
CAN YOU TELL IF IT'S A MALE OR A FEMALE?
THAT SEEMS LIKE A VERY TOUGH QUES-TION!
IT'S ACTUALLY QUITE SIMPLE!
THE MALES HAVE SHARP TEETH RIGHT HERE...
THEY USE THESE TEETH IN COMPETITIONS WITH OTHER MALE HORSES FOR A FEMALE'S ATTENTION.
WHOA
WHOOO
HORSES ARE STRONGER THAN YOU MIGHT THINK!
AND THIS ONE'S FROM ME...
RATTLE RATTLE
ガラガラ
WOW, IT'S HUGE!

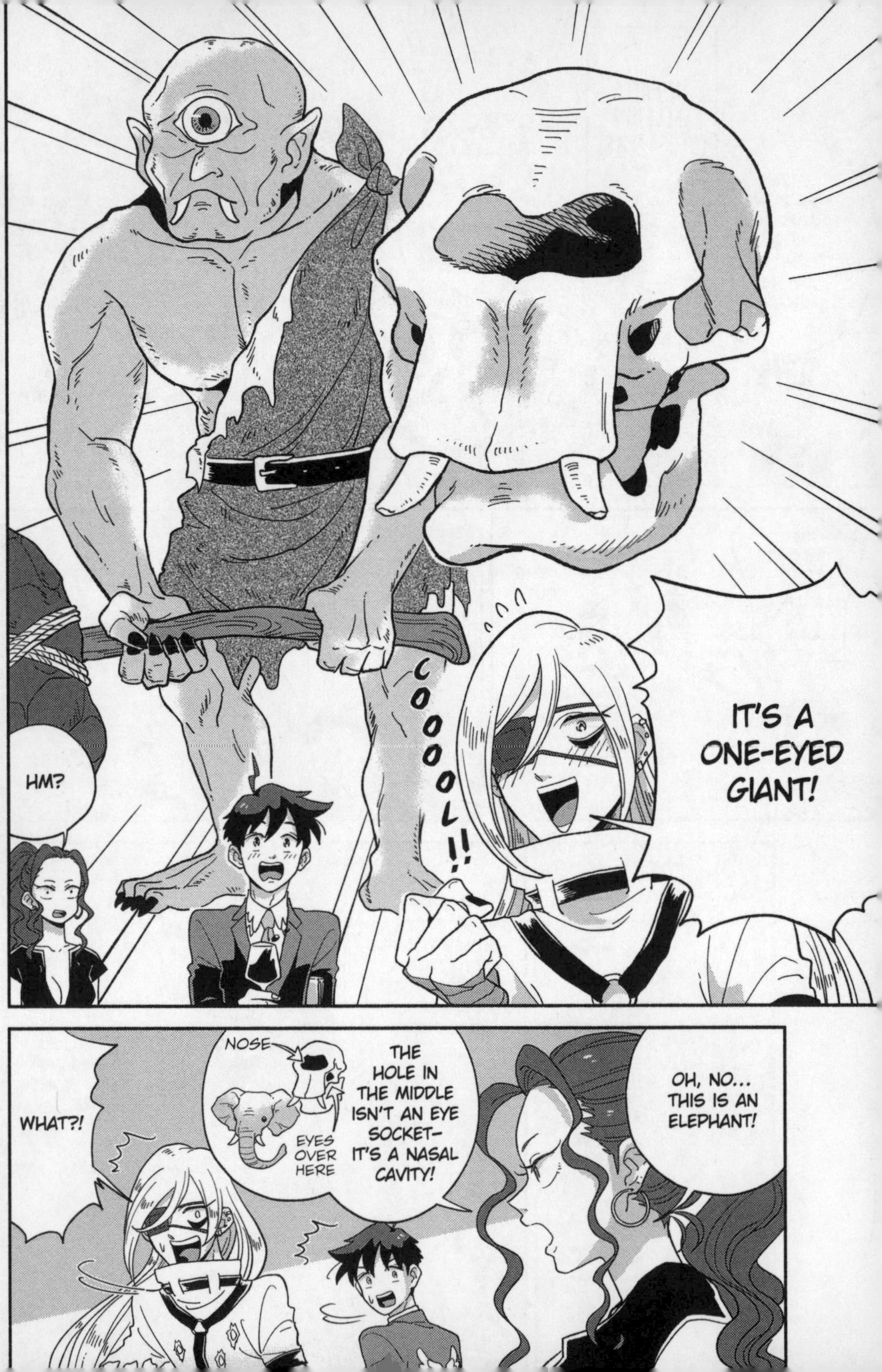
IT'S A ONE-EYED GIANT!
COOOOOL!!
HM?
OH, NO... THIS IS AN ELEPHANT!
THE HOLE IN THE MIDDLE ISN'T AN EYE SOCKET— IT'S A NASAL CAVITY!
NOSE
EYES OVER HERE
WHAT?!

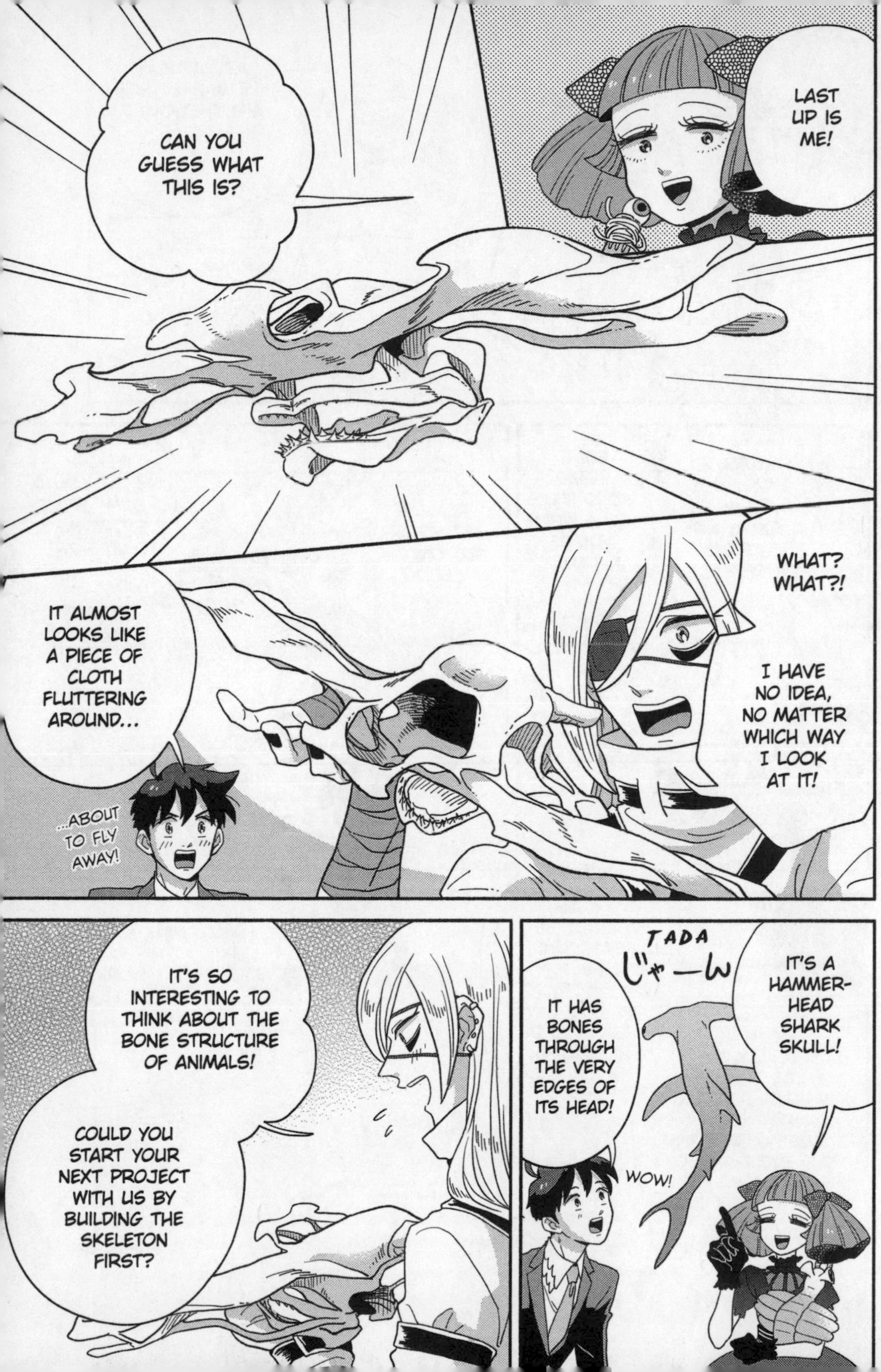
LAST UP IS ME!
CAN YOU GUESS WHAT THIS IS?
WHAT? WHAT?!
I HAVE NO IDEA, NO MATTER WHICH WAY I LOOK AT IT!
IT ALMOST LOOKS LIKE A PIECE OF CLOTH FLUTTERING AROUND...
...ABOUT TO FLY AWAY!
IT'S A HAMMER-HEAD SHARK SKULL!
TADA
じゃーん
IT HAS BONES THROUGH THE VERY EDGES OF ITS HEAD!
WOW!
IT'S SO INTERESTING TO THINK ABOUT THE BONE STRUCTURE OF ANIMALS!
COULD YOU START YOUR NEXT PROJECT WITH US BY BUILDING THE SKELETON FIRST?

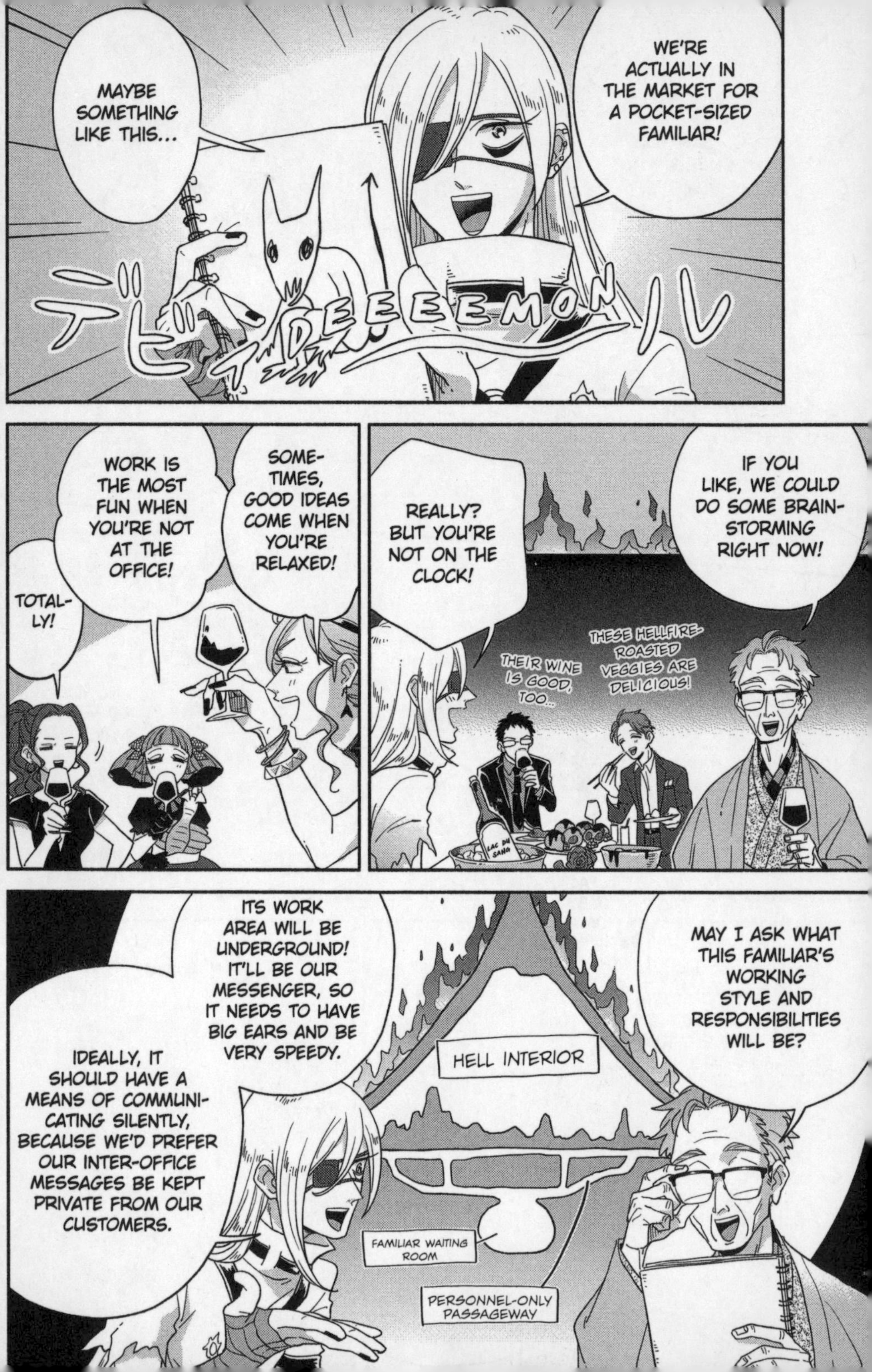
WE'RE ACTUALLY IN THE MARKET FOR A POCKET-SIZED FAMILIAR!
MAYBE SOMETHING LIKE THIS...
DEEEEEMON
IF YOU LIKE, WE COULD DO SOME BRAIN-STORMING RIGHT NOW!
REALLY? BUT YOU'RE NOT ON THE CLOCK!
THESE HELLFIRE-ROASTED VEGGIES ARE DELICIOUS!
THEIR WINE IS GOOD, TOO...
LAC DU SANG
SOME-TIMES, GOOD IDEAS COME WHEN YOU'RE RELAXED!
WORK IS THE MOST FUN WHEN YOU'RE NOT AT THE OFFICE!
TOTAL-LY!
MAY I ASK WHAT THIS FAMILIAR'S WORKING STYLE AND RESPONSIBILITIES WILL BE?
ITS WORK AREA WILL BE UNDERGROUND! IT'LL BE OUR MESSENGER, SO IT NEEDS TO HAVE BIG EARS AND BE VERY SPEEDY.
HELL INTERIOR
IDEALLY, IT SHOULD HAVE A MEANS OF COMMUNI-CATING SILENTLY, BECAUSE WE'D PREFER OUR INTER-OFFICE MESSAGES BE KEPT PRIVATE FROM OUR CUSTOMERS.
FAMILIAR WAITING ROOM
PERSONNEL-ONLY PASSAGEWAY

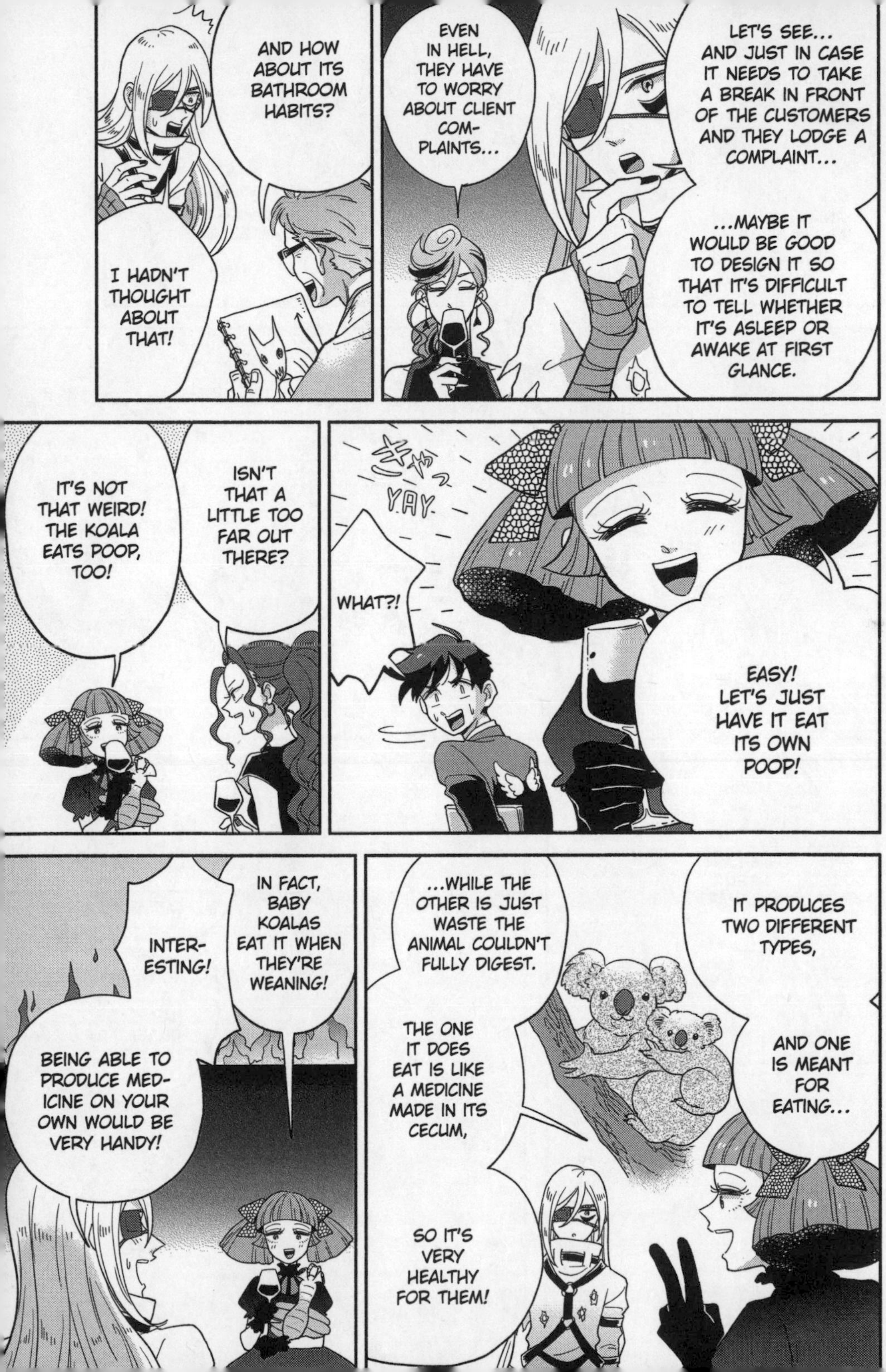
LET'S SEE... AND JUST IN CASE IT NEEDS TO TAKE A BREAK IN FRONT OF THE CUSTOMERS AND THEY LODGE A COMPLAINT...
...MAYBE IT WOULD BE GOOD TO DESIGN IT SO THAT IT'S DIFFICULT TO TELL WHETHER IT'S ASLEEP OR AWAKE AT FIRST GLANCE.
EVEN IN HELL, THEY HAVE TO WORRY ABOUT CLIENT COM-PLAINTS...
AND HOW ABOUT ITS BATHROOM HABITS?
I HADN'T THOUGHT ABOUT THAT!
EASY! LET'S JUST HAVE IT EAT ITS OWN POOP!
きゃっ YAY
WHAT?!
ISN'T THAT A LITTLE TOO FAR OUT THERE?
IT'S NOT THAT WEIRD! THE KOALA EATS POOP, TOO!
IT PRODUCES TWO DIFFERENT TYPES,
AND ONE IS MEANT FOR EATING...
...WHILE THE OTHER IS JUST WASTE THE ANIMAL COULDN'T FULLY DIGEST.
THE ONE IT DOES EAT IS LIKE A MEDICINE MADE IN ITS CECUM,
SO IT'S VERY HEALTHY FOR THEM!
IN FACT, BABY KOALAS EAT IT WHEN THEY'RE WEANING!
INTER-ESTING!
BEING ABLE TO PRODUCE MED-ICINE ON YOUR OWN WOULD BE VERY HANDY!

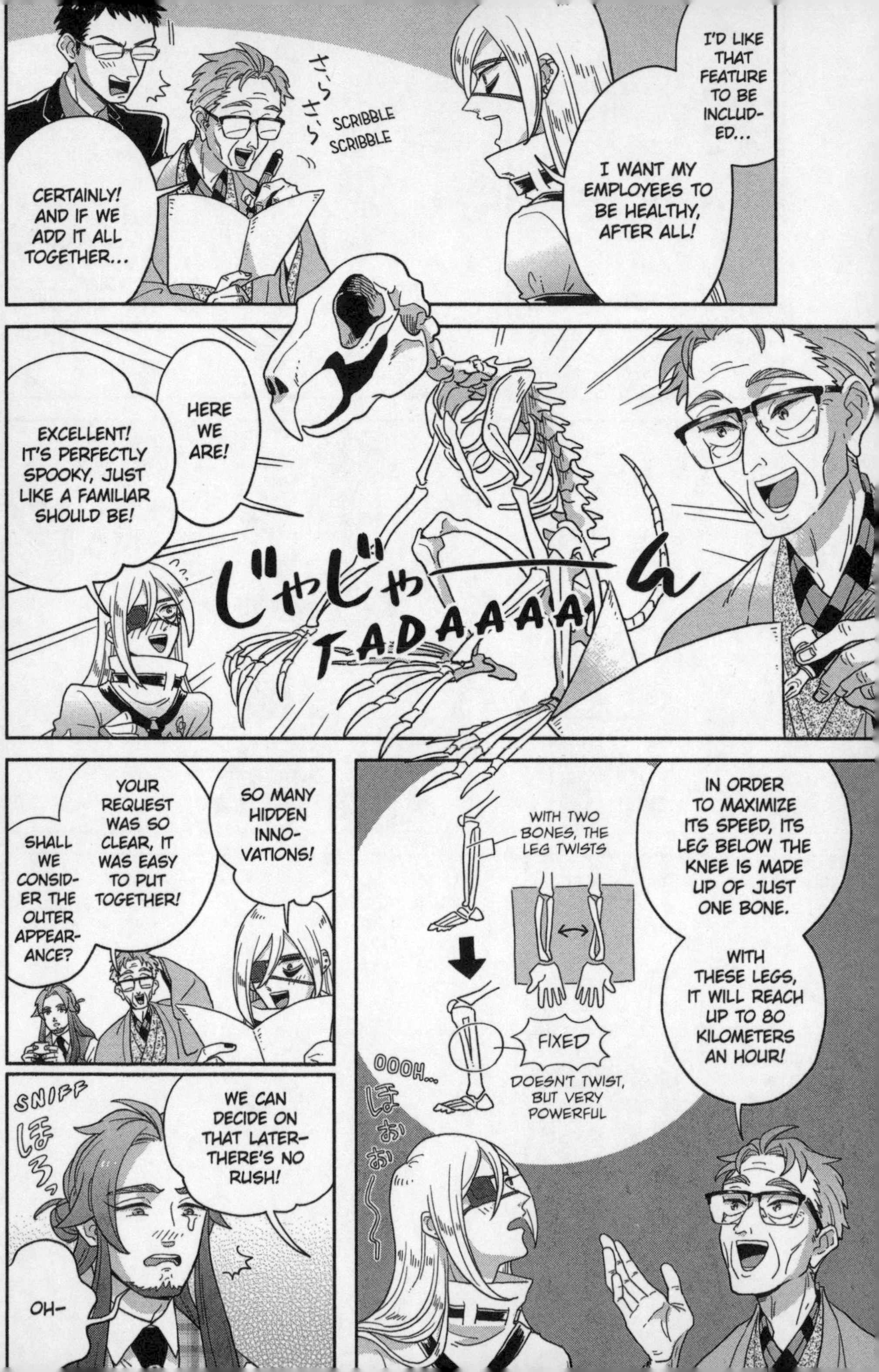
I'D LIKE THAT FEATURE TO BE INCLUDED...
I WANT MY EMPLOYEES TO BE HEALTHY, AFTER ALL!
さらさら
SCRIBBLE SCRIBBLE
CERTAINLY! AND IF WE ADD IT ALL TOGETHER...
HERE WE ARE!
じゃじゃーん
TADAAAAA
EXCELLENT! IT'S PERFECTLY SPOOKY, JUST LIKE A FAMILIAR SHOULD BE!
IN ORDER TO MAXIMIZE ITS SPEED, ITS LEG BELOW THE KNEE IS MADE UP OF JUST ONE BONE.
WITH THESE LEGS, IT WILL REACH UP TO 80 KILOMETERS AN HOUR!
WITH TWO BONES, THE LEG TWISTS
FIXED
DOESN'T TWIST, BUT VERY POWERFUL
OOOH...
ほおお〜
SO MANY HIDDEN INNO-VATIONS!
YOUR REQUEST WAS SO CLEAR, IT WAS EASY TO PUT TOGETHER!
SHALL WE CONSID-ER THE OUTER APPEAR-ANCE?
WE CAN DECIDE ON THAT LATER- THERE'S NO RUSH!
SNIFF
ほろっ
OH-

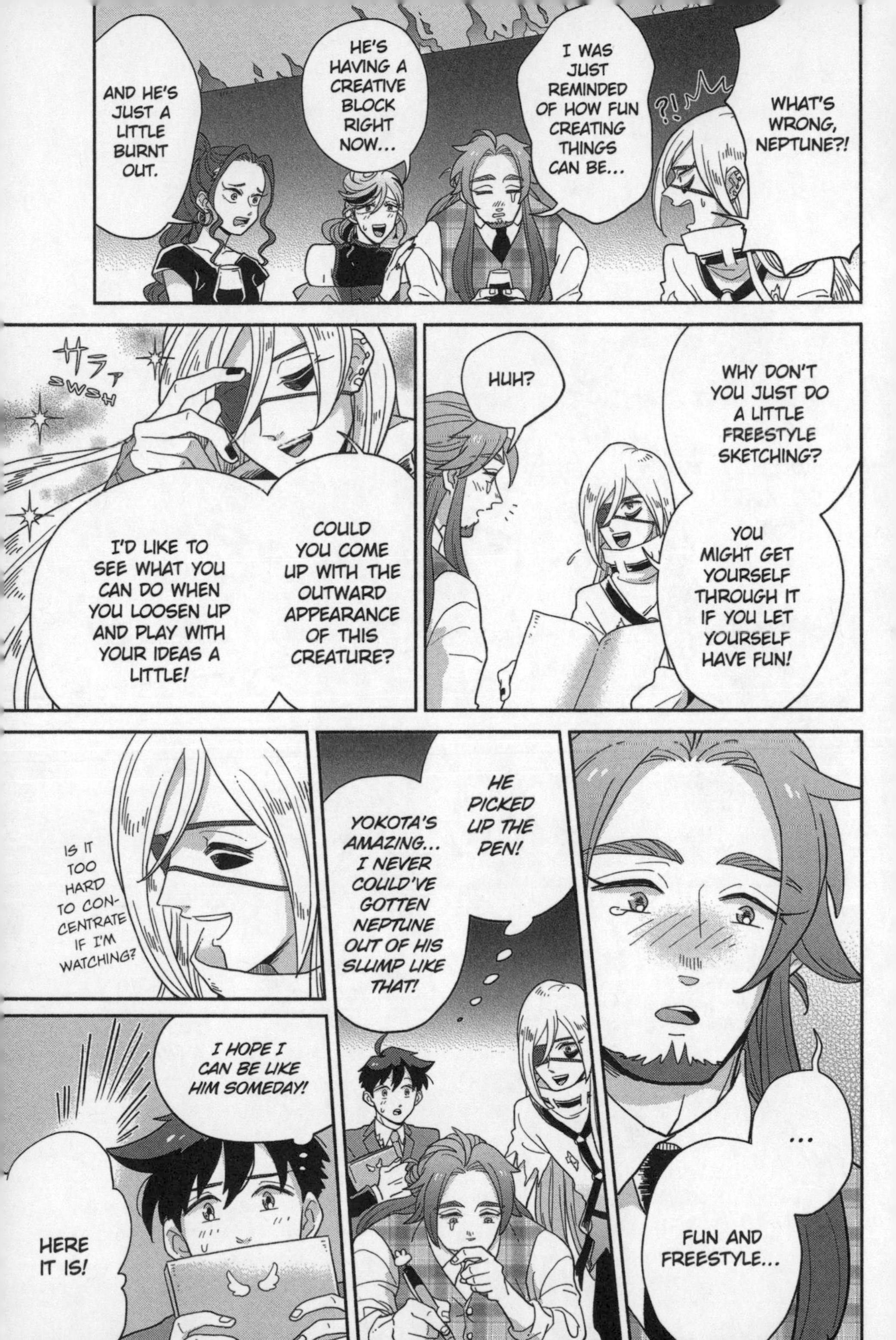
WHAT'S WRONG, NEPTUNE?!
?!
I WAS JUST REMINDED OF HOW FUN CREATING THINGS CAN BE...
HE'S HAVING A CREATIVE BLOCK RIGHT NOW...
AND HE'S JUST A LITTLE BURNT OUT.
WHY DON'T YOU JUST DO A LITTLE FREESTYLE SKETCHING?
HUH?
YOU MIGHT GET YOURSELF THROUGH IT IF YOU LET YOURSELF HAVE FUN!
サラァ
SWSH
COULD YOU COME UP WITH THE OUTWARD APPEARANCE OF THIS CREATURE?
I'D LIKE TO SEE WHAT YOU CAN DO WHEN YOU LOOSEN UP AND PLAY WITH YOUR IDEAS A LITTLE!
...
FUN AND FREESTYLE...
HE PICKED UP THE PEN!
YOKOTA'S AMAZING... I NEVER COULD'VE GOTTEN NEPTUNE OUT OF HIS SLUMP LIKE THAT!
I HOPE I CAN BE LIKE HIM SOMEDAY!
IS IT TOO HARD TO CONCENTRATE IF I'M WATCHING?
HERE IT IS!

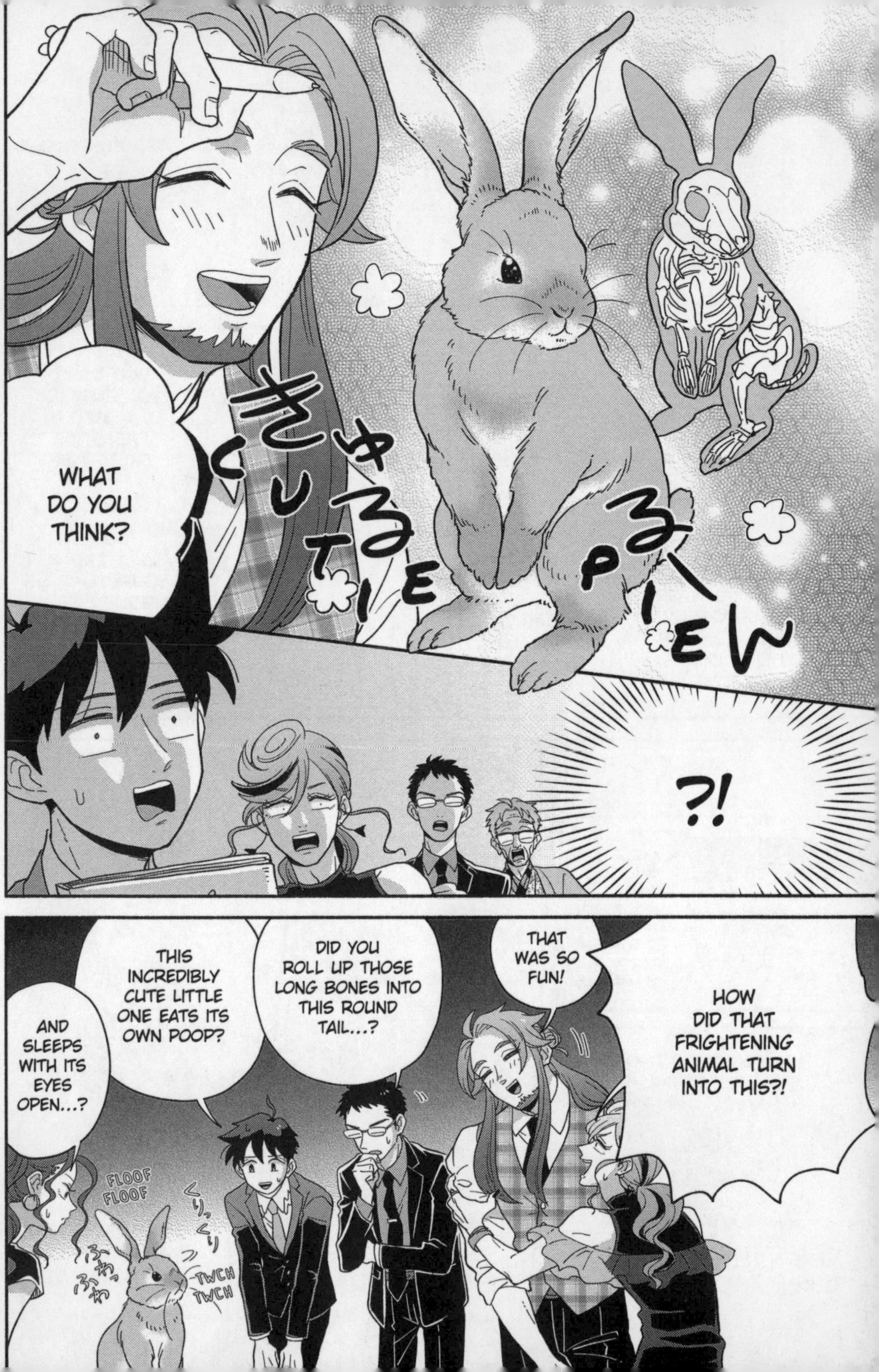
WHAT DO YOU THINK?
?!
HOW DID THAT FRIGHTENING ANIMAL TURN INTO THIS?!
THAT WAS SO FUN!
DID YOU ROLL UP THOSE LONG BONES INTO THIS ROUND TAIL...?
THIS INCREDIBLY CUTE LITTLE ONE EATS ITS OWN POOP?
AND SLEEPS WITH ITS EYES OPEN...?
TWCH TWCH
FLOOF FLOOF

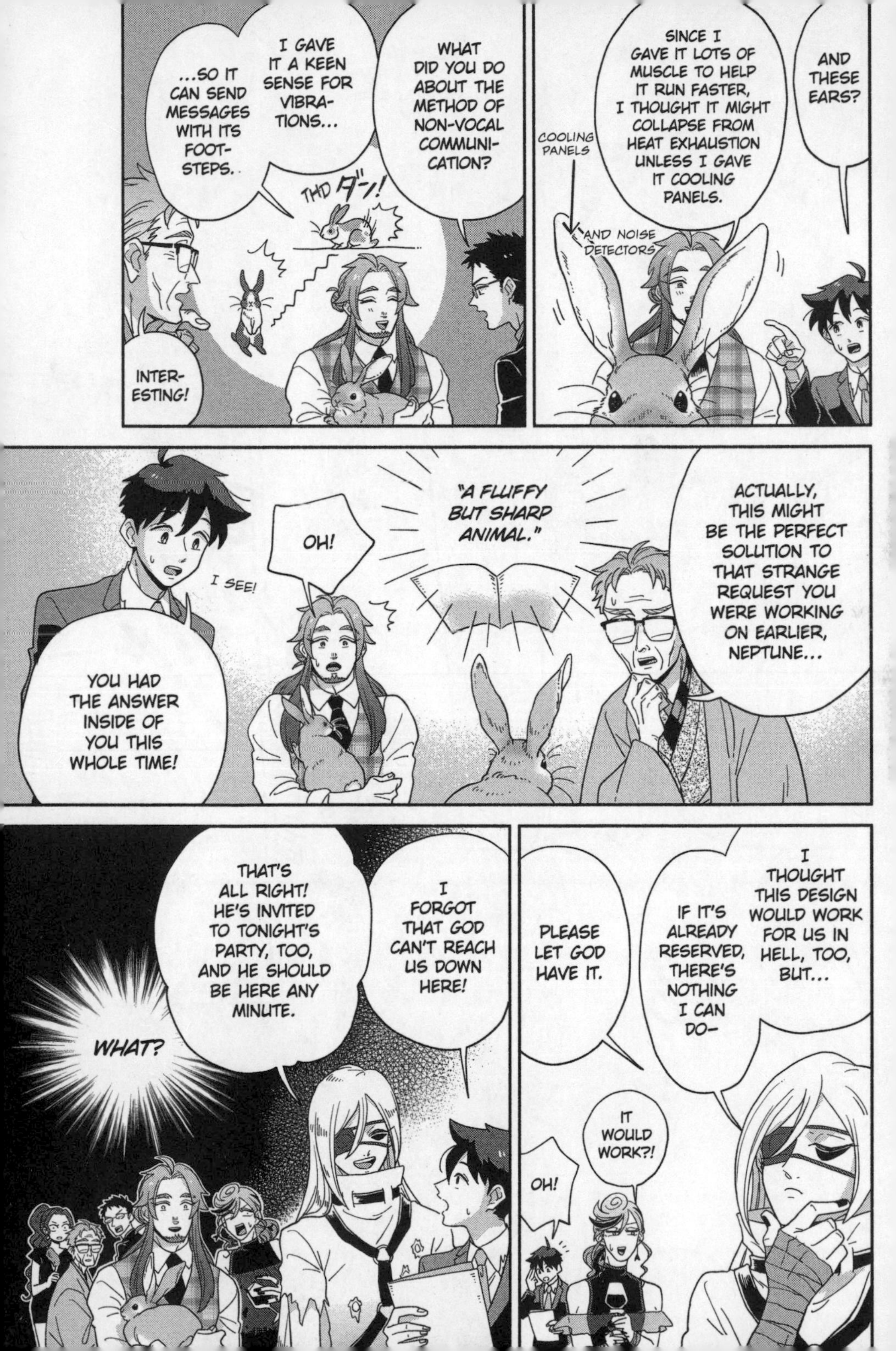
AND THESE EARS?
SINCE I GAVE IT LOTS OF MUSCLE TO HELP IT RUN FASTER, I THOUGHT IT MIGHT COLLAPSE FROM HEAT EXHAUSTION UNLESS I GAVE IT COOLING PANELS.
COOLING PANELS
AND NOISE DETECTORS
WHAT DID YOU DO ABOUT THE METHOD OF NON-VOCAL COMMUNICATION?
I GAVE IT A KEEN SENSE FOR VIBRATIONS...
...SO IT CAN SEND MESSAGES WITH ITS FOOTSTEPS.
THD ダン!
INTERESTING!
ACTUALLY, THIS MIGHT BE THE PERFECT SOLUTION TO THAT STRANGE REQUEST YOU WERE WORKING ON EARLIER, NEPTUNE...
"A FLUFFY BUT SHARP ANIMAL."
OH!
I SEE!
YOU HAD THE ANSWER INSIDE OF YOU THIS WHOLE TIME!
I THOUGHT THIS DESIGN WOULD WORK FOR US IN HELL, TOO, BUT...
IF IT'S ALREADY RESERVED, THERE'S NOTHING I CAN DO–
PLEASE LET GOD HAVE IT.
IT WOULD WORK?!
OH!
I FORGOT THAT GOD CAN'T REACH US DOWN HERE!
THAT'S ALL RIGHT! HE'S INVITED TO TONIGHT'S PARTY, TOO, AND HE SHOULD BE HERE ANY MINUTE.
WHAT?

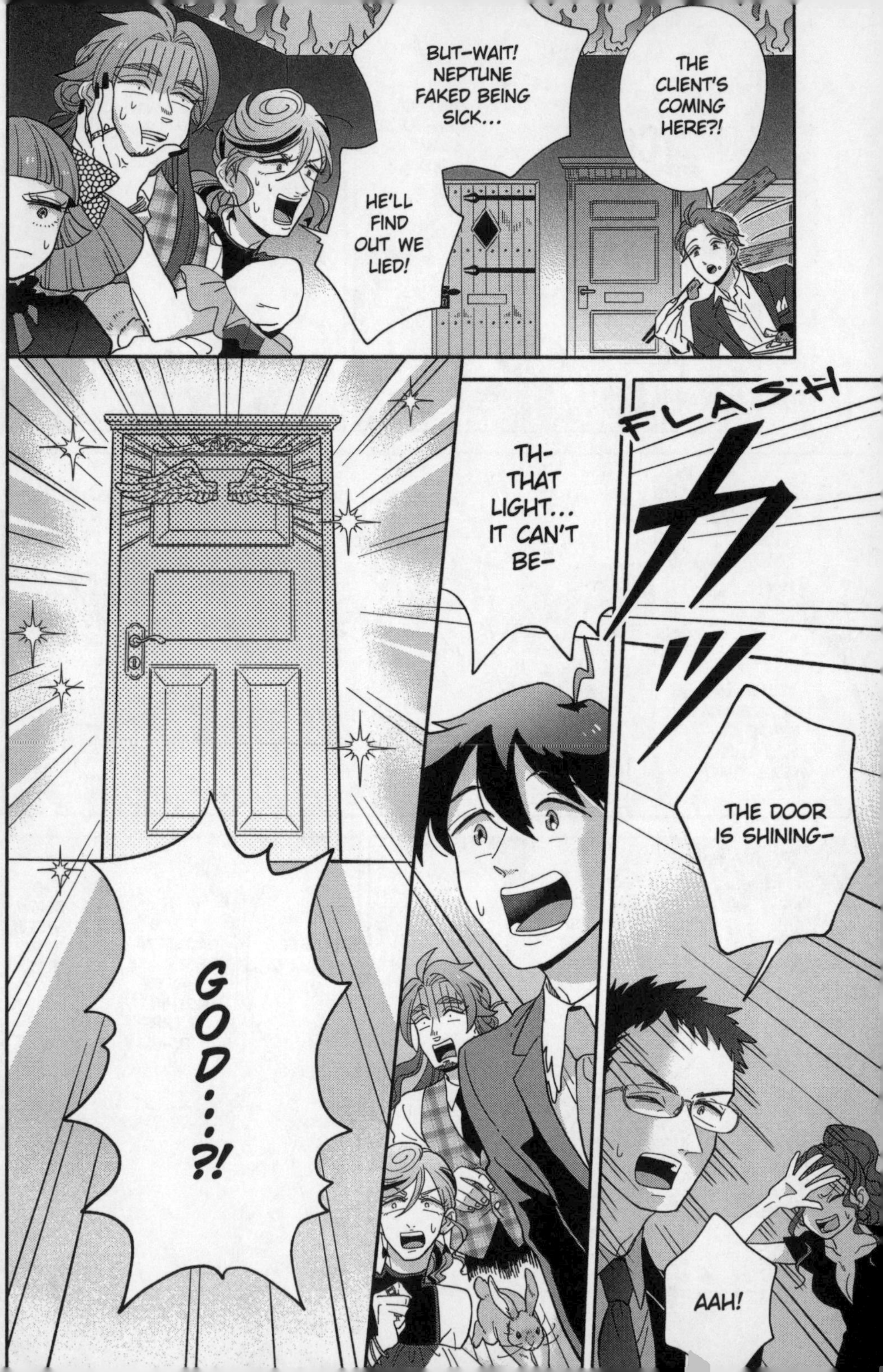
THE CLIENT'S COMING HERE?!
BUT—WAIT! NEPTUNE FAKED BEING SICK…
HE'LL FIND OUT WE LIED!
FLASH
THE DOOR IS SHINING–
AAH!
TH- THAT LIGHT… IT CAN'T BE–
GOD…?!

THE ENCYCLOPEDIA OF REAL ANIMALS 21

ANIMAL 54 RABBIT

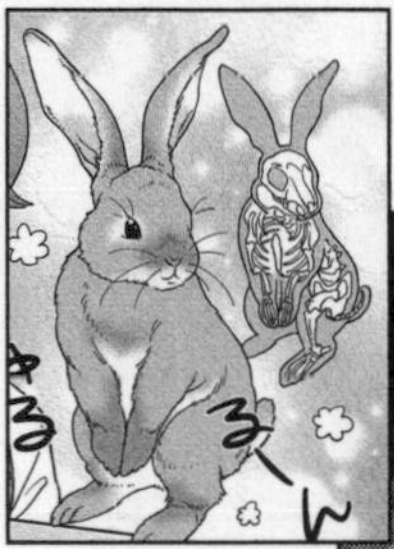

THE REAL THING

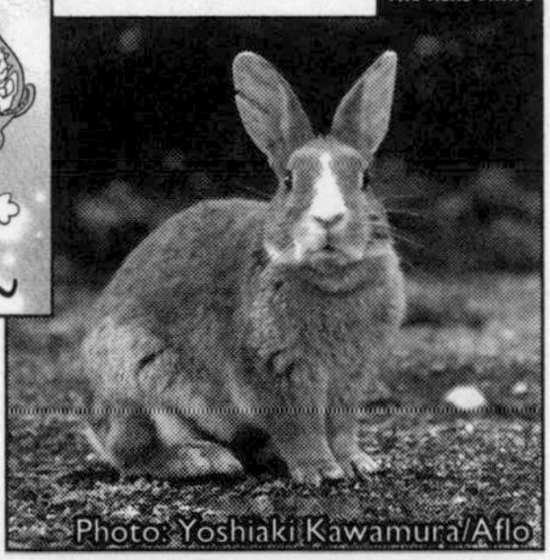

Photo: Yoshiaki Kawamura/Aflo

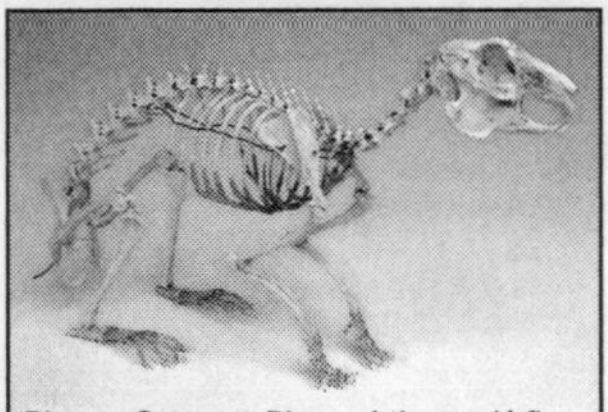

Photo: Science Photo Library/Aflo

A European rabbit and its skeleton.

Just like the one depicted in this chapter, rabbits sleep with their eyes open and communicate by stomping. It also eats its own feces in order to extract the necessary vitamins and nutrients from its food.

Looking at the skeleton, one can see that there are no bones in the ears, which serve as cooling panels and noise detectors. The bones of its tail are deceptively long, but are curled under and make the tail appear short. In order to escape from predators, the rabbit moves both legs at the same time to hop away. For this reason, its hind legs are extremely long and fused from the knee to the ankle. Though it is difficult to guess based on the rabbit's round appearance, its powerful hind quarters are evident in its skeletal structure. The adaptations in the hind legs also help it avoid excessive joint movement when in motion.

[Name]	Rabbit
[Classification]	Class: Maxillopoda Order: Lagomorpha Family: Leporidae
[Habitat]	Africa, the Americas, Eurasia, Japan
[Length]	15-65 cm (6-25.6 in)

ELEPHANT BONES

The skeletal remains of
an African elephant in
Tanzania.
Photo: Ardea/Aflo

It's said that the legend of the giant cyclops was created by people of ancient times after discovering elephant skeletons. The hole that appears to be an eye socket is in fact the elephant's nasal cavity. Through this large opening, the animal can drink large volumes of water. The elephant also uses its trunk to snorkel, take mud baths, eat, and communicate with its fellows.

ANIMAL 55 | WILD WATER BUFFALO

The wild water buffalo's horns are intended more for use in combat than the cow's, and even in captivity, accidental deaths are not uncommon. Living mostly near water, the animal has long been domesticated as livestock and used to plow fields. Because of this, their numbers in the wild are dwindling.

The wild water buffalo's close relative, the African buffalo, is capable of using its horns to defend itself against lions.

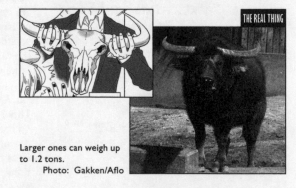

THE REAL THING

Larger ones can weigh up to 1.2 tons.
Photo: Gakken/Aflo

[Name]	Bubalus arnee
[Classification]	Class: Mammalia
	Order: Artiodactyla
	Family: Bovidae
	Genus: Bubalus
[Habitat]	India, Nepal, and Bhutan
[Length]	2.4-3 m (7.9-9.8 ft)

References

Zimen, Erik. *Der Wolf*. Translated by Mineko Imaizumi. Japan: Hakusuisha, 1995.

"Ookami to wa." *Japan Wolf Association*, 2004. http://japan-wolf.org/content/wolf-about/.

Dinets, Vladimir. *Dragon Songs: Love and Adventure Among Crocodiles, Alligators, and Other Dinosaur Relations*. New York: Arcade Publishing, 2013.

Kodansha no Ugoku Zukan MOVE Doubutsu Kenrouban. Supervised by Juichi Yamagiwa. Japan: Kodansha Ltd., 2017.

Toihara, Kazumi and NHK. "Darwin ga Kita!". *Hakken! Manga Zukan NHK Darwin ga Kita! Shinsouban -Yasei no Okite Survival Hen-*. Japan: Kodansha Ltd., 2017.

"Bird Research News February 2007 Edition, Vol.4 No.2." *Tokutei Hieiri Katsudou Houjin Bird Research*, 2007. http://www.bird-research.jp.

Matsuoka, Hiroshige. *Tori no Honetan – Dachou, Pengin, Ahoudori, Tsuru, Taka, Perikan kara Fukurou, Kakkou, Kawasemi, Suzume ni Shitaru Nihonsan Oyobi Gaikokusan Shuyou Chourui no Zenshin Kokkaku Hyouhon to Toukotsu, Kyoukotsu, Tsubasa no Hone, Ashi no Hone nado no Bunkai Hone Color Shashin kara Miru Kokkaku Bird Watching*. Japan: NTS, 2009.

Ito, S. "Seibutsu no Hishou, Yuuei Toki ni Hassei suru Uzu to sono Hansayou no Chikara." *Research Institution for Mathematical Sciences Koukyuuroku 1900* (2014): 26-36.

Strycker, Noah. *The Thing with Feathers: The Surprising Lives of Birds and What They Reveal about Being Human*. Translated by Natsumi Kataoka. Japan: Tsukiji Shokan Publishing Co., Ltd., 2016.

Fogden, Michael, Marianne Taylor, and Sheri L. Williamson. *Hummingbirds: A Guide to Every Species*. Translated by Keiko Ihara. Supervised by Komiya Teruyuki. Japan: Graphic-sha Publishing Co., Ltd., 2015.

Higuchi, Hiroyoshi. *Toritte Sugoi! (Yamakei Shinsho)* Japan: Yama-kei Publishers Co., Ltd., 2016.

"Catching the Wake." *Scientific American*, 2018. https://www.scientificamerican.com/article/catching-the-wake/.

Kodansha no Ugoku Zukan MOVE Tori Kenrouban. Supervised by Kazuto Kawakami. Japan: Kodansha Ltd., 2017.

Yoshimura, Takuzo. *Kyotori ga Ayunda Michi*. Japan: Metamor Publishing, 1990.

"Dachou Mini Zukan" *Dachou Land Okinawa*, 2010. http://dacyou.net/book.html.

Carcinological Society of Japan. *Ebi, Kani no Gimon (Minna ga Shiritai Series 5)*. Japan: Seizando-Shoten Publishing Co., Ltd., 2017.

Sugiura, Chisato, Akira Asakura, and Others. *Sugiura Chisato Hakubutsue Zukan: Utsukushiki Ebi to Kani no Sekai*. Japan: Seizando-Shoten Publishing Co., Ltd., 2012.

Noguchi, Shinichiro. *Rakko no Umi (Monterey Bay California)* – Noguchi Shinichiro Shashinshuu. Japan: Riburopoto, 1995.

Murayama, Tsukasa, Issei So, and Senzo Uchida. *Kaijuu Suizokukan -Shiiku to Tenji no Seibutsugaku-*. Japan: Tokai University Press, 2010.

Nakamura, Hajime. *Rakko no Michishirube -Rakko ga Oshietekureta Tayou na Kachikan-*. Japan: Parol Sha, 2000.

Furukawa, Miyoko. *Rakko no Iru Umi -Ningen ha Ikani Seitaikei wo Kizutsuketekitaka-*. Rippu Shobo Publishing Co., Ltd., 1992.

Miyoshi, T., S. Sodeyama, and M. Kato. "Bunruigun Goto ni Mita Shiiku Doubutsu no Taijuu to Sesshu Energy Ryou no Kankei." *Official Journal of Japanese Society of Livestock Management and Japanese Society for Applied Animal Behaviour* 52, 2 (2016): 98-105.

Widmaier, Eric, P. *Why Geese Don't Get Obese (And We Do): How Evolution's Strategies for Survival Affect our Everyday Lives*. Translated by Michio Imafuku. Japan: Kagaku-Dojin Publishing Company, Inc., 2000.

Yabe, Takashi. *Kodansha no Ugoku Zukan MOVE Hachuurui, Ryouseirui Kenrouban*. Supervised by Hideaki Kato. Japan: Kodansha Ltd., 2017.

Kodansha no Ugoku Zukan MOVE Mizu no Naka no Ikimono. Supervised by Takashi Okutani. Japan: Kodansha Ltd., 2018.

Takeuchi, Kumiko. *Hontou ha Kowai Doubutsu no Kosodate. (Shinchou Shinsho)*. Japan: Shinchosha Publishing Co., Ltd., 2013.

Takeuchi, Kumiko. *Damashiai no Housoku -Ikinuku Tame no "Jiko Boueijutsu"-*. Japan: Kodansha Ltd., 2014.

Narita, Satoko. *Shitatakana Kisei -Nou to Karada wo Nottori Tnkumi ni Ayatsuru Seibutsutachi- (Gentousha Shinsho)*. Japan: Gentosha Inc., 2017.

Ohtsuki, Hisashi. *Kyouryoku to Batsu no Seibutsugaku (Iwanami Kagaku Library)*. Japan: Iwanami Shoten, 2014.

Doubutsu Keitoubunruigaku Dai 7 Kan Jou (Sessoku Doubutsu I). Supervised by Toru Uchida. Japan: Nakayama Shoten, 1964.

Barnes, R. S. K., P. J. W. Olive, D.W. Golding, J.I. Spicer, and P. Callow. *The Invertebrates: A Synthesis*. Third Edition. Translated by Tatsuo Motokawa. Japan: Asakura Publishing Co., Ltd., 2009.

Koukakuruigaku -Ebi, Kani to sono Nakama no Sekai-. Supervised by Akira Asakura. Japan: Tokai University Press, 2003.

Endo, Hideki. *Ushi no Doubutsugaku (Animal Science 2)*. Japan: Tokai University Press, 2001.

Manaberu! Toukotsu Zukan. Supervised by Kenji Furuta. Japan: Futabasha, 2014.

"Visible Interactive Ostrich." *Ohio University WitmerLab*, 2016. https://people.ohio.edu/witmerl/3D_ostrich_htm.

Yuzawa, Eiji and Akinori Azumano. *BONES -Doubutsu no Kokkaku to Kinoubi-*. Japan: Hayakawa Shoten, 2008.

*All websites were accessed on December 25, 2018.

Special thanks:

Editor/Yoshimi Takuwa-san (Institution for Liberal Arts, Tokyo Institution of Technology)

Kamome Shirahama-san
Saba-san
Ame Toba-san
Tomato-san

A Kodansha Comics Trade Paperback Original
Heaven's Design Team 3 copyright © 2019 Hebi-zou&Tsuta Suzuki/Tarako
English translation copyright © 2021 Hebi-zou&Tsuta Suzuki/Tarako
All rights reserved.

Published in the United States by Kodansha Comics, an imprint of
Kodansha USA Publishing, LLC, New York.

Publication rights for this English edition arranged through
Kodansha Ltd., Tokyo.

First published in Japan in 2019 by Kodansha Ltd., Tokyo
as *Tenchi sozo dezainbu*, volume 3.

ISBN 978-1-64651-130-3

Original cover design by SAVA DESIGN

Printed in the United States of America.

www.kodanshacomics.com

9 8 7 6 5 4 3 2 1
Translation and lettering: JM Iitomi Crandall
Additional lettering and layout: Belynda Ungurath
Editing: Z.K. Woodbridge, Vanessa Tenazas
YKS Services LLC/SKY Japan, INC
Kodansha Comics edition cover design by My Truong

Publisher: Kiichiro Sugawara

Director of publishing services: Ben Applegate
Associate director of operations: Stephen Pakula
Publishing services managing editor: Noelle Webster
Assistant production manager: Emi Lotto, Angela Zurlo
Logo and character art ©Kodansha USA Publishing, LLC